ON EQUAL TERMS

ON EQUAL TERMS

THE CONSTITUTIONAL POLITICS OF EDUCATIONAL OPPORTUNITY

Douglas S. Reed

PRINCETON UNIVERSITY PRESS

PRINCETON AND OXFORD

LIBRARY OF CONGRESS CATALOGING-IN-PUBLICATION DATA

REED, DOUGLAS S., 1964–

ON EQUAL TERMS : THE CONSTITUTIONAL POLITICS OF EDUCATIONAL

OPPORTUNITY / DOUGLAS S. REED.

P.   CM.

INCLUDES BIBLIOGRAPHICAL REFERENCES AND INDEX.

ISBN 0-691-08846-2 (ALK. PAPER)

1. EDUCATION — FINANCE — LAW AND LEGISLATION — UNITED STATES.

2. DISCRIMINATION IN EDUCATION — LAW AND LEGISLATION — UNITED STATES.

3. UNITED STATES — FINANCE.   I. TITLE.

KF4137 .R44   2001

344.73'076 — DC21   2001016372

THIS BOOK HAS BEEN COMPOSED IN ELECTRA

PRINTED ON ACID-FREE PAPER. ∞

WWW.PUP.PRINCETON.EDU

PRINTED IN THE UNITED STATES OF AMERICA

1   3   5   7   9   10   8   6   4   2

To Emily and James,

IN THE HOPE THEY WILL LIVE

IN A MORE EQUAL WORLD

CONTENTS

LIST OF ILLUSTRATIONS

Figures

Tables

ACKNOWLEDGMENTS

THIS BOOK LIES at the intersection of several fields: law, education, political science, constitutional theory, and public policy. Any ability I have to speak to these disparate audiences is due to the time, energy, and resources of several organizations and individuals who have supported, taught, and encouraged me during the writing of this book. First, many thanks to the National Academy of Education Spencer Postdoctoral Fellowship program for a year's fellowship. The Spencer Foundation has also supported earlier versions of this work and I am grateful for its support. Georgetown University provided a Junior Faculty fellowship at a critical stage in my writing. In earlier forms, this project has also received support from the Brookings Institution and Yale University.

At Yale, Rogers Smith and David Mayhew provided encouragement and rigorous criticism. At several years' remove, the book still benefits from their comments and insights. At Georgetown, I would like to thank Robert Katzmann, Bill Gormley, and Tony Arend for their unflagging enthusiasm and support. Robert Katzmann is the best mentor a junior colleague could have, providing me with both autonomy and sound advice. While his presence on the federal bench undoubtedly benefits the entire country, I sorely miss his presence at Georgetown. Bill Gormley provided very helpful comments on the manuscript and also set wholly arbitrary, but useful, deadlines for the completion of various sections. His nudging is much appreciated now. Mike Bailey and George Shambaugh gave me much needed advice on the statistical analyses in chapter 6, as did Sarah Binder and Forrest Maltzman on much earlier versions. In their administrative capacities, both Robert Lieber and Eusebio Mujal-Leon have been very supportive of the project, enabling me to take leaves and juggle teaching loads to finish the book. Carrie Menkel-Meadow of the Georgetown Law Center has also encouraged the project. I am also indebted to Jennifer Hochschild and Michael Heise for their incisive and thorough readings of the manuscript for Princeton University Press. Both of them forced me to address difficult issues that I would rather have avoided. The book is better as a result. I am also grateful to Chuck Myers of Princeton University Press for his support of this project. I also thank Robert Meister of University of California, Santa Cruz for introducing me to the perplexities of equality and educational opportunity. While he may have expected the book sooner, I hope it lives up to the standards of engaged scholarship he set for me.

Several unrelated gatherings provided inspiration for different sections of the book, particularly at moments when my own enthusiasm dimmed. I received helpful comments from the Law and Society Workshop at the Georgetown Law Center and at the Fellow's Forum at the National Academy of Education Annual Meetings, which opened up a world of education research for me. Mark Graber and Mark Tushnet's Constitutional Theory Workshop in December of 1998 sparked a flash of insight on constitutional design.

Thomas Regan of the Eagleton Center helped me obtain important public opinion surveys, as did Anne Green of Yale University. I would also like to thank the numerous individuals in state departments of education across the country who helped me obtain school district financing data, often many years old. Julia Riches and Courtenay Daum provided superb research assistance, helping me with the nitty-gritty of cite checking. Maria Toyoda helped out with data entry of the Oklahoma financing data.

In my first year of teaching, I made the fateful mistake of promising my students in Government 232 Civil Rights/Civil Liberties that I would explicitly acknowledge them in this book. Little did I know that several classes would help me think through these issues. So, for the Spring 1996 class and for all my other students who have heard the "school finance lecture," I offer my thanks for their comments, questions, and objections to the ideas in this book.

On a more personal level, I owe my family and friends my grateful thanks for their support and patience. My parents, Don and Caron Reed, always had willing ears to listen to my progress reports, and I always drew strength from their faith in me and from their love. I owe them more than I can say. My wife, Denise Brennan, took time away from her own writing and academic responsibilities to create time for me to work, even when my requests were unreasonable and possibly unfair. Her support, love, and dogged enthusiasm (especially when the hard disk crashed) enabled me to complete the book. Her parents, Arthur and Mary Brennan, provided hours of free baby-sitting so that I could forge ahead amid other demands. Finally, I want to thank my daughter, Emily, and my son, James, for pulling me away from this book and reminding me of life's truly important lessons.

INTRODUCTION

> Today, education is perhaps the most important function of
> state and local governments. Compulsory school attendance
> laws and the great expenditures for education both demonstrate
> our recognition of the importance of education to our
> democratic society. . . . In these days, it is doubtful that any
> child may reasonably be expected to succeed in life if he is
> denied the opportunity of an education. Such an opportunity,
> where the state has undertaken to provide it, is a right which
> must be made available to all on equal terms.
> —*Chief Justice Earl Warren, writing for a unanimous Supreme
> Court in* Brown v. Board of Education

B ROWN *v. Board of Education* looms large in American life. Its meanings resonate far beyond the immediate facts of Southern segregation. It has come to represent not only an entire social movement, but the vitality of America's constitutional promises. Like Rosa Parks's refusal to give up her bus seat and Martin Luther King's "I Have a Dream" speech, *Brown* has been transformed—in our collective imaginings—into an emblem. After the early years of controversy and struggle, *Brown* now symbolizes the moral righteousness of the law and of the capacity of our courts to *do* justice, rather than simply administer it.

Among all of its historical and cultural resonances, *Brown* has left us an institutional one as well. One profound legacy of *Brown v. Board of Education* has been a close, continuing relationship between courtrooms and classrooms. In the 1950s and 1960s, the legal battles to end racial segregation took center stage in the Warren Court's constitutional drama of expanding civil rights. And into the 1970s, as court orders over busing proliferated and judges ruled on issues such as student rights of privacy and expression, controversies in public education flowed in and out of judicial chambers. Educational reformers, aggrieved parents and students, social movement activists, and public interest litigators almost reflexively rely on judicial intervention in public education to transform institutions of learning.[1]

Despite the expansion of issues in education law beyond segregation and integration, these efforts at judicial educational policy-making are still stamped with the experiences of federal courts in the wake of *Brown II*. Charged with carrying out a vague constitutional mandate to desegregate with "all deliberate speed," southern federal judges faced a hostile population and local officials who sought to block or at least delay compliance with the *Brown* decision. That story is now a heroic, almost iconic, one in American political history — a tale in which students, empowered by American promises of equality and backed by judicial decrees, overcame intense political opposition, death threats and harassment, even armed intimidation, to assert their rights of equality under the law. "The Problem We All Live With," the Norman Rockwell portrait of a young black girl named Ruby Bridges walking to school under the protection of federal marshals, with blood red stains of hurled tomatoes marring the wall behind her, captures the symbolic meaning of the Supreme Court's prohibition of state-mandated segregation. That symbolism — almost clichéd by Rockwell's heavy-handed moralism — centers on the individual experience of racial bigotry and the judicial efforts to prohibit the expression of that bigotry in law and segregated institutions. Most fundamentally, these judicial efforts were concerned with undoing the persistent injuries that slavery imposed upon African Americans and upon the entire nation.

Another form of segregation has also marked American public education over the past forty years or so, one far less personal and individuated. The segregation of educational resources has increasingly characterized American schools since the suburban boom of the post–World War II era. This form of segregation results not so much from the explicit confinement of poor students to particular schools, but from the confinement of educational revenues to particular schools. Resource segregation in public education emerges from our system of geographically defined school districts, in which property values vary significantly from one district to another. In the United States, educational resources are generally raised from a combination of local property taxes and state aid. These differences in property values from district to district create a system in which a student in one school district receives far fewer educational resources than a student in another district. While resource segregation does not target individual students, it can circumscribe learning and life opportunities just as efficiently and cruelly as racial segregation. Organized not on the basis of individual student characteristics, resource segregation instead operates on an institutional level and emerges through the confluence of real estate markets, family incomes, and the political geography of public education in America.

Like racial segregation, resource segregation has undergone judicial assault. But the circumstances of this assault are significantly different from those in *Brown* and its aftermath. This assault has been led, not by the U.S. Supreme Court or the federal judiciary, but by state courts across the United States. For nearly thirty years, these courts have ruled that state constitutions require either greater equity in educational funding or greater adequacy of funding for property-poor districts. This book is, in part, about the impact of these decisions on educational financing and the political reactions of voters, interest groups, and legislators to these decisions. The politics that emerge from these decisions are simultaneously familiar and distinctive. They are familiar because they invoke long-standing American norms of equal opportunity, but they are distinctive because they expressly argue that class ought not matter in the distribution of educational advantages. Class-based politics is not unheard of in the United States, but it is rarely initiated by the judiciary and other elites. These cases present that dilemma to state legislators and their constituents, and the resulting clashes often produce intense political fireworks. By exploring court decisions, legislative responses, public opinion, and interest group politics, this book will try to make sense of those fireworks.

In the course of pursuing solutions to unequal educational opportunity, state judiciaries have battled recalcitrant state legislatures, bucked popular opinion, and tried to defuse the advantages of mobilized interests. All of this can be a daunting task, and many state supreme courts have chosen not to undertake these initiatives. Those that have often risk fomenting a popular backlash against their reform efforts. To date, no state has rewritten its constitution to allow for the inequities or inadequacies that state supreme courts have struck down, but some states have seen intense popular agitation over the restructuring mandated by their state supreme courts. This fervent, almost passionate, reaction to such dry material as guaranteed tax bases, hold-harmless provisions, and two-tiered foundation plans reveals the fundamental importance of educational finance and educational politics to state and local governance. As the public spaces that Americans freely share dwindle, efforts to widen educational opportunities to low-income areas are seen as dangerously threatening to the interests of middle- and upper-middle-class students and parents. School finance reform may, at times, be dreadfully dull, but its significance is not lost on an American population that sees local home rule as the last bastion of democratic self-governance. Parents and local residents see local control of fiscal resources as virtually the final saving grace of public education. Fearful of losing control of public schools if money either goes outside their local district or originates from outside that district, many parents, teachers, principals, and superintendents fight vigorously to preserve their advantages within the existing system. Simultaneously, however, growing popular frustration with property taxes has given new life to efforts to reduce the dependence of educational revenues on property taxes. The 1993 Michigan initiative to shift educational financing from property taxes to sales and cigarette taxes highlights this frustration. Of course, every taxation vehicle has its limitations, and residents of Michigan may one day regret their shift to a more volatile tax base. Americans seem, then, divided: they want local control, but they are frustrated with rising property taxes. They are broadly committed to the notion that all children should receive an equal educational opportunity, but they resist efforts to develop a financing system to provide those opportunities.

These, then, are only some of the obstacles facing state supreme courts as they try to navigate the treacherous waters of educational finance. At base, however, the problem of educational financing goes beyond a fickle or inconsistent public. The problem is a structural one, deeply embedded in the organization of state and local politics. American educational finance is built on a foundation of home rule and local property taxes, but the logic of school finance reform litigation aims directly at those two principles. Courts are trying to impose norms of equality and adequacy on a system that is virtually designed to generate unequal and inadequate educational revenues for some districts. The twin assumptions of local control and the educational property tax almost guarantee those outcomes. It is with this structural feature of public education that courts must, ultimately, do battle. And it is these conflicts that form the wellsprings of the judicial politics of educational opportunity.

That said, this book is about more than the judicial politics of class-based educational opportunity; it is also about ways of viewing constitutional commitments to educational opportunity. In the course of exploring how constitutional commitments to educational opportunity manifest themselves, I want to rethink and expand the range of what counts as a constitutional commitment. Scholars who study courts and equality have for a long time focused on doctrinal aspects of constitutional law, most particularly the Fourteenth Amendment. I want to continue those investigations into the judicial understanding of equal opportunity, but I want to extend the scope of constitutional understandings of equality beyond doctrine and into broader discourses. Those broader discourses that I explore touch on judicial policy-making, public opinion, interest group mobilization, and institutional arrangements. All of these, I contend, also represent constitutional commitments to educational equality, even though an exclusive doctrinal focus would place them outside our field of vision.

Another aim of this book, woven throughout its chapters, is to explore how *Brown* and its judicial progeny have profoundly shaped — for good and for ill — what educational opportunity means. The state supreme court opinions I analyze here would not have been written if *Brown* had been decided differently. Both the legal interest-group use of *Brown* and the application of the case by state judiciaries to school financing issues could not have happened without *Brown*'s moral clarity. Nonetheless, the continuing resonance of *Brown* within school financing cases also presents some difficulties. Class disadvantage is not the same as racial disadvantage. They represent two significantly different kinds of power disparity, even when they are located within the same person. Trying to understand the differences between race-

and class-based educational opportunity — and the institutional and political settings that can achieve them — forms a third aim of this book.

Structure of the Book

This book is divided into two parts. Part I, Race, Class, and Educational Opportunity, explores the similarities and differences between racial and class educational opportunity as interpreted by state and federal courts. Chapters 1, 2, and 3 comprise part I.

Chapter 1 provides an overview of the rise of school finance equalization cases within state courts by tracing the development of judicial intervention into public education. The story is one of the progression from federal judicial efforts to remedy racial segregation to state court initiatives to address resource segregation among school districts. The chapter first addresses the linkages between litigation to end segregated schools and the more recent effort to redress economic inequalities in education. It then discusses the parallels (and differences) between *Brown v. Board of Education* and another Supreme Court decision, *San Antonio Independent School District v. Rodriguez*.[2] That decision held that children who lived in property-poor districts were not denied their federal right to equal protection of the laws simply because their schools received unequal funding. *Rodriguez* led, in turn, to state-level litigation aimed at unequal or inadequate educational funding. The chapter concludes by providing an overview of the arguments in the rest of the book.

Chapter 2 examines in detail the impacts of state supreme court rulings on school finance in eight states. Using district-level data, I explore the distribution of educational resources over six- to ten-year time spans. Because adequacy claims stress the relative position of low-spending districts, I examine the range between high and low districts, as well as the median district. Also, I examine the effects of these decisions on the equity of the school financing systems in these states. The results show that state supreme courts generally have significant impact on the distribution of educational resources. Both equity and adequacy of educational finance systems improve — sometimes dramatically — when state supreme courts force state legislatures to adopt school finance reforms.

As a check on these findings, I also explore the equity and adequacy trends of states where supreme courts have upheld the existing finance systems. These states — generally drawn from the same regions, to control for political culture and other regional influences — test the proposition that reforms would have happened in the absence of judicial intervention. In most of these states, equity remains relatively constant, as measured by the

Gini coefficient and the coefficient of variation. Adequacy, as indicated by the changes in the low-spending districts, remains relatively constant as well. Overall, my findings in chapter 2 indicate that state supreme courts are having an independent effect on both the equity and adequacy of educational financing systems in states where they have intervened.

Chapter 3 reexamines the experiences of school desegregation and integration to see what lessons they might hold for state judges as they undertake school finance reform. The aim here is to contrast and compare the judicial and political features of these two reform efforts to understand whether a class-focused effort to achieve educational equality is subject to the same, or different, liabilities as school desegregation efforts.

Part II, The Constitutional Ordering of Educational Opportunity, turns the focus of the book toward state-level experiences of school finance reforms and illustrates how the judicial politics of educational opportunity is a sharp expression of what I term constitutional ordering.

Chapter 4 introduces the notion of constitutional ordering. By examining how constitutional commitments can be expressed in court decisions, in public expressions of normative aspirations, and in institutional designs, this chapter attempts to expand the range of constitutional theory by incorporating extrajudicial forms of constitutional commitment into accounts of judicial politics.

Chapter 5 turns to the nature of judicial involvement in the policy-making process itself. My account examines state supreme court school finance decisions as blueprints for reforms, blueprints that state legislators study very carefully before erecting their reform structures. By looking at these state supreme court decisions in this way, we can understand how judicial decision-making affects both the substance and form of the legislation designed to redress the constitutional infirmities of the existing school financing systems. The lessons from this chapter suggest that judicial errors can also compound the political difficulties state lawmakers face.

In chapter 6, I examine public attitudes toward educational financing by examining polls and election returns that tap into the public sentiment toward school finance equalization and increased spending. This examination is designed to register support for educational opportunity and the cleavages within the electorates of these states over the issue of equality. Because different data are available for different states, I cannot provide a detailed portrait of each state's public attitudes toward school finance reform. But by looking at key states, I can identify important features of public attitudes toward school finance equalization and finance reform in general. In particular, I explore whether citizens in these states have rejected the norms of equality promoted by these state supreme court decisions, or whether the public mood has been more accommodating. Do racial and class differences have an effect on the levels of support for school finance reforms?

And if so, how? Not surprisingly, my findings show profound cleavages within American society over educational funding. Although survey data show that most Americans support greater equality of funding for public schools, there is also significant opposition to specific proposals designed to meet the constitutional standards handed down by state supreme courts. The nature of these cleavages is somewhat surprising, however. As I will discuss, localism is a central feature of most objections to school finance reform. Ideology and race play important, but complex, roles in school finance reform—both within public attitudes toward equalization and in the development of policy proposals. Race—as it is in so many questions of economic distribution within American society—is often conflated with class within the electorate and among policy-makers. In short, even though school finance reform is, in large measure, about unequal wealth distributions among communities, public opposition or support for many reform proposals I study do not break down uniformly along class lines. Sometimes they do (and do so rather neatly), but there is also an enduring ideological and racial dimension to these conflicts, even when class is held constant.

Chapter 7 explores the nature of the institutional-level regime of inequality that courts must engage as they seek to reform public school financing. This institutional analysis focuses on how the structure of local control, local property tax, and economic stratification among school districts forges organized interests that are readily defended within the state legislature. Through a case study of the politics of education in New Jersey, this chapter will explore the relationship between the institutional features of educational financing and the relative strength of various interest groups. It is the responses of these interest groups—teachers' unions, superintendents' associations, educational policy specialists, taxpayers' associations, business groups, urban leaders, minority community activists, to name a few—that profoundly shape the legislative reforms designed to meet the courts' demands for greater educational opportunity. The deployment of these interests and groups within the New Jersey state legislature and within the policy process tells us much about not only the organization of educational interests but also whether a pluralist, policy-making apparatus can respond to demands for greater equity, particularly demands that are cast in a language of constitutional rights and imposed by state supreme courts. In short, the New Jersey case study illustrates how groups and interests respond to the judicial mandate for greater equality and/or greater access to resources and how the existing structure of financing affects the capacity and effectiveness of various groups.

Chapter 8 concludes the book by returning to the themes of race and class tensions in educational opportunity. By showing how racial tensions undergird the resource fights within educational policy, the chapter returns us to the dual dilemmas of educational opportunity in the United States today. Both these forms of disadvantage create environmental obstacles to learning that are obscured when judges and policy-makers pursue a single-minded focus on either class or race inequalities in education. The chapter also proposes a remedy as yet untested within either school desegregation or school finance litigation: a residential property credit for parents of children attending schools that are economically and racially segregated. The proposal strives to incorporate the lessons of the foregoing chapters and still provide some workable policy that might alter the underlying regime inequalities within neighborhoods suffering under miserable educational systems. The proposal itself is modest, and it assumes that judges will continue to pursue vigorously the agenda of educational opportunity they have mapped out over nearly fifty years of litigation.

In 1989 the Kentucky Supreme Court handed down the most ambitious ruling on education in nearly half a century.[3] Not since the U.S. Supreme Court's ruling in *Brown v. Board of Education* has a court sought to restructure so profoundly the provision of education within the United States. Indeed, the Kentucky Supreme Court explicitly invoked the legacy of *Brown*. Writing for the court, Chief Justice Stephens wrote, "The goal of the framers of our constitution, and the polestar of this opinion, is eloquently and movingly stated in the landmark case of *Brown v. Board of Education*."[4] This brief passage shows the continuities between two legal movements. The campaign by the NAACP Legal Defense Fund achieved a tremendous moral victory for constitutional politics in the United States. Likewise, many other less visible litigators are attempting to achieve equality of another sort in American education. The ambitions of numerous school finance activists and plaintiffs echo those of the NAACP, but unlike the NAACP, these activists have fought a more decentralized battle, winning— and losing—on several fronts. The reluctance of the U.S. Supreme Court to declare school finance equity a constitutional right in the *Rodriguez* case has created a decentralized, state-by-state litigation effort. This book is an attempt to discern some of the consequences of that effort and to understand the meaning of this constitutional ordering of educational opportunity within the United States.

PART I

RACE, CLASS, AND

EDUCATIONAL OPPORTUNITY

1

COURTS AND EDUCATIONAL OPPORTUNITY:

THE MOVEMENT FROM RACE TO CLASS

Learning to Divide: Race, Class, and Educational Disparities

ALTHOUGH POPULAR OPINION typically regards *Brown* and its progeny as a symbol of pride in American constitutionalism, the lived reality of school districts in the wake of court-ordered integration has failed to meet the promise of those early decisions. In major metropolitan areas, white flight to the suburbs — already apparent in the 1950s and 1960s — accelerated with court-ordered busing in the North in the early 1970s. With the rise of "chocolate cities and vanilla suburbs," racial homogeneity of urban school districts increased (Farley et al. 1978). In his 1978 book on busing, Gary Orfield wrote that our nation's pattern of fragmented metropolitan areas, combined with continuing residential segregation, made desegregation a difficult task: "The rapid departure of young white middle class families from the central cities, together with the plummeting birthrate, means that an increasing number of cities and some inner suburbs are left with few whites to integrate" (Orfield 1978, 55).

One initial response to this white flight was to include outlying suburbs within the desegregation remedy. In Detroit a federal judge ruled that fifty-three of eighty-five surrounding suburban districts were to be included within a desegregation plan that encompassed most of the Detroit metropolitan area. By designing a metropolitan-wide solution to the problem of interdistrict racial segregation, plaintiffs hoped to reincorporate the white students who had flown beyond the Detroit school district boundaries. The U.S. Supreme Court, however, put a stop to this interdistrict remedy in its 1974 *Milliken v. Bradley* decision.[1] Writing for a slim 5-4 majority, Chief Justice Warren Burger declared that only an interdistrict violation of constitutional rights could justify an interdistrict remedy. The Supreme Court found that a remedy could not be imposed on districts that had not actively segregated their own students. In construing the state-action requirement in this fashion, the Supreme Court ignored the growing reality of suburban-central-city segregation and left district court judges with few tools to integrate schools on a metropolitan-wide basis. As Stephen Halpern has written:

In America's greatest cities, by the end of the decade in which the Court decided *Milliken*, even the limited educational goal that had emerged from the late 1960s — racial integration — was endangered. By 1980, in many of the nation's largest cities, including New York, Los Angeles, Baltimore, Washington, D.C., and Chicago, whites represented a numerical minority of the total public school population and lived in highly segregated neighborhoods, raising serious impediments to achieving racial integration in schools. (Halpern 1995, 94)

This shifting demographic pattern of American cities emerged out of many factors, but the increasing prospects of residential and educational integration clearly played a role. The capacity of local officials to delay school desegregation, in both the North and the South, gave middle-class whites time and opportunity to abandon already shrinking central city school districts. Their departure changed not only the racial dynamics of public education, producing greater racial homogenization within school districts, but it changed the economic bases of education as well. Historically, poverty in America has been largely a rural phenomenon — and in many regions it still is. But the white middle-class abandonment of central cities in the post–World War II era, combined with a wrenching deindustrialization of American cities, helped created an urban poverty that is racially skewed. Declining property values, excess school capacity, and shrinking incomes of the remaining residents hit inner-city districts particularly hard, especially within the Northeast urban corridor. Although the picture was somewhat different in the West and South, because of growing urban populations and more expansive central-city boundaries, wherever multiple school districts existed within metropolitan areas, similar economic, if not racial, segregation occurred.

At about the same time as school desegregation suits turned northward, litigators in a number of areas began filing suits against the funding systems that states used to finance public education. These suits came out of a growing sense among civil rights lawyers that desegregation alone would not get to the heart of unequal educational opportunity. To the extent that blacks and other minorities were disproportionately poor, and to the extent that educational resources were most available to middle-class and upper-middle-class school districts, desegregation was not going to resolve the issues of profound educational disparities between whites and nonwhites. Also, growing frustration with white flight and the reluctance of middle-class whites to send their children to school with minority students led many activists to increasingly doubt the effectiveness of further desegregation efforts. Thus, both as part of the quest for greater educational opportunity and as part of a growing frustration with desegregation as a remedy for the educational inequalities suffered by blacks and other minorities, educational legal activists increasingly turned their attention to the financing disparities among school districts. As a result, lawsuits began to emerge that challenged the distribution of educational resources.[2]

These suits, arising first in California, Texas, and New Jersey, sought to fuse two significant elements of the Warren Court's political and jurisprudential commitments to equality. First, school finance litigators hoped to transform the Warren Court's rulings on behalf of equal educational opportunity for blacks and whites into a broader commitment to equal resources for education. Second, they hoped to extend a series of Warren Court–era rulings that suggested class was a constitutionally impermissible basis for public policy. In earlier decisions such as *Edwards v. California*,[3] the Supreme Court had suggested that the poor might merit special judicial protection because of their limited access to political channels. The Warren Court took that burden seriously, and in cases such as *Griffin v. Illinois*[4] and *Gideon v. Wainwright*[5] struck down the provision of rights according to wealth. The Warren Court was particularly responsive if a claimant's indigence prevented the exercise or enjoyment of a fundamental right. In California the state supreme court applied precisely this reasoning in the 1971 school finance case *Serrano v. Priest*.[6] In *Serrano* the California High Court declared that poverty was a suspect classification under the equal protection clause of the Fourteenth Amendment and that public education was a fundamental right under the U.S. Constitution. A few months later, a federal district court in Texas adopted that logic in *Rodriguez v. San Antonio Independent School District*.[7] The U.S. Supreme Court accepted the Texas decision for review on appeal, and by 1973 the judicial stage was set for an important ruling by the Supreme Court on inequality in public school finance.

The Fundamental Lessons of Rodriguez

In retrospect, there were clear signs that the Supreme Court would not look too favorably on the lower court rulings on school finance coming out of Texas and California. Although the Warren Court's aura of judicial activism still glowed, the Court was under increasing political pressure to scale back its agenda. Importantly, President Nixon had appointed three politically moderate or conservative judges in the early 1970s: Chief Justice Warren Burger and Associate Justices William Rehnquist and Lewis Powell. The Burger Court clearly consolidated a number of Warren Court doctrines — most notably within the area of school busing[8] and the right to privacy,[9] but the notion of poverty as a suspect classification under the Fourteenth Amendment was not among those consolidations. Indeed, in an early Burger Court decision, *Dandridge v. Williams*,[10] Justice Potter Stewart explicitly chose not to construe Maryland's limitation on welfare benefits to large families as a violation of constitutional rights. Instead, he viewed the regulation as simply one of any number of rational policies a state might employ in the administration of its social policies. This test, known as the rational basis test, simply requires that there be a logical nexus between the policy and a legitimate government interest.

With the *Rodriguez* case, the plaintiffs hoped that the important position of public education within American political and economic life would lead the Court to declare education a fundamental right, thereby forcing the Court to examine much more carefully any wealth-based discrimination in the provision of public education. Certainly, the Court's position in *Brown v. Board of Education* supported the view that education was, implicitly at least, of central importance to governance and citizenship. After all, Chief Justice Earl Warren had written for a unanimous Court that "education is perhaps the most important function of state and local governments," adding, a few lines later, that educational opportunity, "where the state has undertaken to provide it, is a right which must be made available to all on equal terms."[11] But what had been "the most important function of state and local governments" under the Warren Court in 1954 became somewhat less important under the Burger Court in 1973. This transformation of education's centrality—combined with a reluctance to view wealth as a suspect classification—led the Supreme Court to deny, by a narrow 5-4 margin, the claims of Demetrio Rodriguez and his fellow plaintiffs. Instead, Justice Lewis Powell contended that a healthy respect for federalism and the importance of local control in educational financing virtually required the Supreme Court to find the admitted disparities as outside the Court's purview.

The facts of *Rodriguez* are simple enough. The state of Texas funded its public schools as most states do, through a two-tiered system of local property taxes and state aid. The bulk of a district's educational revenues came from local property taxes, which made the revenues highly dependent on the property wealth within the area. Districts with high property values could generate greater sums at lower tax rates than those with low property values. The mechanism for distributing state aid took these different capacities into account, but only to a very modest degree. As a result, districts across Texas allocated widely varying per pupil expenditures. The question before the Court was whether this two-tiered system generated inequalities prohibited by the Equal Protection Clause of the Fourteenth Amendment.

Justice Lewis Powell, writing for the majority, had to disengage two critical issues in *Rodriguez* from earlier Supreme Court rulings. First, the *Brown* decision strongly implied that education is a fundamental right in America. Second, if education is a fundamental right, then the line of wealth discrimination rulings suggested that wealth was a constitutionally suspect classification by which to distribute that right. Together, these two claims formed the foundation of the plaintiffs' claims in *Rodriguez*.

Powell aimed first at the fundamental status of education. He wrote that "[T]he importance of a service performed by the State does not determine whether it must be regarded as fundamental for purposes of examination under the Equal Protection Clause" Powell further noted that "Education, of course, is not among the rights afforded explicit protection under our Federal Constitution. Nor do we find any basis for saying it is implicitly so protected."[12] The Supreme Court's retreat from the fundamental — or at least quasi-fundamental — status of education was, in itself, a marked departure from the normative commitments of the Warren Court. Next, Powell also engaged the question of whether the poor — as a class — are an identifiable minority whose interests ought to be safeguarded because they are particularly vulnerable to attack or neglect by the state.

Powell rejected the notion that the Fourteenth Amendment's Equal Protection Clause requires the Court to regard poverty as a "suspect classification," for two reasons. First, the Texas school children living in poor districts were not clearly definable as a class of "poor," and second, they did not suffer "an absolute deprivation of the desired benefit."[13] In support of the first contention, the Court argued that it is not clear that poor school children — as measured by family income or per capita income — were clustered in poor districts, as measured by property wealth.[14] Thus, according to Powell, it is hard to link the poverty of a district and its limited resources to the poverty of the individual students. The Court did not accept an implicit and important contention of the appellees: that land-poor districts contain cash-poor students.

Even if he had accepted this view, Powell's second reason for rejecting the suspect status of a poverty classification would have prevented the Court from finding for Rodriguez. Powell wrote:

> The argument here is not that the children in districts having relatively low assessable property values are receiving no public education; rather, it is that they are receiving a poorer quality education than that available to children in districts having more assessable wealth. . . . [A] sufficient answer to appellees' argument is that, at least where wealth is involved, the Equal Protection Clause does not require absolute equality or precisely equal advantages.[15]

An absolute equality, Powell argues, cannot be obtained. Instead, the court can only ask if the education received in property-poor districts is "adequate." The state of Texas argued that it was, and the Court agreed.

The claims made by Demetrio Rodriguez in *San Antonio Independent School District v. Rodriguez* provide an illuminating contrast to those made by Linda Brown in *Brown v. Board of Education*. In both cases, the plaintiffs contended that the laws governing the administration of education yielded grossly unequal educational opportunities. In Mr. Rodriguez's case, those disparities emerged from differences in wealth among communities. Educational resources, in other words, were segregated by place. In Ms. Brown's case, the disparities emerged from differences in skin color, with students segregated by race and then provided different resources accordingly. These similarities, however, belie important differences between the two claims, differences that a majority of the Supreme Court could not ignore. A number of political reasons — independent of jurisprudential rationales — stood in the way of a Supreme Court intervention to reduce the class biases of public education, despite the precedent of *Brown*. First and foremost, *Brown* was fundamentally different because it emerged from a lineage of slavery. The racial hierarchy implicit within Jim Crow and racially segregated institutions obviously echoed the power dynamics of slavery. The legal systems that mandated racial segregation controlled and dominated former slaves and their children, and it arose as a mechanism of social control not long after the physical controls of involuntary servitude were abolished in the Thirteenth Amendment (Woodward 1974). Thus, as a moral issue, if not a legal one, judicial involvement in the dismantling of racial segregation was much more readily justified. There is no historical parallel in the practice of economic or class segregation. Indeed, American society prides itself on its ideology of individual economic advancement, even if the reality of our economic disparity is often more bleak than the nation's sunny economic optimism would ever admit.

Second, public education historically has been the province of state and local governments. Despite *Brown's* precedent, the Supreme Court has been loathe to impose a federal presence on such a decentralized and localist institution, especially without express constitutional language to uphold the federal right at issue. In the *Rodriguez* decision, the court recognized and admitted profound financing disparities among school districts in Texas, but contended that the U.S. Constitution could provide no relief for such inequalities. Although the Court implicitly condemned the Texas financing scheme, it found no federal constitutional violation.[16] Instead, any wrong that existed was a function of an unfair taxation scheme — a matter best left to states and local governments to work out. As Justice Powell wrote:

> The consideration and initiation of fundamental reforms with respect to state taxation and education are matters reserved for the legislative processes of the various States, and we do no violence to the values of federalism and separation of powers by staying our hand.[17]

The federal judiciary, the Court stated, is the wrong place to seek the reform of "tax systems which may well have relied too long and too heavily on the local property tax." School financing goes to the heart of state taxation policies and is best resolved, the Court contended, through local efforts: "[T]he ultimate solutions must come from the lawmakers and from the democratic pressures of those who elect them."[18]

This reliance on local solutions was premised, of course, on the notion that education is not a national right, at least not one conferred by the U.S. Constitution. Despite *Brown's* strong language about the importance of education, the Supreme Court declined to declare equal education a right enforceable in federal court. That reasoning, however, left an opening for state courts and state constitutions, an opportunity that school finance equity activists were quick to exploit. Many state constitutions contain equality provisions, and virtually all contain explicit language about the structure of public education. These direct references could, many constitutional scholars noted, provide a doctrinal foundation for striking down unequal or inadequate financing systems under *state* constitutional provisions.[19] If a judge can demonstrate that a state constitution holds "independent and adequate" state grounds for greater educational equity, his or her decision lies beyond the reach of federal courts.[20] Because of this federal deference to state constitutional issues, state supreme courts were largely free to rule on these cases as they saw fit. They could offer the final word, free from the possibility of federal court reversal.

The "New Judicial Federalism" and School Finance Reform

Thirteen days after *Rodriguez* came down, the New Jersey Supreme Court offered its own ruling on school finance, *Robinson v. Cahill.*[21] That decision was based on the state's educational clause, which requires the state to provide all schoolchildren with a "thorough and efficient" education.[22] Unlike the U.S. Supreme Court, the New Jersey Supreme Court chose not to view the case as a violation of constitutional principles of equality, but as a violation of the state constitution's educational provisions. But like the U.S. Supreme Court's experience in the *Brown* decision, the New Jersey Supreme Court confronted major obstacles to the implementation of its decree. Ultimately, the New Jersey Supreme Court forced a nine-day shutdown of New Jersey schools in 1976 in order to compel the state legislature to fund the reform legislation adequately (for details, see Lehne 1978). That initial clash of wills between state legislature and state court has proven, over the years, to be a recurring pattern within the judicial politics of school finance equalization. The judicial rulings requiring either greater equality of educational expenditures or a greater adequacy of funding for poor districts often pit judges against elected officials in a battle of wills over educational policy-making. Surprisingly enough, state supreme courts win their fair share of battles, but the institutional context ensures that none of the battles are short lived. School finance struggles are political and legal wars of attrition.

The New Jersey experience with court-mandated school finance reform was the first of many post-*Rodriguez* decisions in which state supreme courts declared existing school finance mechanisms constitutionally invalid. Over the twenty-five years between 1972 and 1997, thirty-two state supreme courts have ruled on school financing lawsuits. Sixteen of those decisions have struck down the existing systems of funding schools and sixteen have upheld them. These lawsuits did not emerge, however, out of thin air. Inspired at first by judicial successes in New Jersey and California, school finance litigators also relied on judicial and academic theories about state constitutional interpretation. Beginning in the mid-1970s, lawyers and state court judges began using state constitutions to protect individual rights and liberties.[23] The increasingly conservative nature of the federal judiciary (particularly in the Reagan and Bush years) helped bolster what has become known as the "new judicial federalism." Since 1977, when Supreme Court Justice William Brennan published the "Magna Carta" of state constitutionalism, the new judicial federalism has grown steadily and been applied to an array of issues.[24] State rulings on search and seizure, the right to die, the right to privacy and free speech have expanded individual liberties in areas where the Supreme Court has limited its reach or not yet ruled.[25]

Most of these rulings that reinterpret state constitutional obligations have not, however, forced a systematic and wholesale revision of state institutions.[26] For example, a state supreme court may recast the scope of the exclusionary rule, but the general framework of law enforcement remains intact. In contrast, the school finance decisions aim to sharply restructure educational policies at the state level. Indeed, these decisions go to the heart of two central features of state government: education and taxation policies. As a result, these rulings are far more controversial and are of far greater consequence than other developments within the new judicial federalism. The movement of educational financing lawsuits from federal court to state courts — combined with the increasing robustness of state constitutional protections — has, in many states, effected a substantial transformation in educational financing, as we will see in chapter 2.

The Logic of It All: How (and Why) Do Courts Strike Down School Finance Systems?

But just what are the provisions of state constitutions that enable state supreme courts to restructure the distribution of educational resources? By what guiding principles do these state courts make these decisions? In *Brown*, the logic of the U.S. Supreme Court was clear: Separate is inherently unequal. It is more difficult to summarize the rationale of state supreme court rulings that strike down school financing systems. Different courts have offered different rationales for their decisions and some constitutions are more amenable to school financing suits than others. For example,

Montana's constitution stipulates that "Equality of educational opportunity is guaranteed to each person of the state."[27] In contrast, the Alabama Constitution proclaims that the state shall "foster and promote the education of its citizens in a manner and extent consistent with its available resources . . . but nothing in this Constitution shall be construed as creating or recognizing any right to education or training at public expense."[28] Clearly, a lawyer in Missoula has much more to work with than a lawyer in Mobile.

In general, however, we can group state supreme court rulings that strike down existing school finance systems into two major groups: those that rely on a principle of equity and those that rely on a principle of adequacy.

Equity decisions: Generally built on a foundation of U.S. Supreme Court equal protection rulings, equity decisions substitute state equality provisions for the Fourteenth Amendment of the U.S. Constitution. Many state constitutions do not expressly provide for "equal protection of the laws," but contain other equality provisions — some dating back to the Jacksonian Era and others more recent adoptions of state equal rights amendments.[29] Within the context of school finance, these equality provisions have been used to argue that gross inequalities in educational financing violate state constitutions. For example, the early school finance decision in California, *Serrano v. Priest*, anchored its analysis firmly within the framework of federal equal protection analysis, declaring wealth a suspect classification under the California Constitution and declaring education a fundamental right for California citizens.[30] Other courts, however, have been less enthusiastic about viewing school finance litigation through the lens of equal protection. Declaring education a fundamental right, they have argued, could bring a wave of lawsuits over disparate police and fire protection, water services, even housing needs.[31] Also, many state courts have traditionally interpreted state equality provisions as coextensive with the U.S. Constitution's equal protection clause. Reluctant to break this "lockstep" interpretation, some state courts have applied the *Rodriguez* rationale to the state context, holding that equality in educational spending does not fall under the purview of state equality provisions.[32] In general, state supreme court decisions based wholly or in part on state equality provisions are becoming increasingly rare, as state supreme courts have more recently relied solely on state educational clauses to strike down existing school finance systems.[33]

Adequacy decisions: When plaintiffs make a claim under a state educational clause, they are typically seeking a judicial declaration that the state is not providing an adequate education within public schools. In short, they want the court to assert that the state is not meeting its constitutional obligations within public education. Commonly, this would be remedied by a new financing structure that would provide greater assistance to the worst-off districts so they could provide students with an adequate education. In adequacy cases, plaintiffs are typically not so concerned with establishing a strictly equitable distribution of funds among school districts, but with simply securing more resources for the poorest districts. Of course, determining that an existing finance system cannot generate sufficient revenues for an adequate education within all districts forces courts to address all kinds of thorny issues about what constitutes an "adequate" education and even whether the court can discern its elements. Thus, courts that face an adequacy claim must closely examine the meaning of a state constitution's educational clauses. Unfortunately, these provisions provide only the roughest definitions. The language in these clauses ranges from simple declarations that create a system of schools to broad assertions about the fundamental importance of education within the state. For example, the Oklahoma education clause reads, "The legislature shall establish and maintain a system of free public schools wherein all the children of the State may be educated,"[34] while the Washington Constitution asserts that education is the "paramount duty of the state."[35] Between these two extremes lies the more common educational clause that stipulates a particular level of educational opportunity to its students. States in this middle ground must provide their students with a "thorough and efficient"[36] education or a "general and uniform"[37] education throughout the state.[38]

Mingling equity and adequacy: Over the past few years, school finance litigators have come to rely increasingly on these general education provisions to sustain their adequacy claims. Indeed, William Thro has argued that school financing decisions have come in three waves, culminating in an almost exclusive reliance on educational clauses rather than equality provisions (see Thro 1990; 1993; 1994). The first wave, Thro argues, began with suits that relied on the equal protection provisions of the U.S. Constitution; of course, that wave crashed to the shore with the *Rodriguez* decision. The second wave of rulings, beginning shortly after *Rodriguez* and continuing until 1989, relied on both state equality provisions and state education clauses. In the third and current wave, state supreme courts, according to Thro, are basing their decisions exclusively on state education clauses, ruling that the existing financing systems do not provide students with an adequate education. The remarkable string of successes enjoyed by adequacy claimants has led some to argue that equality claims no longer play a central role in school finance litigation (see, for example, Enrich 1995). Recent decisions coming out of Arizona, Vermont, and Ohio, however, indicate that the abandonment of equity claims is not complete — for two important reasons. First, equity claims are still viable, independent vehicles for school finance litigators, and second, adequacy claims often implicitly involve equity issues. This can lead to mixed rulings that intermingle equity with adequacy concerns.

The 1997 ruling in Vermont nicely illustrates the first point, the continuing viability of equity claims. In that decision, the state supreme court ruled that "the present system has fallen short of providing every school-age child in Vermont an equal educational opportunity." Indeed, the Vermont Supreme Court explicitly held that "to fulfill its constitutional obligation the state must ensure substantial equality of educational opportunity throughout Vermont."[39] Clearly, within Vermont, equity claims are still quite robust. And in Arizona the state supreme court recently struck down the existing system of financing school facilities, concluding that the "general and uniform" requirement of the Arizona Constitution held an implicit norm of equality. The court ruled, quite simply, that the state's obligation under the education provision would be met only if the "[f]unding mechanisms provide sufficient funds to educate children on *substantially equal terms*."[40]

The Arizona case also illustrates how adequacy claims often become tangled up within egalitarian language, making the distinction between equity and adequacy difficult to discern. Although many adequacy rulings are based expressly on educational provisions of state constitutions, norms of equal distribution nonetheless surface within cases that merely seek to demonstrate inadequate funding. This is true even for older rulings that some analysts have seen largely through the lens of adequacy. For example, the Kentucky Supreme Court ruling in *Rose v. Council for Better Education*[41] held that

> The system of common schools must be substantially uniform throughout the state. Each child, *every child*, in this Commonwealth must be provided with an equal opportunity to have an adequate education. Equality is the key word here. The children of the poor and the children of the rich, the children who live in the poor districts and the children who live in the rich districts must be given the same opportunity and access to an adequate education.[42]

Is this decision about equity or adequacy? It is about both, and to argue that norms of equality did not figure in the court's construal of what constitutes an "efficient" school system is to ignore the language of the decision itself.[43]

The point here is that equality claims are still integral components of school finance decisions, even if judges are basing their decisions on state educational provisions rather than state equality provisions. As the Vermont experience shows, courts still can, and do, base their decisions on norms of equality, but their egalitarian impulses are often infused with notions of adequacy. This is due to a number of factors. Judges often view adequacy in light of relative resource levels rather than absolute levels, lending support to the argument that the constitutional inadequacy of a school financing system stems from its overall inequality. In other words, a judge may see a system as inadequate or inefficient simply because it generates significant resource inequalities. Also, judges may define "equality of educational opportunity" in terms not of perfect equality of resources or education, but in terms of fairness, which requires a rough parity of resources. Part of state supreme courts' tendency to conflate adequacy and equity may, in fact, arise from confusion over what equality actually means. As I will discuss in chapter 5, equality comes in various forms and if judges do not specify carefully what *kind* of equality the state constitution requires, they may be asking state legislatures to enact contradictory policies.[44] All of these factors lead state supreme court justices to sometimes mingle equity issues with adequacy issues in their rulings. Courts often draw freely on the multiple and possibly conflicting arguments made by plaintiffs' lawyers, and lawyers, being lawyers, are more than happy to provide courts with multiple ways to reach similar conclusions. As a result, judges — who are generally not specialists in the technical aspects of school financing formulas — blend arguments and sometimes conflate issues that are analytically distinct, but enjoy a political or rhetorical affinity.

The jurisprudential routes to school finance reform are varied, but they vary within fairly specific constraints. State equality provisions define one boundary while state educational clauses constitute another. Within those boundaries, claims are often mingled; the routes to reform often crisscross. Clearly, claims made under state education clauses are increasingly effective, but equity claims still suffuse — either explicitly or implicitly — school finance reform litigation. As state supreme courts increasingly look at class disparities among classrooms, the judicial notion of equal educational opportunity shifts from a race-based conception to a class-based notion. This is true whether one sees these state supreme court decisions as efforts to achieve equity or adequacy or both. In either case, these courts have both initiated a judicial politics of educational opportunity and extended and redefined a judicial tradition begun in *Brown v. Board of Education*. The next chapter assesses the success of that project.

2

THE JUDICIAL IMPACT ON SCHOOL

FINANCE REFORM

MANY POLITICAL SCIENTISTS who study courts and social movements in a broad sense have, over the past few years, been concerned with a puzzling dilemma. *Brown v. Board of Education* is, at a popular and constitutional level, one of the most significant Supreme Court decisions of the twentieth century. But when one looks at what *Brown* actually accomplished, its effects are, at best, indirect. Until recently, the conventional wisdom of legal academics and political scientists has been that *Brown* helped spur a revolution in American social life, first pulling a reluctant South into the national mainstream, and then focusing the entire nation's attention more broadly on the harms of racial prejudice and discrimination. From this perspective, the Supreme Court was both a moral and institutional leader in race relations, articulating a vision of a shared political and public life between blacks and whites and effectively realizing those ends. That, at least, was the conventional wisdom.

In 1991 Gerald Rosenberg published a book entitled *The Hollow Hope*. He argued that courts can achieve significant social transformations only under very carefully specified conditions.[1] Because courts lack the institutional tools to undertake major social restructuring, the success of their agendas depends, significantly, on other branches of government and popular support. In a careful, but nonetheless criticized, analysis of *Brown*'s impact, Rosenberg argued that the Supreme Court and lower federal courts achieved little in terms of direct integration of schoolchildren. Instead, it was not until the 1964 Civil Rights Act—a major national legislative achievement that placed the powers of the federal government squarely behind the forces of integration—that judicial actors could count on support from other branches of government. Thus, Rosenberg contends, *Brown* and its progeny in lower federal courts were politically inert and ineffective until other actors provided meaningful political support for their aims.

Surely, though, *Brown* represented a major moral victory for civil rights activists, inspiring other actors and providing greater indirect support for the aims of racial integration. The legitimating force of *Brown*, one would think, must be significant. According to Rosenberg, this is not the case. In a controversial chapter, Rosenberg found little evidence that *Brown* affected the subsequent course of the civil rights movement.[2] Analyzing media coverage of the civil rights movement before and after *Brown*, the incidence of protest actions within the South before and after *Brown*, and the elite and mass attitudes of Americans, Rosenberg argues that *Brown* barely caused a blip in American political consciousness and activity. In sum, Rosenberg contends that neither its direct effects on school desegregation, nor its indirect effects on the civil rights movement support the conventional view of a transformative Supreme Court, supervising a judiciary bent on fundamentally reworking the institutional and political life of the United States. Rosenberg goes on to analyze other movements — the women's movement and the environmental movement, in particular — in his effort to argue for the limited nature of judicial capacity, but none of his case studies pierce the conventional wisdom quite as sharply as his treatment of *Brown*. There has been a growing scholarly refutation of Rosenberg's argument, but his book has reoriented the field of inquiry into courts, social movements, and judicial impact.

In part, this book is a rejoinder to Rosenberg. In particular, this chapter aims to demonstrate the meaningful effects courts have had on school finance reforms. And this judicial project is no small endeavor. If all expenditures on public primary and secondary education were removed from the hands of state and local governments and turned over to the federal government, it would be the largest item in the national budget, comprising 22.3 percent of the federal budget, larger than both national defense and social security (Witte 2000, 19). As a percentage of GDP, expenditures on elementary and secondary education in 1998 amounted to 4.4 percent of total economic activity in the United States (Digest of Education Statistics, 1999, table 31). A large-scale redistribution of these resources would represent social and political change of the highest order. The agenda of court-based efforts to change the basis and distribution of educational revenues certainly aims at that end. The question is whether state supreme courts have been effective in their efforts to achieve that transformation.

The evidence presented in this chapter indicates that courts have been rather successful — surprisingly so, given the intensity of opposition to reforms within some states. Indeed, the degree of change in school finance over the past twenty-five years in states where supreme courts have struck down the existing systems is rather substantial, especially given the constraints under which courts must operate. However, as later chapters will more fully develop, these reductions in the level of inequality have not substantially altered the institutional contexts of educational finance. Thus, while the changes in resource inequality and inadequacy suggest that Rosenberg's view of judicial limitations is overstated, the obstacles that courts still face in restructuring educational finance indicate that the inegalitarian pressures within the system are still quite acute, despite these judicial interventions. In sum, courts can achieve substantial and meaningful redistribution of educational resources despite intense political opposition, but the institutional pressures that produced that inequality in the first place remain more or less intact. As a result, continuing judicial pressures will be necessary to preserve the improvements in educational opportunity this legal campaign has won.

How Do We Know Things Have Changed?
The Problem of Case Selection and Assessing Impact

Two central questions guide the inquiry in this chapter. First, I want to answer whether winning court decisions matters to the distribution of educational resources, and second, whether some state supreme courts are more successful than others in their efforts to redistribute educational resources. These two questions require comparisons of two different sets of decisions. By comparing changes over time in educational resources in states where plaintiffs have won to states where plaintiffs have lost I can determine the effects of decisions that strike down the existing systems. The second question seeks to understand the differing capacity of state supreme courts to achieve their reform goals. This question — are some state supreme courts more successful than others? — requires a comparison of judicial outcomes in those states where plaintiffs have won.

There are, however, some important methodological difficulties with school financing data. To test effectiveness, I need to trace the impacts of these decisions over a long time period. As a result, the most recent decisions of school finance reform are of little help to me. Reforms must be allowed to ripen in order to see their effects. Also, I cannot lose sight of my primary arguments: I need to study states where plaintiffs have both won and lost, and I need to study enough states to give some flavor of the variability in state supreme court effectiveness. This is no mean task. When one examines all the state supreme court decisions concerning school finance, not too many meet all the relevant criteria. I have, however, selected eight study states that meet the needs of my inquiry. These states and the year of the state supreme court decision are listed in table 2.1.

The eight states are clustered into three groups — each representing a distinct combination of geographical region, political culture, and type of poverty. Group 1 states are distinguished by a Northern, urban, central-city poverty, largely affecting racial minorities, while the rural white poverty of the Southern mountain region predominates in Group 2. Group 3 includes Southwestern states with significant rural poverty. By holding constant the region, the nature of poverty, and local political culture, we can see whether these factors are related to the success of judicial efforts to restructure public school finance. In large part, these groupings are useful because they can

TABLE 2.1

States Included in School Finance Impact Analysis, Organized by Direction of
Ruling, Region, and Predominant Form of Poverty

	School Finance System Struck Down	School Finance System Upheld
Group 1: Affluent Northern states with racially identified urban poverty	Connecticut, 1977 New Jersey, 1990	Illinois, 1992*
Group 2: Southern mountain states with significant rural poverty	Kentucky, 1989 Tennessee, 1993	North Carolina, 1987
Group 3: Southwestern states with rural poverty	Texas, 1989	Oklahoma, 1987

*Date of district court ruling. Decision later upheld by state supreme court.

help organize and systematize comparisons among state supreme court outcomes. By examining outcomes within clusters I can determine the extent
to which winning lawsuits can actually produce results, and by examining
political reactions among winners across the groups, I can more carefully
identify the significant political features of school finance reform efforts
amid varying demographic and poverty contexts.

Equality and Adequacy: From Concept to Measurement

Before we can assess the effects of judicial intervention on school finance,
we need to clarify what we are looking for. The jurisprudence of school
finance decisions centers on two basic principles of equality and adequacy,
and here I want to explore how analysts have understood these two principles, looking at them first in theoretical terms and then through an empirical lens.

Equality and Equity in School Finance

Equality is a notoriously fickle concept. Because equality can assume multiple, even contradictory forms, its achievement is complex and, at times,
counterintuitive. A relationship between two entities may be equal under
one set of assumptions, but grossly unequal if those assumptions change. As
a result, if I am to argue that school resources were more (or less) equal
after a court ruling than prior to that ruling, I must first clarify my assumptions concerning equality. Douglas Rae and his coauthors have provided a

useful "grammar" of equality that can sort through the varieties and forms of equality. Rae et al. urge us to "think of equality as a series of conflicting forces, related in abstract conception yet contradicting one another in practice" (Rae et al. 1981, 2). Thus, equality is not a unitary concept, but a complex principle of allocation by which any number of goods, resources, powers, or benefits may be distributed to various individuals or groups. The configuration of that allocation will necessarily vary according to the assumptions built into one's notion of equality. Thus, a definition of school finance equality must specify such things as the boundary of the distribution range (those included within the bounds of equality), the relevant recipient unit within that distribution range (individuals, groups, blocs, etc.), the nature of the good to be distributed (divisible or unitary). In the context of school finance, it matters a great deal whether we are talking about equality among school districts as geographical and political entities, or equality among pupils. Similarly, it matters whether we are discussing equality of resources or equality of welfare.[3] Also, it matters whether we are discussing equality of curriculum or equality of opportunities to learn.[4] Seemingly minor differences among these positions can yield substantially different determinations of equality within a distribution of resources.

For the purposes of this chapter, I am concerned with the following elements of school finance. First, I take the relevant recipient unit to be pupils, not school districts. Because school district enrollments vary widely within a state, the size of the district matters a great deal when one calculates the level of equity within a state. Accordingly, I weight my analyses of per pupil revenues and expenditures within a district by the size of the district.[5] Second, I am explicitly concerned with resource inputs — particularly the per pupil dollar amounts of revenues and expenditures within districts.[6] One possible objection to my exclusive concern with dollar amounts is the claim that more money does not necessarily provide a better education. Clearly, sound educational environments are built with more than mere dollars. Indeed, the debate among educational researchers over the value of greater monetary resources to educational achievement is a long and loud one.[7] For my purposes, I regard monetary inputs as a necessary, but not sufficient condition for educational achievement.[8] Well-funded school districts may be poor educational environments, but poorly funded districts will rarely be centers of excellence. Certainly, factors such as parental involvement in a student's education, the educational attainment of parents, the socio-economic background of families, the expectations placed upon children, the level of safety in schools, the leadership exerted by principals, and teachers' skills all matter significantly to learning and academic achievement. But without sufficient resources, academic achievement becomes much more unlikely, perhaps impossible. Third, I am concerned with students who are similarly situated. That is, I aim to track what is known within school finance parlance as "horizontal equity."[9] Horizontal equity is achieved when students in all districts receive equal funding. If full horizontal equality exists, there will be no difference in the per pupil expenditures for the students who do not have special needs.[10] Thus, in the language of political theory, I am less concerned with equality of welfare than I am with equality of resources. To be sure, certain students (or even certain districts) may require additional funds to achieve the same level of learning, but that welfare-based argument is in no way obviated by a prerequisite effort to ensure an equality of resources. I see equality of resources — horizontal equality — as a necessary precondition for equality of welfare.[11] Before we can respond adequately to students with special needs, we need to ensure that all students achieve equitable resources. In this regard, I see special needs as residing "on top of" the common needs of all students.

In order to translate these theoretical distinctions among forms of equality into empirical accounts of changes in equity, we need a measure of equity that reflects the theoretical dimensions of equality. The Gini coefficient — long used in studies of income inequality in economics — is well suited to the task because it registers changes in revenue levels for all districts within a state, not simply those at the top or bottom of the distribution.[12] The results presented here were confirmed by another measure, the coefficient of variation (defined as the standard deviation of a population divided by the mean of that population). For all practical purposes, the Gini coefficient and coefficient of variation measures produced the same results, but for space considerations I present only the Gini coefficient here. Given the theoretical constraints laid out above, the Gini coefficient is the best measure to reliably track the horizontal equity of a school finance system over time.[13]

Adequate School Financing: What Do Courts Want?

But equality is not the only standard by which state supreme courts have judged school financing systems to be constitutionally infirm. State supreme courts have also ruled that some school financing systems do not provide "adequate" educational resources and opportunities. By what standard or standards have courts made this determination? Generally, a court concludes a financing system is inadequate after a plaintiff has demonstrated a thoroughgoing failure of the educational system to meet the basic needs of students in the worst-off districts. Most often, this takes the form of judicial fact-finding and relies on testimony of relevant officials, students, parents, and teachers, rather than a statistical analysis of adequacy per se. For example, the Ohio Supreme Court ruled that the system of educational financing in Ohio did not meet the "thorough and efficient" clause of the Ohio Constitution. As the Court wrote:

[I]t is imperative to consider the record as presented to us. In doing so, we find that exhaustive evidence was presented to establish that the appellant school districts were starved for funds, lacked teachers, buildings, and equipment, and had inferior educational programs, and that their pupils were being deprived of educational opportunity.[14]

Based on its examination of the trial record, the court ruled that the inadequacies of the system put the state in violation of the constitution's thorough and efficient clause.[15] But findings of inadequacy do not necessarily imply that courts have a coherent or consistent definition of adequacy in educational funding. Adequacy is a highly subjective term, and rulings that declare school finance systems constitutionally inadequate have been criticized for their failure to define the term rigorously. As the Florida Supreme Court recently wrote:

[T]he courts cannot decide whether the Legislature's appropriation of funds is adequate in the abstract, divorced from the required uniformity. To decide such an abstract question of "adequate" funding, the courts would necessarily be required to subjectively evaluate the Legislature's value judgments as to the spending priorities to be assigned to the state's many needs, education being one among them. In short, the Court would have to usurp and oversee the appropriations power, either directly or indirectly, in order to grant the relief sought by Plaintiffs.[16]

As the Florida High Court noted, any definition of adequacy within school finance must necessarily be contextual and refer to some external standard or standards of educational needs. In general, these external standards are not specified within constitutional language. As a result, courts that do strike down existing systems on the grounds of inadequacy most often view the issues through a lens of judicial common sense: Does this system produce funding — or educational — outcomes that meet the basic needs of students and society?[17] Unlike equity — which can be determined independent of external, contextual considerations — adequacy is, ultimately, in the eye of the beholder. To be sure, statutory language often guides that interpretation,[18] but as the Florida Supreme Court indicated, the process of defining and then identifying adequacy within an educational system holds few judicial landmarks.[19]

Similarly, there are few empirical benchmarks to determine whether a school finance system is more adequate at one point in time than another. Because decisions that focus on adequacy typically focus on the absolute level of the least affluent districts within a state, it is plausible to discern changes in adequacy by reference to the expenditure and revenue levels of the worst-off districts within the system. Presumably, adequacy improves when the districts with the fewest resources gain more resources. Certainly adequacy is not harmed by this change. Alternatively, we could look at the revenue and expenditure level of the median district. If we want to examine how the "average" district is faring, we can chart the median expenditure and revenue levels within a state over time. Improving median levels would imply an improvement in adequacy. Of course, there is no absolute point at which a state "achieves" adequacy. We can only determine whether a system is more or less adequate at two points in time.[20] In the empirical findings presented below, I examine both the median resource levels and the resource levels of the worst-off districts.

Finally, it is important to note that adequacy and equity are analytically distinct. A state may fund its schools with complete equity and nonetheless produce a horribly inadequate system. Equal funding at very low levels — although rare, for political reasons — is a logical possibility.[21] Likewise, a system may produce an adequate level of resources for all students, but still exhibit high levels of inequality. There is no necessary connection between equality and adequacy — despite what a number of courts have claimed. As we shall see, the political responses to constitutional findings of inadequacy or inequality are roughly similar, but the policy changes required to remedy the two conditions are substantially different.

Findings from Eight States

What Happens When You Win? Findings from Five States Where School Finance Reform Litigants Won

Let's now look at the experiences in five states in which plaintiffs won at the state supreme court level. I first want to examine changes in the per pupil revenues of the median and worst-off districts — a useful measure of the adequacy of a school financing formula. The range can also help us understand the dimensions of the equity gaps within a state. That is, the range can give us a good snapshot of the magnitude of inequality of resources within a state, but it is not terribly good at showing changes in equality over time.[22] Nonetheless, the range is useful to see the dimensions of resource inequalities within a state. Clearly, reducing a large range is a much larger political (and judicial) task than reducing a narrow one. Thus, despite its methodological shortcomings, the range can illustrate, in graphic terms, the dimensions of an inegalitarian distribution.

Figures 2.1 through 2.5 show the high per pupil revenue, low per pupil revenue, and median revenue in the five states for the relevant years.[23] The story these figures tell is somewhat surprising. First, when we examine the absolute range of revenues[24] (in inflation-adjusted dollars) between the topmost and the bottommost districts in these states, we see that the range has actually increased over the relevant time periods. That is, the gap between

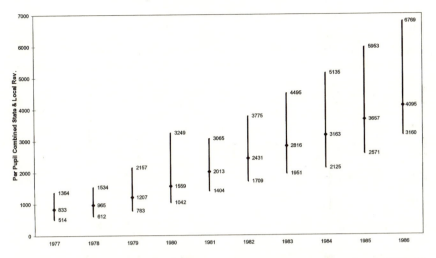

FIGURE 2.1. Connecticut school finance revenue ranges and medians, 1977–86: high, low and median per pupil combined state and local revenues.
(K12 Districts; Thomaston figures omitted for 1978–79 because of exceptionally high federal aid. All values weighted for district enrollment and expressed in constant 1986 dollars. Data source: Connecticut Public Expenditure Council Annual Reports, 1977–86.)

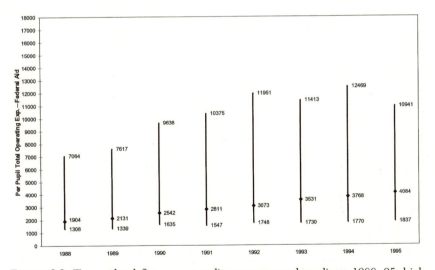

FIGURE 2.2. Texas school finance expenditure ranges and medians, 1988–95: high, low, and median per pupil total operating expenditures minus federal aid.
(K12 districts > 100 pupils and expenditures > $100 per pupil. For 1994, Benavides, Lancaster, and Sudan ISDs omitted because of data errors. All values weighted for district enrollment and calculated in 1995 dollars. Data source: Texas Education Agency, March 1994 and July 1996.)

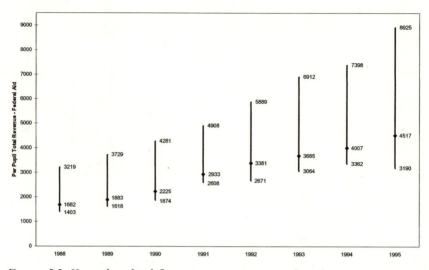

FIGURE 2.3. Kentucky school finance revenue ranges and medians, 1988–95: high, low, and median per pupil total revenues minus federal aid.

(K12 districts only. All values weighted for district enrollment and calculated with constant 1995 dollars. Data source: Kentucky Department of Education, March 1994 and December 1996).

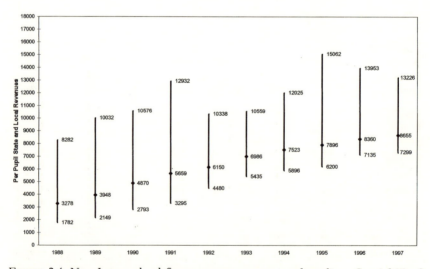

FIGURE 2.4. New Jersey school finance revenue ranges and medians, Special Needs and I & J districts only, 1988–97: high, low, and median per pupil combined state and local revenues.

(K12 and hypothetical K12 districts constructed from regional high schools and K8 and K6 districts. All values weighted for district enrollment and calculated with 1997 dollars. Data source: New Jersey Department of Education, January 1994 and January 1997.)

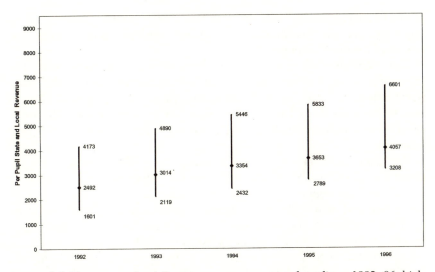

FIGURE 2.5. Tennessee school finance revenue ranges and medians, 1992–96: high, low, and median per pupil combined state and local revenues.
(K12 districts only. All values weighted for district enrollment and calculated with constant 1996 dollars. Data source: Tennessee Department of Education, April 1997.)

these two points is, in general, larger in the later years than it is immediately prior to the court decisions. Simultaneously, however, we see that the level of resources for all districts — top, median, and bottom — has generally increased quite dramatically. In Connecticut, the real median per-pupil combined state and local revenues more than quadrupled over a ten-year period, increasing from $833 to $4,095; in Texas and Kentucky, the real median figures more than doubled over eight years; in New Jersey, it doubled within six years, nearly tripling within nine. Tennessee's median state and local revenues did not climb as dramatically, but nonetheless the figure grew 63 percent — in real dollars — over five years.

Also interesting is the level of revenues at the low end of the scale. In Connecticut, Kentucky, New Jersey, and Tennessee, we see significant increases in revenues among the lowest-spending districts during the relevant years. In contrast, expenditures in Texas's low-spending districts remain relatively constant, but the highest districts show a noticeable decline, in constant dollars, since 1992. The former states seem to have emphasized increased revenues among low-end districts in their school finance reforms, while Texas has, it appears, sought to cap the high-end district expenditures. In all these states, however, the median districts had significantly more resources at their disposal after the court decisions than they did prior to the decisions. Moreover, in most states the lowest-spending districts have also seen their revenue levels increase dramatically. Whether the goals of the school-finance litigation suits in these states were greater adequacy or equity, they appear in meaningful ways to have produced, on the whole, more resources for most districts.[25]

The distribution of these resources, however, still remains at issue. The increasing ranges between the top and bottom districts suggest that these new funds were not distributed with a concern for equity, but that disparity may be misleading. As I have indicated, other measures besides the range can give us a more accurate picture of changes within the top and bottom extremes.

The Gini coefficient provides a measure of equality that takes into account transfers from all districts in the revenue distribution, not just those at the top and the bottom ends of the scale. The Gini coefficient ranges between one and zero, with zero indicating perfect equality. Thus, the lower the Gini coefficient, the more equal the revenue distribution. Looking at figures 2.6 through 2.10 as a whole, we see that all states indicate increasing equity (whether modest or great) after the state supreme court decisions that invalidated the existing school finance system. In one case, Connecticut, that trend toward increased equity was small and partially reversed (see figure 2.6) but on the whole we can see that inequality decreased significantly in most states in the wake of these decisions. For example, New Jersey saw its Gini score drop from 0.100 to 0.062 over a three year period, a 38.0

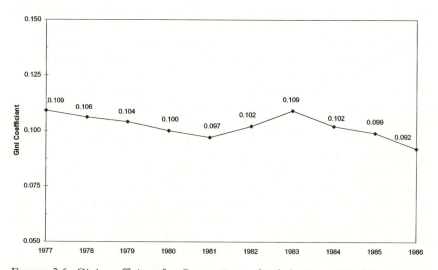

FIGURE 2.6. Gini coefficient for Connecticut school districts 1977–86: per pupil combined state and local revenues.
(K12 districts. Thomaston figures omitted for 1978–79 because of exceptionally high federal aid. All values weighted for district enrollment and calculated with constant 1986 dollars. Data source: Connecticut Public Expenditure Council Annual Reports, 1977–86.)

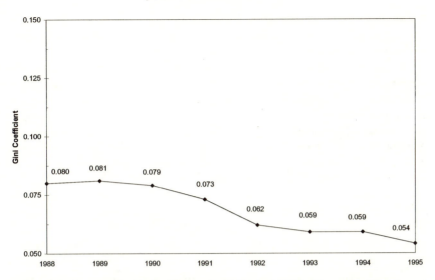

FIGURE 2.7. Gini coefficient for Texas school districts, 1988–95: per pupil total operating expenditures minus federal aid.

(K12 districts > 100 pupils and expenditures) $100 per pupil. For 1994, Benavides, Lancaster, and Sudan ISDs omitted because of data errors. All values weighted for district enrollment and calculated in 1995 dollars. Data source: Texas Education Agency, March 1994 and July 1996.)

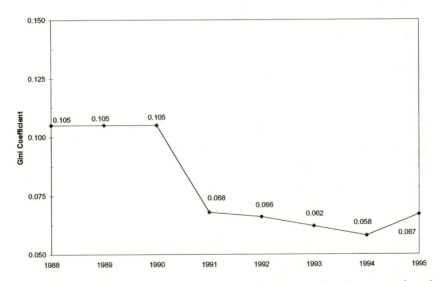

FIGURE 2.8. Gini coefficient for Kentucky school districts, 1988–95: per pupil total revenue minus federal aid.

(K12 districts only. All values weighted for district enrollment and calculated using constant 1995 dollars. Data source: Kentucky Department of Education, March 1994 and December 1996.)

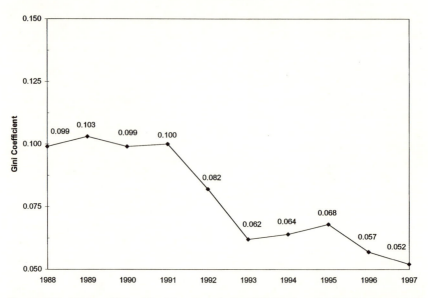

FIGURE 2.9. Gini coefficient for New Jersey's Special Needs and I & J districts, 1988–97: per pupil combined state and local revenues.
(K12 and hypothetical K12 districts constructed from regional high schools and K8 and K6 districts. All values weighted for district enrollment and calculated using 1997 dollars. Data source: New Jersey Department of Education, January 1994 and March 1997.)

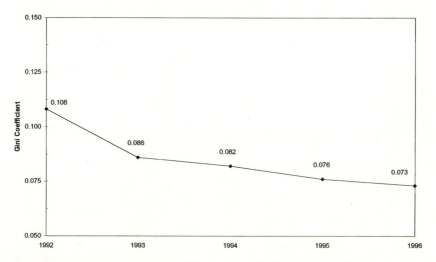

FIGURE 2.10. Gini coefficient for Tennessee school districts, 1992–96: per pupil combined state and local revenues.
(K12 districts only. All values weighted for district enrollment and calculated using constant 1996 dollars. Data source: Tennessee Department of Education, April 1996.)

percent improvement in the equity between affluent, suburban districts and thirty "special needs" districts.[26] Over a seven-year period, that figure dropped further, for a 48 percent reduction in the level of resource inequality. Over seven years, Texas saw its inequality drop from the 0.080 range down to 0.054 in 1995, an improvement of 32.5 percent. Kentucky's level of inequality dropped dramatically from 0.105 to 0.058 over a five-year period, a remarkable 44.8 percent drop in resource inequality. Even in Connecticut, where the change in equity was comparatively small, the level of inequality dropped by nearly 16 percent, although the trend proved erratic. Tennessee's level of inequality dropped a more modest, but meaningful, 15.1 percent.

Together, these changes — with the possible exceptions of Connecticut and Tennessee — represent sizeable and enduring changes in the level of inequality among the relevant school districts. These changes are not one-time dips, but sustained and relatively robust redistributions of resources among school districts. The average decline in inequality among the five states is 29.38 percent. Some of the dips are gradual, but Kentucky's and New Jersey's are steep and abrupt. Taken together these changes tell a story, in most instances, of persistent and meaningful decreases in inequality over time. Clearly, the states exhibit significant variation — in both the slope of the decline and its duration. Despite these differences, the lesson we should learn from court-initiated school finance equalization is that it generally achieves results. With the exception of Connecticut, school financing in these states was invariably more equal after the courts became involved than it was before. Moreover, the fact that the top-spending districts did not decline significantly (except in Texas) over these time periods (as shown in figures 2.1 through 2.5) indicates that, contrary to many critics' fears, state legislatures are usually able to raise the revenues of low-wealth districts rather than simply cap resources in affluent districts.

What Happens When You Lose? Findings from Three States Where School Finance Reform Litigants Lost

These trends in the level of equity and adequacy of school finance systems, while impressive, could be dismissed as part of a general trend — one that had little to do with court decrees and state supreme court rulings. It is possible these changes would have occurred without judicial interventions. To claim that courts were central to this reform process, I must also examine cases in which the courts were not involved. Only by comparing changes in adequacy and equity in states where courts were not involved and where courts were involved can we begin to determine the scope of judicial influence on school finance reform. The three states studied in this section — Oklahoma, North Carolina, and Illinois — were chosen because their local political cultures and their political geographies of poverty are roughly similar to states studied in the first part of this chapter. Thus, we can compare North Carolina outcomes to outcomes in Kentucky and Tennessee because all three are Southern or border states in which Appalachian rural poverty constitutes a significant feature of school financing inequalities. In contrast, Illinois's urban, predominantly black poverty is roughly comparable to the inequalities experienced in Connecticut's and New Jersey's central cities. Finally, Oklahoma and Texas are both Southwestern states with significant rural poor populations — although central-city poverty is present in Texas as well. The aim was to find similar states in which the judicial outcomes were different.

So how do these states compare? Figures 2.11 through 2.13 illustrate trends in the ranges of revenues and the median revenues.[27] Oklahoma's median revenues have seen significant growth since the 1987 Oklahoma Supreme Court decision, but the bottommost districts have not joined in that revenue growth. As a result, Oklahoma's range has expanded significantly. In contrast, North Carolina's median expenditures have nearly tripled in real dollars, and the bottommost districts have likewise spent significantly greater funds. Illinois median revenues have grown modestly, but the bottommost districts actually received fewer resources in 1993 than they did in 1990 — a contraction of almost 4 percent. In sum, the median revenue

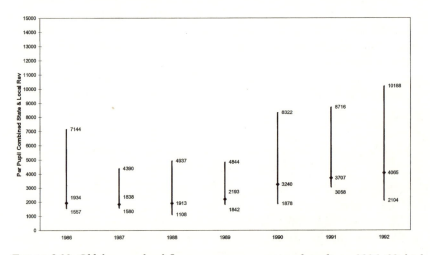

FIGURE 2.11. Oklahoma school finance revenue ranges and medians, 1986–92: high, low, and median per pupil combined state and local revenues.
(K12 districts > 100 pupils; Red Rock and Frontier districts omitted because of exceptionally high industrial property values. All values weighted for enrollment and calculated in 1992 dollars. Data source: Oklahoma Department of Education, Annual Reports, 1985–86 to 1991–92.)

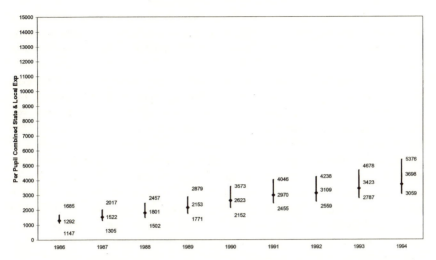

FIGURE 2.12. North Carolina school finance expenditure ranges and medians, 1986–94: high, low, and median per pupil combined state and local expenditures.
(K12 districts only. All values weighted for district enrollment and expressed in constant 1994 dollars. Data source: North Carolina Department of Education, April 1997.)

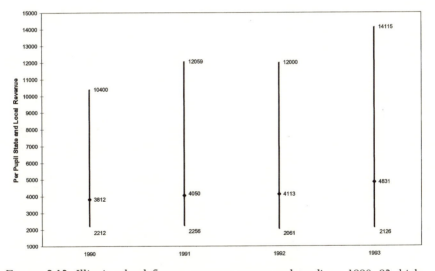

FIGURE 2.13. Illinois school finance revenue ranges and medians, 1990–93: high, low, and median per pupil combined state and local revenues.
(K12 districts only. All values weighted for district enrollment and calculated with constant 1993 dollars. Data source: National Center for Education Statistics, Common Core of Data CD-ROM, October 1996 edition.)

and expenditure figures for these three states show significant increases, but at somewhat smaller rates of growth than the five states where state supreme courts have ordered the state legislatures to redesign the school finance system.[28]

More dramatic differences, however, can be seen in Figures 2.14 through 2.16, which show the changes in the level of equality. In Oklahoma, five years after the state supreme court ruling declaring the school finance system constitutionally acceptable, inequality was 13.6 percent *worse* — a Gini index shift from 0.066 to 0.075. In North Carolina, the level of inequality was basically flat, seeing a slight worsening of inequality within two years after the decision, but virtually identical inequality within five years. In Illinois, the level of inequality from the filing of the lawsuit to one year after the district court decision was 19 percent worse, jumping from 0.079 among K12 school districts to 0.094. In total, these three states saw on average a 9.2 percent decline in the level of equality. In all three cases, equality was either worse or the same after the court decision.

Taken together, these two groups of states show a significant and meaningful effect of judicial involvement on school finance reform. The range and the Gini coefficient across these states and years give us a fairly good picture of the changes in the distribution of educational resources in the

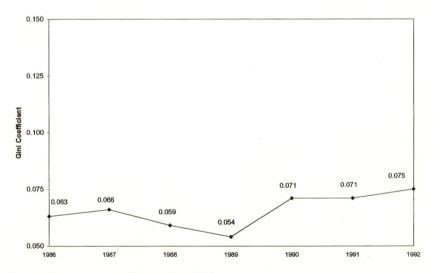

FIGURE 2.14. Gini coefficient for Oklahoma school districts, 1986–92: per pupil combined state and local revenues.
(K12 districts with enrollment greater than 100 students. All values weighted for district enrollment and calculated using 1992 dollars. Data source: Oklahoma Department of Education, Annual Reports, 1985–86 to 1991–1992.)

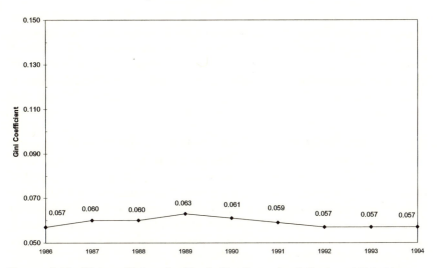

FIGURE 2.15. Gini coefficient for North Carolina school districts, 1986–94: combined state and local expenditures only.
(K12 districts only. All values weighted for district enrollment and calculated using constant 1994 dollars. Data source: North Carolina Department of Education, April 1997.)

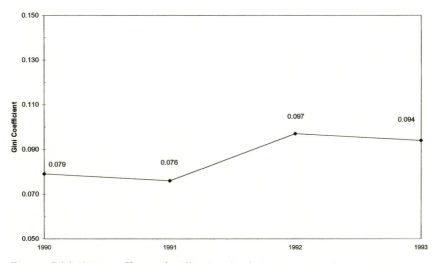

FIGURE 2.16. Gini coefficient for Illinois school districts, 1990–93: per pupil combined state and local revenues.
(K12 districts only. All values weighted for district enrollment and calculated using constant 1993 dollars. Data source: National Center for Education Statistics, Common Core of Data CD-ROM, October 1996 edition.)

wake of these state supreme court decisions. We see that improvements in equality typically follow state supreme court decisions that order improvements in equality, and that little change or worsening inequality follows from decisions upholding the existing school finance systems — even in states that face roughly comparable forms of poverty and exhibit similar political cultures.

The Research of Other Scholars on the Impact of School Finance Cases

Based on this evidence, then, it would seem that a meaningful relationship exists between judicial intervention and changes in the revenues available to school districts. But what have other scholars found? Is there any consensus on the impacts of these decisions? A review of the limited studies that have been conducted in the field show that other research confirms the basic findings presented here. Murray, Evans, and Schwab's (1998) examination of changes in school financing between 1971 and 1996 found that court reforms reduced within-state inequality by 19 to 34 percent, depending on the measure of inequality used. Because the data used in Murray et al.'s study are collected by the U.S. Census Bureau every five years, they do not register the yearly fluctuations that this analysis does. Nonetheless, the Murray study has the singular virtue of including all fifty states within its analysis. Despite these differences in data collection and analysis, both Murray et al.'s and my analysis come to remarkably similar conclusions: Courts *have* been effective at directing additional revenues to low-wealth school districts, without substantially reducing resources to high-wealth districts. As Murray et al. write: "Our estimates suggest that court-ordered reform raises spending in the poorest districts by 11 percent, raises spending in the median district by 8 percent, and leaves spending in the wealthiest districts unchanged" (1998, 804).

Other studies also come to similar conclusions. In a recent Ph.D. dissertation, Marci Kanstoroom uses a sophisticated statistical technique to explore the economic and political dimensions of funding reform in states where courts have struck down the existing school financing systems. Analyzing all fifty states and controlling for the effects of such factors as Democratic party control, per capita income, and private school enrollment, she concludes that state supreme court decisions do have a meaningful effect on equity in school financing, producing, on average, a 14 percent decline in expenditure inequality (Kanstoroom 1998, 125).

Some scholars, of course, raise objections. Michael Heise, for example, disputes the notion that court decisions have forced states to pick up a greater share of total educational expenditures or that aggregate educational spending has increased in the wake of equity decisions. At best, he contends, the record is mixed.[29] Heise's data, however, raise some concerns about his conclusions. His use of state-level data could fail to register aid that is directed to property-poor districts. It may be that a state's overall share of educational expenditures remains fixed, while property-poor districts receive a larger share of state aid and affluent districts receive less. If equity suits are working as their plaintiffs hope, then additional state monies are being channeled to property-poor districts and not to property-rich ones. Relying on aggregate data could potentially obscure the changes in that intrastate distribution. Thus, Heise's state-level data and analysis could be overlooking the dramatic effects that this study, and others, are clearly registering.

Conclusion

In sum, a number of studies clearly support the notion that courts can effectively change how money is distributed to schools. Winning court decisions matters largely because courts can and do change the distribution of educational dollars. This conclusion is important because it shows that courts can direct more money to the education of children who would not otherwise receive those resources, and, importantly, that those financial changes are meaningful and durable. With this conclusion, a new puzzle emerges: Why are courts effective in the realm of school finance, but apparently less effective in school desegregation? What accounts for this apparent judicial success story? In the next chapter I place the impact of the school finance cases in the context of the school desegregation cases of earlier years. This comparison will begin a discussion that will be with us for the remainder of this book: How does class differ from race within the realm of educational opportunity? Can courts redress class-based disadvantages more or less effectively than they can reach race-based denials of educational opportunity? Is race "harder" than class? And does the confluence of poverty among racial minorities fundamentally challenge the American sentiment favoring equal educational opportunity?

3

RACE, CLASS, AND THE LIMITS OF JUSTICE

A S WE BEGIN TO THINK about why courts have enjoyed success in changing the distribution of educational resources, it may be useful to consider some of the disagreeable features of these cases, those things that render them only qualified successes for even the most ardent egalitarian. The first fact that leaps out is that school finance litigation is nearly endless. The lawsuits themselves are protracted, the legislative efforts to provide remedies are often stymied, and as a result, years, even decades, may pass before additional resources are delivered to schools in need. It is not uncommon to learn that a child who at age eight or nine was a plaintiff in a school finance case has graduated from high school before a final resolution of her or his claims. Second, the end results in these cases often please no one. Parents in affluent (and not-so-affluent districts) are unhappy about possibly higher taxes and reduced services at schools, judges are tired of overseeing complex litigation, plaintiffs feel their fundamental claims have not been addressed, and legislators fear the punishment of the voters who are receiving less but paying more. Third, the courts' efforts to redress inequality in educational resources touch only one facet of broader inequities in American life. The growing gap between high- and low-income households and the shrinking number of social spaces in which money is irrelevant both illustrate our society's increasing tolerance for class inequality.

All this points to the keen difficulties confronting courts that seek to address either inadequate or unequal levels of educational resources. Perhaps we should not be asking why some courts are more successful than others, but why *any* court is successful, given these daunting obstacles. Barriers to judicial reform are not unique, however, to school finance litigation. Prison reforms, housing lawsuits, and, especially, school desegregation all have witnessed, at times, glacial progress. This chapter seeks to understand both the opportunities and limitations of court-ordered reform by exploring the obstacles facing federal courts as they seek to desegregate public education and then contrasting those limitations with state court initiatives to reduce financial disparities in public schooling. This investigation will hinge on the differences between race and class cleavages in American politics and demonstrate that these two forms of inequality create different political dynamics that courts must acknowledge.

Some Lessons from School Desegregation

The year 2004 is the fiftieth anniversary of *Brown v. Board of Education*. Few Supreme Court decisions hold social and cultural relevance for nearly half a century, but *Brown* clearly has. Its continuing significance to American life stems, in no small part, from its sharp moral clarity, but we return almost ritualistically to *Brown's* message for another reason as well: its demonstrated inadequacies and inabilities to resolve fully the problem of educational segregation. While it is undoubtedly unfair and perhaps irresponsible to expect a single court decision to redress 250 years of racial subordination, none other than Thurgood Marshall told a *New York Times* reporter shortly after the *Brown* decision that "by the time the 100th anniversary of the Emancipation Proclamation was observed in 1963, segregation in all its forms would have been eliminated from the nation" (quoted in Rosenberg 1991, 43). While such enthusiasm is understandable coming from a man who had just spent nearly twenty years on a legal crusade to end segregation, we should perhaps cast a more gimlet eye on the situation. Segregation, obviously, still exists; *Brown* could not cure the nation's racial ills. But is that the fault of *Brown*? Surely schools are not as segregated now as they were before *Brown* and the integration struggles of the 1960s and 1970s?

The answer to that simple question is complex. In some parts of the country, especially the Deep South, segregation is *far* less extensive than it was in the 1960s, but it has recently increased. The percentage of black children attending majority-white schools in the South jumped from 2.3 percent in 1964 to 36.4 percent in 1972. In a mere eight years, the South saw the initial promise of *Brown* partly realized. The percentage of African American students attending majority-white schools in the South peaked in 1988 at 43.5 percent, but has since declined to around 35 percent (Orfield and Yun 1999, 13).

In contrast, segregation in the Northeast has increased substantially over the same time period. For example, in 1970 the typical black student in Connecticut attended a school that was 44 percent white. By 1996 the typical black student attended a school that was only 34 percent white. In New Jersey, that same percentage dropped from 32.4 percent white to 25.2 percent (Orfield and Yun 1999, 22). Similar patterns are found in Rhode Island and New York. Consequently, those regions that used to be among the least segregated are now among the most. Today, black students in the Northeast and the Midwest, particularly Michigan and Illinois, face substantially greater segregation than black students in the South and West. By two separate measures, New York, Michigan, and Illinois run the three most segregated school systems in the country (Orfield and Yun 1999, 23).

Part of this change is due to a declining percentage of white students

within the public school system as a whole (due to immigration and changing demographics of the nation), but much is due to the changing nature of
segregation in our nation's schools. We have a different kind of separation
today than we did forty years ago. As Charles Clotfelter has written, most of
the nation's segregation today "is due to racial disparities between districts
rather than segregative patterns *within* districts" (Clotfelter 1999b, 502). The
significance of this finding should not be understated because it highlights
the ways that our nation's program of desegregating schools has failed. With
segregation increasingly the result of students being concentrated by race in
separate school districts, the only meaningful remedy is movement across
district lines. As Steven Rivkin notes, "even comprehensive district desegregation plans will do little to increase the enrollment of Whites in predominantly Black schools if few of the district's students are White" (Rivkin
1994, 285). He concludes that "only the movement of students across district boundaries, either through interdistrict integration programs or changes
in housing patterns can significantly reduce the racial isolation of Black
students."

Yet the Supreme Court, as we learned in chapter 1, prevented precisely
that kind of school desegregation remedy in *Milliken v. Bradley* in 1974. In
effect, the continuing problems of public school segregation in our country
are not due, directly, to the failings of *Brown*, but to the success of *Milliken*.
By exempting entire districts from involvement in school desegregation remedies, the Supreme Court created islands of immunity that relied on residential and class segregation to achieve what was no longer possible within
school districts. It is no surprise, then, that school segregation is increasing
at greater rates in those areas (i.e., the Northeast and Midwest) that have
fragmented jurisdictions and multiple school districts within metropolitan
areas. That fragmentation maximizes the likelihood that white parents can
isolate their children from minority students. Chief Justice Warren Burger
contended in *Milliken* that the local autonomy of school districts preserved
important values in public education:

> No single tradition in public education is more deeply rooted than local control
> over the operation of schools; local autonomy has long been thought essential
> both to the maintenance of community concern and support for public schools
> and to quality of the educational process. . . . Thus, in *San Antonio School
> District v. Rodriguez* . . . we observed that local control over the educational
> process affords citizens an opportunity to participate in decisionmaking, permits
> the structuring of school programs to fit local needs, and encourages "experi-
> mentation, innovation, and a healthy competition for educational excellence."[1]

Unfortunately, the subsequent history of Detroit and other major metropolitan school districts shows that racial homogeneity is a by-product, if not
an implicit goal, of an educational system premised on local control. By

elevating local control to an important constitutional value, the Supreme Court truncated the reach of *Brown* and trimmed the capacity of the federal judiciary to effect meaningful racial desegregation. If there is a legal bogeyman in the judicial quest for greater racial equality in public education, it is *Milliken*.

It is important to note that persistent white flight is not merely a product of the 1970s integration struggles; it continues today. As Charles Clotfelter amply illustrates, white flight "was still at work in the 1990s" (Clotfelter 1999a, 25). Clotfelter's analysis of every public school in 238 U.S. metropolitan areas shows that white enrollments are typically steady until the interracial exposure rates reach about 0.25, or until 25 percent of the students within a district are nonwhite. Moreover, the ability to flee to a neighboring, whiter district accelerates white flight. As he writes, the white enrollment trends over the 1990s "were influenced both by the 'push' of interracial contact and the 'pull' of nearby whiter school districts" (Clotfelter 1999a, 18).

A puzzling question remains, however: Why do white parents feel a need to isolate their children from black, Hispanic, and Asian children? The perceived need for this isolation is even more striking when we consider the level of support that whites express for the *notion* of integrated education. According to numerous surveys, white Americans have never been more supportive of desegregated education. For example, Christine Rossell has shown that the percentage of whites voicing support for the principle of integration in national surveys increased from roughly 50 percent at the time of *Brown v. Board of Education* to 93 percent in 1985 and has more or less stayed at that level. Indeed, she writes, "One could easily believe that only the lunatic fringe — about 6 percent of the white population — is opposed to the principle of school integration" (Rossell 1998, 123). Yet when white school children are actually exposed to nonwhite school children, and their parents are presented with an easy exit option to a nearby whiter school district, the devotion to those principles of integration wanes considerably.

What explains this conundrum? While it is not possible to reach a definitive answer here, we can review some possible factors that may be at work. First, it is quite possible that white flight occurs because of white racism, albeit cast in a different form. A number of studies show that white opposition to busing is not based on the possible harms one (or one's children) may suffer under a busing plan, but by the symbolic meaning of busing.[2] Those who engage in symbolic racism, rather than overt prejudice, insist that some of the political demands made by minorities threaten traditional American values. The result, according to David O. Sears is "a blend of anti-black affect and the kind of traditional American moral values embodied in the Protestant Ethic" yielding a "resistance to change in the racial status quo based on moral feelings that blacks violate such traditional American values as individualism and self-reliance, the work ethic, obedience, and discipline" (Sears 1981, 416). The logic of symbolic racism connects black claims for governmental protection or support with attacks on the values of individual self-reliance and self-discipline. Similarly, white parents may perceive a shift in the educational values promoted within schools as the percentage of nonwhite students increases, a shift that threatens their own educational values. These struggles over values could be proxies for racialized conflict and may then induce greater white flight from desegregated schools, especially as whites see themselves less likely to win those contests. White parents may not see their child necessarily harmed educationally by attending schools with nonwhites, but they may fear that their preferred educational values will be sacrificed in an integrated setting. In short, symbolic racism's perception of black claims as damaging to core American (and possibly educational) virtues could account for the disjuncture between the attitudes of white parents and their actions.

Another possible explanation is that white parents feel that their children are receiving inferior educations in an integrated setting. Richard Pride's study of public perceptions of school performance in Nashville highlights a connection between integrated schools and perceived academic decline — even in the face of academic improvement. Reading test scores for Nashville–Davidson County from 1971 to 1993 show that "on average in Nashville both black and white children learned more rather than less with busing for racial balance in place" (Pride 2000, 209). While this finding does not indicate that busing produced higher test scores, it does show that busing did not necessarily produce a worse education in Nashville. Pride then went on to examine why respondents opposed busing, and most survey respondents contended, despite the documented increase in Nashville's educational performance, that busing had either decreased or had no effect on the educational achievement of both black and white youngsters. Indeed, beside the respondent's race, the most significant predictors of opposition to busing in Nashville were the perceptions that busing had harmed either black or white academic performance (Pride 2000, 218–19). Clearly, busing is seen as a threat to educational performance even when the demonstrated effects on test scores indicate otherwise.

The perception that education is threatened by integration may have emerged out of early social science studies that showed desegregation had little effect on academic achievement of African Americans. The 1966 Coleman Report, officially titled *Equality of Educational Opportunity* and commissioned by the U.S. Department of Education, found that school settings had little to do with the educational attainment of students. Instead, student family backgrounds and socioeconomic status were the best predictors of academic success (Coleman et al. 1966). In terms of the integration struggle, one implication of the Coleman Report was that integration, by itself, did not produce higher academic achievement in the short run. The benefits that accrued to black students attending predominantly white schools stemmed from their association with students who had higher family incomes, not from the fact that their fellow students were white. Since then, however, there have been numerous studies showing the long-term effects of school desegregation on the career opportunities, earnings, college achievement, and social networks of black students (Braddock and Dawkins 1981, Crain 1970, Crain and Mahard 1983, Schofield 1989, Trent 1997, Wells 1996, Wells and Crain 1994). This conclusion was also drawn by a comprehensive meta-analysis of studies of black students' achievement commissioned by the National Institute of Education in 1984 (Cook et al. 1984). In addition, more recent studies indicate that although socioeconomic status is the best predictor of test scores, higher concentrations of minority students in a school produces, independent of socioeconomic status, worse educational achievement, particularly in elementary school (Bankston and Caldas 1996, Bankston and Caldas 1997, Caldas and Bankston 1998, Entwisle and Alexander 1992). Combining the long-term benefits of desegregation with recent evidence about the persistent negative effects of segregation on academic achievement, the picture becomes increasingly clear: desegregation improves educational outcomes for minority students. There is also little evidence that desegregation lowers test scores of whites (Entwisle and Alexander 1992, Schofield 1989, ix).

So why the persistent perception among whites that desegregated schools produce worse educations for their children? Two possible answers emerge, one distressing, the other perhaps less so. The first answer returns to the theme of racism. We know that many parents choose schools for reasons other than academic performance. Two separate studies of private school enrollment that took into account public school academic performance in Florida and Texas (Smith and Meier 1995, Wrinkle et al. 1999) come to virtually the same conclusion:

> Poorly performing public schools are not a determinant of private school enrollment. The record of public schools has virtually no impact on the dependent variable. . . . Catholic population and the percent of public school enrollment that is black, however, are significant predictors. The results suggest that people are not buying quality education from private schools. They are instead purchasing religious services and racial segregation. (Smith and Meier 1995, 470–71)

Another study of private school choice in upstate New York that controlled for such school characteristics as funding levels and teacher qualifications came to the conclusion that "the extent to which white and minority students differ in their propensity to attend a particular school largely depends upon the racial composition of the school" (Lankford and Wyckoff 2000, 13). The pull of racially (and possibly religiously) homogeneous educational environments appears to be very powerful for whites who are currently sending their children to school with minority students. Even the same or stronger academic performance within schools that have significant minority enrollments cannot overcome that attraction. From this perspective, the excuse that integrated schools lead to worse educations appears to be only that, an excuse for racism.

On the other hand, we should not ignore the fact that black suburbanization has been increasing (Farley and Frey 1994) and that blacks are also fleeing central-city schools. This suggests a possibly more hopeful explanation of the nature of flight — both black and white — from central cities. The primary finding of the Coleman Report highlighted the family background and class differentials in educational attainment. These are not surprising and they have held up in numerous studies. Simultaneously, central cities have faced an increasing concentration of poverty as jobs and residents have left. As a result, the peers of urban middle-class students are poorer than they were a generation ago, and parents, being parents, perceive rather strongly the peer effects of increasing poverty on their children. To the extent that remaining in an urban school district means associating one's child with poorer children, middle-class parents — of all races — may seek alternatives, either flight to neighboring suburbs or private schools. In this sense, urban flight may, in some respects, be a flight from poverty and a desire to rub one's child's shoulders with the shoulders of more affluent children. Indeed, one study of magnet schools contended that one magnet school appealed to "many middle-class and ambitious working-class parents [who] sought a school where their children would be with the children of the highest social class and achievement level possible" (Metz 1986, 208). While social climbing may not itself be attractive, as a possible explanation for continued white flight it certainly has greater normative appeal than outright racism.[3]

No matter what its cause, white flight has not gone unnoticed by the federal courts, which appear to have lost any appetite for busing programs. Since 1981 federal courts have ordered compulsory student reassignment plans only twice, both in rural Mississippi (Rossell 1998, 122). Instead, courts have pursued voluntary or "controlled choice" plans to remedy school segregation. And over the course of the 1990s, legal developments have made it far less likely that courts will reverse their trend. Since the early 1990s the U.S. Supreme Court has made it easier for school districts to end their busing programs or to eliminate other programs designed to foster racial mixing, such as magnet schools and "controlled choice."[4] In addition, educators, politicians, and parents have renewed their calls for neighborhood schools — often for a variety of nonracial reasons, including transportation costs, a desire for greater parental involvement, or even simple convenience.

These educational changes take place, however, in a context of segregated housing markets and will necessarily result in greater segregation. Because Americans typically do not live in integrated neighborhoods, our educational institutions will be segregated to the extent that they reflect our housing patterns.[5] Municipal and school district boundaries function rather effectively as racial and economic sorting mechanisms, and abandoning efforts to overcome those sorting processes necessarily yields greater school segregation.[6] Yet in its most recent decisions, the Supreme Court has declared that school authorities are not responsible for addressing these informal processes of segregation.[7] Rather than remedying the varied causes of current housing and educational racial segregation — built, clearly, through a blend of both private and public action — the federal courts are increasingly inclined to ignore plaintiff claims that official state action has harmed them. As an attorney for the American Civil Liberties Union has noted, "In my view, the principal explanation for the change in judicial attitudes toward school desegregation cases in the last few years is simple exhaustion. Courts . . . are simply giving up" (Hansen 1993).

The project of school desegregation, begun by the Supreme Court in *Brown* and carried on by federal district courts through busing programs and other remedies, is largely moribund today. School reforms currently being touted and enacted, such as school vouchers and school choice, will, most likely, lead to even greater segregation than what currently exists. But it is important to remember the underlying causes of today's segregation: the physical separation of white and minority students into separate districts. The older segregation of the pre-*Brown* days took place within districts. With *Milliken* and the values of local control still firmly in place, remedying our current situation will take an energetic effort to change residential segregation, something far beyond what the Supreme Court envisioned when it ruled in favor of Linda Brown and her coplaintiffs.

Is School Finance Reform Different?

These experiences with court-ordered school integration should give us pause as we begin to contemplate judicial intervention into the financing of public schools. To the extent that court involvement in school integration has not fully achieved its primary aim, and to the extent that other court decisions like *Milliken* made that aim more difficult to achieve, we may want to consider closely whether judges should decide how money is raised and spent on our schools. Although, as an issue of justice, judicial intervention to overcome entrenched de jure and de facto segregation may have been necessary, as an issue of public policy, judges may have produced less-than-optimal results. It is necessary to ask, then, why would we expect anything different from school finance reform.

The Important Differences: How Court-Ordered School Finance Reform Is Different from Court-Ordered Integration

Despite the analogy made here between race and class, there are some important reasons to argue that the experience of pursuing equal educational opportunity through financing reform may be better, or at least different, than school desegregation.

A *single arena of reform*: An important difference is that school finance decisions aim at different targets. Because the right to an equitable or adequate education is a statewide right, the decision requires that the financing system for all school districts be rethought and redesigned.[8] This statewide reform effort, in contrast to the districtwide racial integration efforts, ensures that the legislative reforms apply more or less uniformly to all districts within a state. This does not mean that all districts will have the same funding levels, only that any similarly situated district will be eligible for the same amount of state aid. In contrast, school desegregation suits were filed only against those school districts with substantial numbers of segregated minority students, leaving out of the judicial framework the all-white districts that were in many cases adjoining suburbs of the central city schools undergoing integration. Thus, the patchwork of judicial decrees across school districts literally created spaces that were (relatively) immune from judicial intervention. This maximized the potential and lure of white flight. The school finance decisions differ significantly because the entire state is subject to the reforms, creating few incentives for parents to move away from their local district in the wake of reforms or to exit the public school system entirely.[9]

A *single agent of reform*: Similarly, the form of legal relief in the typical school finance decision ensures that one legislative body, not multiple school boards, must produce the reforms mandated by the court. If a state supreme court rules the existing scheme unconstitutional, it charges the state legislature with removing the constitutional deficiency from the educational system, but it generally does not impose the means. For example, the New Hampshire Supreme Court, after declaring that "in New Hampshire a free public education is at the very least an important, substantive right," insisted that the Court does not "define the parameters of the education mandated by the constitution as that task is, in the first instance, for the legislature and the Governor." The Court added, a few lines later, that "we are confident that the legislature and the Governor will fulfill their responsibility with respect to defining the specifics of, and the appropriate means to provide through public education, the knowledge and learning essential to the preservation of a free government"[10] Having plopped this issue squarely in the laps of the state legislators, it was clear who was responsible for developing a comprehensive, statewide response to the decision. The typical decision also generally establishes a timetable for introducing a remedy, but does not indicate what will happen if that timetable is not met. The result is that a single body of lawmakers is responsible for assuring that the declared constitutional rights are respected within a relatively clear timetable.

The exit option is less visible and less viable: In part because there is both a single arena of reform and a single agent of reform, individuals living through the changes have decreased opportunity to flee the reform process. Because of the statewide nature of reforms, parents only have two ways to avoid the court-ordered changes: move out of the state or enroll their children in private schools. While relocating may be feasible in some metropolitan areas in which multiple states abut (like the New York, New Jersey, and Connecticut area), it nonetheless presents a very significant disruption of one's life for a rather vague payoff. In short, the transaction costs are too high for too diffuse a benefit. Unlike school integration, in which a short move across a district line could insulate a white family from attending schools with blacks, school finance reform presents no clear exit option, other than private school attendance. While that may be a possibility for some families, it also is beyond the financial reach of many residents. Moreover, in many places the private schooling infrastructure simply cannot accommodate a mass exodus from public schools. In sum, changes in school financing simply do not present the same opportunity or incentives for flight as school integration did.

Money changes everything: Jesse Unruh, the powerful speaker of the California Assembly in the 1960s, is credited with the expression, "Money is the mother's milk of politics."[11] In many ways, the school financing controversies of the 1990s prove him right. Educational revenues and their distribution are the central conflicts facing state legislatures in court-ordered school finance reforms. In short, cash must be spread around. That creates both obstacles and opportunities that do not exist within school desegregation conflicts. Because money is both fungible and divisible, it facilitates compromises that are simply not possible within the realm of race relations. It is far easier to compensate an affluent community for lost educational revenues while giving that money to a property-poor district than to appease white supremacists while integrating schoolyards. Money is liquid and can be redirected; it allows for politics to proceed. Moreover, halfway measures are far more likely in policy problems that are denominated in dollars rather than skin color. Although racial tokenism certainly marked the first twenty years of integration efforts, once large-scale school busing was approved by the U.S. Supreme Court, halfway measures were no longer viable options for many cities, particularly those in the South. In contrast, disputes about money will always be amenable to compromise, especially since annual or biannual budget allocations create regularized opportunities to reconfigure the distribution. The possibilities of tinkering are endless. And while that could create incentives for affluent districts to seek to undo changes that harmed them, it also creates opportunities to phase in substantial redistributions over time, thus linking school finance reform to another hallowed tradition within American politics: incrementalism. In short, the fact that school financing inequalities are about the distribution of money translates the policy dilemma into something that legislatures are accustomed to dealing with and are relatively good at. The problem for courts within this setting, however, is to ensure that changes are durable and not a thin coat of financial paint over widening chasms of distributional inequalities within school finance.

State courts are different institutions from federal courts and state constitutions are different from the federal constitution: The institutional forum of reforms matters. In the school integration suits of the 1960s and 1970s, opponents of busing (and integration in general) blasted federal judges as "outsiders," responsible to the federal judicial hierarchy and not in touch with local needs and sentiments. Of course, those "local needs" produced massively unequal and segregated educations, but the criticism that outside interests were meddling in local schools was an effective rhetorical tool for building resentment and hostility toward any desegregation effort. In contrast, state judges are typically seen as much more in tune with the political environment and political possibilities within a state. As a result, both state lawmakers and the public often view state court interventions in school finance as the result of real problems within a state's educational system. Typically, lawmakers will regret that the policy problem has been "legalized," but they will not deny the existence of the problem or attribute the judicial decision to the meddling of "outside interests." This is perhaps most sharply revealed by the fact that despite intense and vociferous fights, no state has amended its state constitution to allow for greater inequalities or inadequacies in the wake of a state supreme court decision or stripped the state judiciary of its jurisdiction over school financing. Moreover, the fact that state supreme court justices are popularly elected in many states potentially allows for the venting of democratic steam if public opposition to the reform mandate is too intense. Surprisingly, though, state supreme court justices are rarely punished by voters for their stances on school financing cases.[12] In contrast, state legislators are frequently taken to task by voters for either raising taxes to generate sufficient revenues for the reforms or reducing state aid to affluent districts. In short, state supreme courts are not seen as the cause of the policy dilemma, but simply as the messenger of the constitutional infirmities of the system, infirmities that policy-makers and citizens readily acknowledge.

Once designed, reforms are easier to administer: Despite all the public wrangling over school finance reform, the truth is that the policies necessary to achieve the court's mandate are not technically difficult. In many respects, school finance reform is simply a matter of bookkeeping and billing. It is an administratively easy task to accomplish, even though politically it may be exceptionally difficult. The complicating aspects of school finance reforms emerge when lawmakers introduce elements into the financing formulas in order to anchor support among constituents, appease various interests, surmount the political obstacles to reform, or delay the costs of compliance. But once that political solution is arrived at, the state's administrative machinery can, relatively easily, collect the taxes, determine each district's aid eligibility, and write the checks. In contrast, school integration often became *more* difficult to administer after the plan was adopted. Public protests, white flight, violent confrontations within schools, and continued harassment of minority students all required continuing investment of administrative overhead and surveillance of reforms.

In sum, while I have tried to show the analogies between judicial interventions into racial and class disparities within educational opportunities, the fact remains that class is different from race and that the policy tools available to legislatures to remedy class inequities are different from those available to redress racial injustice. There is, then, at least the hope that state supreme court interventions into public school finance will not produce the same set of unanticipated and unwanted consequences that school desegregation lawsuits did. To be sure, these interventions into class inequalities in educational opportunity will produce their own set of unanticipated consequences — perhaps just as dire — but we can say with some confidence that they will at least be different. The two issues present distinct policy contexts and they will be resolved by distinct policy solutions.[13]

The Sobering Similarities: How Court-Ordered School Finance Reform Is the Same

We can, then, make some meaningful distinctions between the two forms of judicial intervention on behalf of educational opportunity. They are not the same problem and they do not present identical policy features. That said, however, inequalities in American life build on one another. At a certain point, the origins of power inequities, whether race based or class based, become irrelevant and all one knows is that one has little power and the cause of that inequality does not really matter. Consider the inequalities a schoolchild suffers for being poor and black in an inner city. Is she getting a lousy education because she is black? Is it because her entire community is black? Is it because she is poor? Is it because all the families around her are poor? Is it because the property values in her community are low? All of these factors merge into a complex regime of inequality that fuses individual and collective racial and class disparities.

Like segregation, class-based inequalities in educational opportunity are linked to broader hierarchies of power: Segregation in the South, prior to *Brown*, did more than classify and assign students according to race. Segregation was the cornerstone of a racial hierarchy that organized the political, social, economic, and ideological life of the South and, indirectly, the nation. Southern whites resisted the dismantling of segregation so strongly because it was both the manifestation and mechanism of dominance in the region. Without segregation, Southern whites could not be assured of their economic and political standing; the threat that integration posed to their power could not go unresisted. The point here is that an organized system of power controlled and regulated the life options of blacks. Similarly, another organized system of power, while not nearly as oppressive or dominant, regulates class inequalities within educational financing. That structural or institutional organization of class inequalities within educational opportunity is premised on four factors: (1) the funding of public education through local property taxes; (2) the preservation of home rule among local school districts; (3) the economic stratification of housing markets, often according to municipal geopolitical boundaries; (4) the political influence of interests who benefit from the preceding three factors. Together, these institutional and economic factors structure the revenues that a school district has at its disposal, and, by extension, they define the educational opportunities available to a public school child within that system. This institutional arrangement about how schools are financed then proceeds to confer other, additional advantages and liabilities on the actors within the regime. And, like the pre-*Brown* South, the winners within that system seek its preservation and enhancement in order to assure that their children will benefit from the inequities of the regime. Within a class framework, all this is cast as the normal trajectory of upward mobility: members of the middle class seeking advancement move to good neighborhoods in good towns with good schools, so their kids have a better shot at a good college. It is, in many ways, the American Dream, but it is also a regime of inequality that is premised upon a few simple principles of tax and educational autonomy for school districts that are economically stratified by jurisdictional boundaries. The result is segregated educational resources. And when a judiciary espousing ideas of equality, noble as they may be, threatens that nexus between good towns with good schools, these affluent communities have sophisticated political skills to use in their defense. The result is a kind of geopolitical regime that like de facto school segregation is exceptionally difficult to overcome because it is generally accepted as a necessary element of state and local politics. In short, this regime structure and the easy American acceptance of its normative implications present courts with their most formidable obstacle in the reorganization of educational financing.

Substantial public agreement on the goal, but not the methods of providing equal opportunity: At the same time that we see inequality organized by institutional forces, we see, on an individual level, substantial agreement with the principle of equal educational opportunity. As we will explore in more depth in chapter 6, the public at large generally supports the notion of financing education equitably. Typically, over 70 percent of respondents in state-level polls support equal educational opportunity. This figure in many ways corresponds with current public support for sending one's child to an integrated school, and they may also belie to a similar extent the very real opposition to equal educational opportunity when it threatens one or more aspects of the local, home-rule regime. Indeed, as we will see, support for equality drops substantially when it comes into conflict with local autonomy for public education. The linkage here between race and class inequality lies in our tremendous support for the principle, but our profound reluctance to adopt the means necessary to achieve that principle.

Conclusion

Whatever their differences and similarities, court-ordered school financing reforms and court-ordered school integration are eclipsed by a larger context: Both sets of cases are important episodes in the American struggle over the definition of equality. Over the past half-century, our public debates and political fights over the meaning of equality — whether concerned with race or class — have been sustained by and rooted in a rich legal and constitutional idiom. The expansive quality of equal protection under the Fourteenth Amendment and social movements' reliance on constitutional litigation to pursue equality have given courts in the United States a central role in the production of equality's meaning. For the remainder of this book, I explore in greater depth various facets of that production of meaning. Because these forms of meaning emerge out of a legal context, they are, in some ways, stamped with the institutional and jurisprudential commitments of courts, but they also intersect with prevailing normative visions and institutional forms of equality and equal opportunity. By examining how these rulings intersect and interact with other forces in American political life, we can simultaneously arrive at a richer understanding of the constitutional commitments we hold, and locate equality's place among those commitments.

PART II

THE CONSTITUTIONAL ORDERING OF

EDUCATIONAL OPPORTUNITY

4

HOW DOES A CONSTITUTION MEAN?

CONSTITUTIONAL ORDERING AND THE LESSONS

OF EDUCATIONAL OPPORTUNITY

COUNTING DOLLARS, counting districts, counting school-children. That, plus a little division and adjusting for inflation, is what chapter 2 did, in more or less fancy ways. In that chapter, we traced the effects of state supreme court rulings concerning educational opportunity through a careful counting and tallying of resources. The simple story was, of course, that state supreme courts matter. They can and do redistribute resources, directing additional dollars to poorer school districts in the wake of their rulings. But that story is far too simple, too linear, too narrow to encompass the full range of political meanings these decisions represent. As with any complex story, the story of equal educational opportunity has more characters and more plots than first meet the eye. True, the financial impact of school finance decisions on the poor school districts around the country is an important part of our story, but by no means the only part. In order to appreciate fully the lessons of these educational opportunity decisions, we need to explore other facets of the cases and the politics they generate. For the purposes of this book, perhaps the most central aspect of these decisions is that they are, in different and various ways, *constitutional* decisions.

This chapter will explore the implications of that fact. What does it mean for a school finance decision to be based on a constitution? In what ways does that constitutional status affect the course and trajectory of the responses to the decision, in both a political and a policy sense? And how does it matter that these are state constitutions we are expounding, to borrow a phrase from Chief Justice John Marshall? To what extent are our constitutional meanings bound by the texts and to what extent are they defined outside those texts, by our own political imaginations, by our normative commitments, or by the existing institutional and economic contexts? In short, I want to explore in this chapter *how* a constitution means in the context of class-based equal educational opportunity.

Traditional scholarship on constitutional meanings has focused almost exclusively on Supreme Court interpretations of the U.S. Constitution, but for this project, the conventional view cannot encompass the full range of constitutional meanings and politics present in these cases. Part of the insufficiency emerges from a growing recognition that the established scholarly view of constitutional law and politics is inadequate to our practical and historical experiences with constitutionalism. The notion of constitutionalism as consisting solely in textual interpretation by nine Supreme Court justices is becoming an increasingly untenable explanation of how constitutional law and politics play out in American life. Scholars such as Sanford Levinson, Wayne Moore, Mark Graber, Stephen Griffin, Keith Whittington, and Mark Tushnet show us that definitive and meaningful constitutional law can emerge and thrive either in tension with Supreme Court doctrines or in their absence.[1] The common thread of these accounts of nonjudicial forms of constitutional interpretation (or "construction," as Whittington terms it) is an unwillingness to cede to the Supreme Court the final authority to determine the Constitution's meanings. Instead, the meanings of the Constitution that have binding force as law often emerge not merely as Supreme Court decisions, but through political clashes and popular redefinitions of our Constitutional mandates. As Whittington writes, "Examination of political efforts to construct constitutional meaning reveals that the governing Constitution is a synthesis of legal doctrines, institutional practices, and political norms" (Whittington 1999, 3). Similarly, Moore contends that individual citizens, often through their constitutionally authorized forms of political participation, can endow the Constitution with new and binding meanings: "By interpreting and exercising these prerogatives [of political participation], individuals have also been able to create and reinforce unofficial constitutional norms that have been integral components of the law of the land" (Moore 1996, 54). In sum, this extrajudicial school of constitutional meaning-making understands the term "constitutional" in ways incomprehensible to Chief Justice John Marshall when he claimed the power of judicial review and strictly delineated the line between higher "constitutional" law and more pedestrian forms of lawmaking.[2]

Turning more directly to the constitutional status of education in American life, we confront even more objections to viewing constitutionalism strictly as a product of Supreme Court reasoning. There is no mention of public education in the U.S. Constitution, and until the mid-twentieth century, the federal government had no role in the provision of education. In early cases in which the Supreme Court defended the right to an education, it cast the issue in terms of protecting private education from public attack. In *Pierce v. Society of Sisters*, the Supreme Court struck down an Oregon initiative that required all children between the ages of eight and sixteen to attend only public schools. Justice James McReynolds argued that the law unreasonably interfered "with the liberty of parents and guardians to direct the upbringing and education of children under their control."[3] Thus the federal understanding of the right to education was defined in the early twentieth century not in terms of a governmental obligation to provide education, but in terms of familial autonomy from a state educational monopoly. *Brown v. Board of Education* later suggested that education may be a fundamental right, but in 1973 the Supreme Court rejected that line of reasoning and explicitly declared in *San Antonio Independent School District v. Rodriguez* that there is no fundamental right to education under the U.S. Constitution. So, the question remains: Is it possible to speak of a *constitutional* politics of education in the United States? It is easy to conceive of a distributional or interest-based politics of education, but that perspective does not produce the foundational claims necessary for a constitutional vision of education.

It is clear, then, that the traditional American framework of higher law constitutionalism, premised on judicial interpretative supremacy, lacks the conceptual apparatus to discuss education as a substantive right protected by the federal Constitution, akin to the right to vote or the right to an abortion. Instead, the most salient considerations under the national constitutional law of education are the limits on state programs of education. Both *Brown* and *Rodriguez* require that federal perspectives on the right to an education be filtered through the lens of state and local decisions to provide that education. It is important to remember that key phrase in *Brown*: Educational "opportunity, *where the state has undertaken to provide it*, is a right which must be made available to all on equal terms."[4] Thus, from the higher law perspective, education is not profoundly different from any other governmental service that states and localities provide. The limits of federalism, rather than any substantive individual right, are the Court's primary concern. The higher law tradition sets boundaries on states' educational policies, but has little to say about any substantive right to an education. To insist on an independent *constitutional* politics of education, we must look outside the parameters of the U.S. Constitution and its interpretation by the U.S. Supreme Court.

A much firmer basis for the constitutional politics of education can be built on the American state constitutions, which are the textual bases for any governmental obligation to provide public education. Forty-nine of fifty states have an education clause that specifies some required level of public education; many, in fact, declare public education to be a fundamental state right. These provisions, as I noted in chapter 1, have a broad range, but they are nonetheless more specific than any possible guarantee of education under the U.S. Constitution. Direct comparisons, however, can be misleading, and we should be careful before we simply insert state constitutional language into our claims about the constitutional nature of educational opportunity. State constitutions are far different beasts than the U.S. Constitution and operate in a kind of constitutional no-man's-land between statutory requirement and constitutional obligation.[5] Until the early 1970s, state constitutions were the neglected stepchild of American constitutional-ism, more likely to be a legal embarrassment than a respected source of higher law obligations. Then, at the close of the Warren Era, partly inspired by Supreme Court Justice William Brennan, many state supreme court judges began to interpret their own state constitutions as independent grounds for protecting individual rights.[6] The movement, dubbed the new judicial federalism, then expanded to include broader forms of constitu-tional litigation, such as the school finance cases. Until now, most analysts of the new judicial federalism and its protection of individual rights have treated state supreme courts and state constitutions as direct analogues to the U.S. Supreme Court and the U.S. Constitution. But partly because of the different contexts of constitutional interpretation at the state level and partly because of the reconceptualizations of American constitutionalism that authors like Levinson, Whittington, Griffin, and Moore have urged upon us, this direct transfer of interpretative frameworks from the national to the state constitutional contexts is not tenable.

The reasons for this are relatively straightforward. First, the interpretative project facing state supreme court judges is substantially different from that facing U.S. Supreme Court Justices. States are generally assumed to have plenary powers, and, as a result, state constitutions, unlike the U.S. Consti-tution, are often lists of prohibitions or enumerations of things that state governments cannot do (Tarr 1998, 6–9). Thus, unless specifically pre-vented from acting, state lawmakers enjoy an implicit authority to enact any variety of social policy. Within the policy domain of public education, the sometimes vague language of the education provisions in the state constitu-tions have led lawmakers, prior to these court decisions, to organize public education as they saw fit, without much constitutional reference. This legis-lative approach also comports with the highly localist organization of public education and generally translates into a judicial deference to the policy-making expertise of state lawmakers under a separation of powers doctrine. In addition, state constitutions are far more responsive to democratic major-ity sentiments than the U.S. Constitution, and state supreme court justices are, more often than not, either elected to office or subject to voter approval at the end of a fixed term. This electoral dimension can place profound constraints on a judge's willingness or ability to strike down the existing system of educational finance.

Given these differences, our first order of inquiry, then, is to understand how and in what sense these state supreme court interpretations of state constitutions are *constitutional*. This line of analysis is demanded, rather straightforwardly, by the nature of the interpreters and the nature of the texts themselves. While some may dismiss the state constitutional interpretations of education and equality provisions under state charters as nothing other than naked judicial policy-making, I contend there is a clear constitutional dimension to these decisions. It is revealed most clearly in judges' reliance on the popular constitutional meanings of *Brown* and their efforts to impose higher law obligations on their state citizenry in light of *Brown's* vision. State supreme court judges are not blind to the cultural significance of *Brown* and its redefinition of educational opportunity, and they themselves have relied on that constitutional understanding within their own decisions to spell out the constitutional obligations of state lawmakers and educational officials. While the legal doctrines of *Brown* and the school desegregation cases may not directly inform these decisions, the hope and promises of *Brown* do.

The constitutional meanings of the school finance cases are not confined, however, to the judicial interpretations that sustain them. The popular dimensions of these decisions help reveal the lived meaning of educational opportunity within the United States. The public reaction to these decisions, and the politics that flows from that reaction, enable us to see the relative importance of equal educational opportunity within American political values. The legislative and political fights over these decisions help define the constitutional meanings of educational opportunity, while simultaneously highlighting the foundational importance of educational opportunity to the communities and states involved. Clearly, one aspect of the constitutional meanings of these cases lies in the extent to which these court decisions on equal educational opportunity reflect and articulate the public's attitudes and beliefs. The gap between the judicial view and the public view may be wide or narrow, but the public dimension cannot be ignored if we are to fully encompass the range of constitutional meanings these cases present.

Lastly, these cases clearly present a challenge to the existing array of interests and resources within particular communities. Indeed, they seek to disrupt many of the political assumptions about public education and its organization. As a result, the organizational dimension of these cases is profoundly important to understanding their constitutional meanings. One aim of the following analysis is to understand how these decisions intersect with the existing arrays of power and resources that define the scope and boundaries of equal educational opportunity. To do so requires an examination of how these decisions target particular institutional arrangements that perpetuate and entrench existing inequalities in educational opportunity. Dismantling these systems of inequalities is, in some respects, the most ambitious goal of these decisions and their most difficult task. Understanding both their lines of attack and the responses of the institutions under attack is essential to understanding the constitutional politics of school finance reform.

Guided, then, by the absence of a substantive federal right to public education, by the distinctive nature of state constitutions, and by new conceptions of American constitutionalism, I want to explore three ways of thinking about *how* a constitution means: First, we can conceive of constitutional meaning as the product of judicial interpretation. Second, we can see how a constitution means by exploring it as a reflection of important normative commitments of the polity. And, finally, we can understand how a constitution means by envisioning it as a mechanism of designing institutions and organizing power and resources. Taken together, these three ways of understanding how a constitution means comprise the central features of what I call *constitutional ordering* — the definition, refinement, and articulation of texts, beliefs, and structures that organize power and resources for particular ends, in this case the ends of education and equality. Constitutional ordering assumes that judicial interpretation will be a central element of American constitutionalism, but by no means the only element. Instead, it seeks to explain how our normative commitments — expressed in public debates and through public opinion — fuse with questions of institutional design to produce a constitutional politics that incorporates judicial interpretations of constitutional texts into lived conflicts and debates over fundamental questions about our collective lives. Exploring the fights of educational opportunity through the framework of constitutional ordering enables us to see the democratic and institutional features of our constitutional conflicts, as well as their judicial roots.

How a Constitution Means:
Lessons from *Brown* and School Desegregation

This notion of constitutional ordering will be more clear if we can explore it in a more familiar, yet related, legal context. To flesh out these lines of inquiry, I want to assess some of the various meanings that *Brown v. Board of Education* holds within our political and judicial contexts. The multiple ways that legal and political actors (as well as lay citizens) use and rely upon *Brown* rest ultimately on differing ways of conceiving of the U.S. Constitution — and constitutionalism more generally. Those multiple meanings — and the richness of those meanings — highlight the interplay between judicial and extra-judicial constitutional interpretation. Because *Brown* clearly cannot be cabined to its location within the jurisprudence on racial equal protection, it is a very fruitful case with which to begin the inquiry suggested by the oddly phrased question of this chapter's title: "How does a constitution mean?"

First, let us locate the meaning of *Brown* within the U.S. Supreme Court's own understanding of its constitutional position. As a matter of judicial interpretation, the central doctrinal concern of *Brown* focused on the then-existing framework of "separate but equal." That understanding of the equal protection clause of the Fourteenth Amendment had constitutionalized Jim Crow laws and allowed an extensive system of compulsory legal segregation to thrive in the American South over the first fifty years of the twentieth century. Thus, the logic of *Plessy* had to be directly confronted if the Supreme Court was to begin unraveling the fabric of segregated education in the South. Thurgood Marshall and the Legal Defense Fund of the NAACP provided part of the needed framework for reversing *Plessy* through its litigation campaign on segregation in higher education and professional schools. By focusing on the effects of segregation, Marshall and his fellow attorneys at NAACP-LDF demonstrated how "separate but equal" educational institutions never could be made truly equal. The mere act of segregation rendered schools unequal. The Supreme Court pursued this line of logic in *Brown* by focusing, in part, on the effects of segregated education on schoolchildren. Segregated education, Chief Justice Warren wrote, generates within students "a feeling of inferiority as to their status in the community that may affect their hearts and minds in a way unlikely ever to be undone."[7] The Warren Court undid *Plessy* by rejecting its conclusion that the state did not intend to demean blacks or stamp them as inferior when it required the separation of blacks and whites in public facilities. In this sense, the constitutional meaning of *Brown* is that state action that generates an impermissible racial hierarchy in a lived sense cannot be constitutionally rationalized through the logic of "separate, but equal." Both the real disparities in education and the obvious intent of Southern majorities were all too apparent.

That understanding of the constitutional meaning of *Brown* has consequences, of course, for any effort by the state to take race into account as it formulates public policy. *Brown* implicitly established the categories of analysis for future decisions on race-conscious policy-making: state action, intent, and impact all must be considered as elements of equal protection of the laws. These categories of analysis emerged as the central features of racial equal protection jurisprudence in the second half of the twentieth century. Just as the *Plessy* era defined race relations through its formal construct of "separate but equal," the post-*Brown* jurisprudential era has translated claims about race-conscious policy-making into a tri-polar debate about (1) the definition of state action; (2) whether beneficial intent can salvage race-conscious decision making; and (3) whether impact alone can justify race-conscious policies. Through its implicit creation of these categories of analysis, *Brown* shifted the terrain of constitutional contestation within racial equal protection. Any future argument about race and the Constitution, within this vision of constitutional meaning, has to be waged within the framework of these three terms — at least until the next transformative ruling on racial equal protection.

Contrast that form of constitutional meaning of *Brown* with the meanings assigned to it by Rev. Martin Luther King Jr. and the authors of the Southern Manifesto. On the third anniversary of *Brown v. Board of Education*, King delivered a speech calling for voting rights legislation. He began that speech with the following:

> Three years ago the Supreme Court of this nation rendered in simple, eloquent and unequivocal language a decision which will long be stenciled on the mental sheets of succeeding generations. For all men of goodwill, this May 17th decision came as a joyous daybreak to end the long night of human captivity. It came as a great beacon light of hope to millions of disinherited people throughout the world who had dared only to dream of freedom.[8]

A little over a year earlier, a group of nineteen senators and eighty-one representatives from the South signed a document known as the "Southern Manifesto." Consider, in contrast, the meaning they assigned to *Brown*:

> This unwarranted exercise of power by the Court, contrary to the Constitution, is creating chaos and confusion in the states principally affected. It is destroying the amicable relations between the white and Negro races that have been created through ninety years of patient effort by the good people of both races. It has planted hatred and suspicion where there has been heretofore friendship and understanding. . . .
>
> With the gravest concern for the explosive and dangerous condition created by this decision and inflamed by outside meddlers:
>
> We reaffirm our reliance on the Constitution as the fundamental law of the land.
>
> We decry the Supreme Court's encroachments on rights reserved to the states and to the people, contrary to established law and to the Constitution.
>
> We commend the motives of those states which have declared the intention to resist forced integration by any lawful means. . . .
>
> We pledge ourselves to use all lawful means to bring about a reversal of this decision which is contrary to the Constitution and to prevent the use of force in its implementation.[9]

These understandings of *Brown* highlight profoundly different dimensions of the case. Tightly bound to individual ideological commitments and political identities, they are personalized "legal" interpretations that exist more or less independent of doctrine. The salience of *Brown* here emerges from its aspirational and transformative ambition, not its concern with *Plessy's* formulation of the equal protection clause. This capacity of a single decision to inspire and motivate activists (both within the civil rights movement and among those deeply opposed to the movement) taps into the normative beliefs and commitments of citizens and political actors alike. The popular understanding of *Brown* transcends its judicially defined constitutional content, encountering an existing array of values and beliefs within communities and individuals. *Brown* as symbol, *Brown* as rhetoric, *Brown* as promise, *Brown* as threat—all these meanings emerge from the decision's potential to impose a norm of equality on public institutions within the South. One's relative normative commitment to equality, then, provides the context that gives meaning to the *Brown* decision. In order to understand what *Brown* means, in this sense, we need to understand how its primary aim — greater equality—intersects with other normative commitments of individuals within a particular community. This kind of investigation into the meaning of *Brown* takes us far from the casebooks and into a realm of attitudes, values, beliefs and norms. Clearly, not all cases decided by the Supreme Court reach this level of constitutional meaning. Many are not so politically resonant, nor do they have *Brown's* transformative aspirations, but some cases hold such intense personal relevance that the Supreme Court decision can be individually threatening or inspiring. To ignore this mode of meaning is to ignore a powerful dual force of American constitutionalism: the capacity of court decisions to reshape our political commitments and the simultaneous ability of personal responses to court decisions to delimit the institutional strength of the judiciary.

Yet another way of conceiving *Brown's* meaning emerges from a reading of *Brown II*, the remedial component of *Brown v. Board of Education*. That decision, although decried for its restrained formula of "all deliberate speed" in the remedial phase, nonetheless set the Supreme Court and the federal judiciary on a task of dismantling and restructuring educational systems that were premised on racial inequality. The constitutional meaning of *Brown* in this context is defined by the decision's efforts to undo the effects of state-mandated segregation. Accompanying that mandate was an implicit injunction to dismantle institutional arrangements that produced a racial hierarchy and distributed educational resources and educational opportunities so as to preserve and entrench advantages for white students.[10] In short, *Brown II* aimed at undermining the constitutional regime of racial inequality. Unequal public education formed a cornerstone of that regime, and the profound resistance among various actors in the South to *Brown* emerged partly from their recognition that a system of organizing power in Southern communities would be destroyed if *Brown's* promise were fulfilled.[11] The constitutional import of *Brown*, from this perspective, lay in the decision's aspiration to reshape a regime of power and to devise a new one, one which would, ideally, substitute a new array of winners and losers in the distributional battle over educational resources. Just as constitutions themselves are blueprints of governance, so too are constitutional judicial interpretations sometimes blueprints for reform, for restructuring, and for reorganization. In order to break down this regime of inequality, educational systems had to be reconstructed and reorganized—and even then, it was not a certainty that racial equality, or even a measure of racial justice, would emerge from these reform efforts. The complexities and difficulties of organizational and institutional change at this level are enormous, and it was clear that *Brown* could only launch that effort at institutional design. *Brown* only hinted at the direction of those reforms; it required enormous efforts on the part of lower court judges, school district officials, plaintiffs, and the U.S. Department of Justice to hammer out new institutional forms.

That project of institutional change and reform—the construction of a new educational regime, in short—has taken far longer than many within the civil rights movement and the federal judiciary ever anticipated,[12] and in some places, the federal courts, with the acquiescence of the U.S. Supreme Court, have given up on the task.[13] Part of our disillusionment with *Brown* and its progeny lies in their inability to revamp the existing regime of educational opportunity. That regime, although no longer premised on a de jure racial hierarchy, still allocates educational opportunities in a disparate fashion, often consigning poor and inner-city children to clearly inadequate and inferior schools. *Brown* produced changes in the constitutional regime of educational opportunity, but not all the changes in that regime have produced greater equal educational opportunity. Yet we could not understand the full meaning of *Brown* without attention to this regime-level effort of reform.

School Finance, State Constitutions, and Equality of Opportunity

To isolate only one form of these meanings is to misapprehend how we endow *Brown* with its power as a constitutional text. The decision owes its status as a foundational constitutional commitment to its capacity to *mean* on many different levels and in many different forms. Thus in order to understand *what* a constitution means, we have to explore *how* that constitution means. But as we turn away from *Brown* and toward questions of class and the distribution of educational resources, our understanding of the constitutional commitment to equal educational opportunity shifts as well. Our understanding shifts in part because, as Americans, we approach class inequalities, in constitutional and political terms, much differently than we do racial inequalities. The scar of slavery has rendered us more sensitive to policies that expressly discriminate on the basis of race than we are to policies that treat the poor differently from the rich, or even the poor from those in middle-class comfort. Indeed, many American public policies—such as the homeowner's interest mortgage deduction—favor propertied citizens over nonpropertied. Living out the American dream—getting ahead, gaining fabulous wealth—is not seen as incongruous to the norm of political or civil equality, even though private wealth may confer enormous political and social advantages. In contrast, racial inequality is seen as a profound threat to the American dream; it violates the very notion that all comers have a chance to succeed. Governmental policies and private powers that distribute material benefits according to one's skin color violate the American dream; governmental policies and private powers that distribute benefits according to the size of one's bank account *define* the American dream.

As a result, within American politics and culture, we view the social and political acceptability of racial and economic discrimination very differently, and those differences shape our debates over school finance and educational opportunity. Racial inequality is seen, typically, as unequivocally bad. It is not generally seen as necessary for the achievement of other educational goals. In contrast, some contend that resource inequality is often a necessary by-product of the achievement of other goods within public education: efficiency, low taxes, local control of school districts, academic excellence within "lighthouse" districts, prevention of flight to private schools, democratic self-governance, economic competitiveness within a region, to name but a few. The inevitability of trade-offs becomes readily apparent when we consider the policies that are necessary to remedy class-based inequalities among students and school districts, and the existence of those trade-offs sharply influences how the constitutional provisions concerning equality are interpreted. The U.S. Supreme Court rejected Demetrio Rodriguez's claims, in part, because it concluded that the pursuit of equality would impair Texas's ability to pursue other, desirable goals for its school system. Within this context, the commitment to equality was trumped by other values, namely federalism and "efficiency" within education. The likelihood that egalitarian claims will be trumped by other values is much greater with the context of economic inequality than in the context of racial inequality.

These differences in our understanding of the relative harms of race and class inequities also have a profound influence on the nature of our state constitutional commitments to equality, especially as they relate to educational opportunity. As I discussed in chapter 1, the shift from race to class within educational opportunity debates parallels a shift from the federal judicial arena to the state arena. That shift means that judges must apply different texts to constitutional claims about economic equality than they applied to racial segregation. The bases for these claims, the equality and educational provisions of state constitutions, differ significantly from the Fourteenth Amendment's equal protection clause. And in the context of economic equality, they produce profoundly different jurisprudential outcomes than federal decisions.

But the differences in constitutional meaning at the state level extend beyond simply textual interpretations. The moral or aspirational meanings of these decisions are quite different from the federal racial equality decisions. Partly because class differences do not have the same moral salience in American life as racial differences and partly because state constitutions do not inspire the same reverence as the U.S. Constitution, the capacity of these decisions to sustain and motivate political movements is far more attenuated. Nonetheless, these decisions, as we will see, do intersect with strong normative commitments within public opinion and attitudes. State-level publics hold strong views about equality in education, but those views are complicated by competing commitments to localism and ideological beliefs.

Finally, these state-level decisions also take on different meanings than their federal counterparts because of the institutional and political contexts of state constitutions. The constitutional and institutional contexts in which plaintiffs and citizens make claims about class inequalities within education matter tremendously to the salience and resonance of those claims. State constitutions are not miniature versions of the U.S. Constitution, and we cannot expect them to take on meaning in precisely the same ways as the federal document gains meaning. The institutional linkages between state and local government are profoundly different from the institutional connection between the national government and states, and because state legislatures have explicit authority to organize public education, these decisions have a far greater salience to questions of institutional design and political competition than *Brown* did. These equality and adequacy decisions loom over state legislatures and local school districts partly because they represent a legitimate threat to the existing forms of educational organization within a state.

The next three chapters are devoted to understanding how these state constitutional decisions gain meaning in the context of claims about equal resources in public education. The central claim for this chapter (and the point of departure for the remaining chapters) is that constitutional ordering — at either the state or federal level — is a complex affair. Constitutional ordering occurs through judicial interpretation and articulation of texts, public expressions of beliefs and attitudes concerning those interpretations, and the sometimes intense political fights over the institutional forms that constitutions specify. By viewing educational opportunity from these three perspectives, we can understand how constitutions richly order our political lives and how we generate their meanings through living (and fighting) within their institutional forms and normative commitments.

5

A BOUNDED AMBITION: THE JUDICIAL ORDERING

OF EDUCATIONAL OPPORTUNITY

> The goal of the framers of our constitution, and the polestar of
> this opinion, is eloquently and movingly stated in the landmark
> case of Brown v. Board of Education: "education is perhaps the
> most important function of state and local governments."
> — *Chief Justice Robert F. Stephens, Kentucky Supreme Court,
> majority opinion*, Rose v. Council for Better Education

> After you have brushed the foam off the beer, the plaintiffs'
> argument concerns only one item — money.
> — *Associate Justice Alva P. Loiselle, Connecticut Supreme Court,
> dissenting*, Horton v. Meskill

AS ONE FIRST BEGINS to read the cases on educational finance, one
is immediately struck by the duality of the decisions: they are both
high-minded displays of rhetorical flourish and numbing treatments
of formulae, statistical measures, and technical definitions. In these cases,
we see both the aspirations of jurists as normative political theorists and the
reality of their role as the policy plumbers of the administrative state. At the
high-minded end, we see judges trumpeting either the American ideals of
equality and opportunity, or the need to respect the institutional integrity of
state government. At the opposite end, we must endure exceptionally dry,
sometimes unfathomable prose that delves deep into the belly of the school
finance beast, parsing out ADM and ADA, determining the constitutional
necessity of foundation aid plans with hold harmless provisions or guaranteed tax base plans with local add-ons. The contrast is not only striking, but
important, because it is within the school finance cases that we find out
whether the institutional and policy aims of American states enhance or
erode American commitments to more equal educational opportunity. The
lofty language and the pedestrian policy-speak represent two sides of every
state supreme court decision on school finance. The formulae and statistical
measures are, in fact, the nitty-gritty stuff of educational opportunity, and to
ignore or downplay them is to ignore the means by which we translate
constitutional commitments into programs and policies that affect the lives

of millions of schoolchildren, parents, and teachers. The two faces of school finance opinions are inextricably bound, because a court cannot espouse a desire for greater equality without discussing the institutions and programs that inhibit or deny that equality. This chapter is about the relationship between those aspirations and the sometimes intensely technical means by which they are fulfilled within public policy.

The argument, in a nutshell, is that state supreme court decisions on school finance profoundly shape the policy options of state legislators, but that different courts play different roles within the policy-making process. A central dilemma faces all courts that seek to restructure school financing: The institutional and political logics of school finance in the United States exert strong pressures for inequality. Thus, judges find themselves arguing and fighting for greater educational opportunity in political contexts where inequality is a central structural element of the school financing regime. These judicial quests for greater educational opportunity (defined as either adequacy or equity) come into conflict with the political incentives and structures that favor inequality. The lessons of these battles are not lost on judges, but they emerge slowly, over time, and through repeated litigation campaigns and judicial rulings on school financing inequities. As a result, these court decisions influence the structure of school finance in a developmental fashion, as courts and legislators volley decisions and financing reforms back and forth. The political and judicial development of school finance emerge through an iterative process in which judges and legislators attempt to reconcile professed public commitments to educational opportunity with political realities and policy options. In the course of this reconciliation, different courts put different developmental stamps on the policy-making process, depending on their priorities and their perceptions of the judicial role and the state's constitutional commitments. This combination of a judicial policy-making arena and the political constraints on legislatures produces a protracted, almost glacial, policy-making setting in which legislators see advantage in delay and judges are limited by their own institutional commitments and priorities. The slow unfolding of reforms can limit a court's ability to reach the underlying inequality in public education. As a consequence, courts are often forced to emphasize the details of financing rather than broader regime questions of governance and power within public education. Moreover, when a court does seek to address larger regime-level issues of educational opportunity, it is typically restrained by a professional and political deference to the representative function of the state legislature and the primacy of democratic institutions in taxation and public education.

In these respects, the judicial campaign against class inequalities in public education echoes the inabilities of federal courts to overcome larger regime issues of racial inequality in public education. In both instances, courts have been constrained by political and economic forces that buttress inequality. The result is a narrower vision of what constitutes equality — whether it be defined in racial or class terms.

This chapter examines four different ways the judicial process structures school financing reforms, each present in varying degrees within the body of school financing decisions handed down over almost thirty years. In short, state supreme court justices stamp the policy process through (1) their construction of "policy templates"; (2) their expressed respect for democratic decision making; (3) their capacity for political learning; (4) their perceptions of the higher law obligations of their respective state constitutions. Of course, not all state high courts will influence the reform of school finance in all of these ways, but these four forms of influence largely define the boundaries of the judicial project of expanding educational opportunity.

School Finance Decisions As Policy Templates

Although the vast majority of school finance decisions employ declaratory relief, they typically do much more than simply declare or assert that the plaintiff possesses a right to an equitable or adequate education.[1] While the finding of that right is important, these decisions cannot be cabined to the simple declaration of a right. Instead, these decisions are important documents within the policy-making process. The substance of these decisions, the rationales judges use to arrive at them, and the deadlines judges impose on legislators all matter tremendously to policy-makers who must struggle to design and then fund a remedy. Often, state lawmakers enact legislation in the shadow of the court's ruling, invoking it and fearing it simultaneously. For example, in Connecticut the state legislature debated whether the proposed reforms would meet with the state supreme court's approval. Their biggest fear lay in allowing the judiciary to assume the role of school finance reformer. They sought to retain control of the reform effort, and to do so required meeting some as-of-yet unknown judicial standard. In introducing the legal context of the act to the state House of Representatives, Rep. John Pier (D-15th) stated:

> We are all very conscious of structuring a legislative proposal to meet three important tests: a political test, a legal test and a moral test. In other words, can it pass the legislature, will it meet the Court's mandate and will it be the best proposal under the circumstances for the whole State of Connecticut? (Connecticut General Assembly 1979, 3696)

In Pier's opinion, the proposed reform (HB 7586) could meet all three tests, but only without modification. It was, in his words, a true political compromise containing or eliminating things many of us find difficult to accept. It is a delicately balanced constitutional compromise. . . . But the bill can only stand in its totality. Any attempt to weaken any part of it, to split it into various parts, to fail to equalize the categorical grants, seriously flattens in my opinion the constitutionality of the whole proposal. (Connecticut General Assembly 1979, 3698–99)

And then he added a doleful warning: Those who attempted to make such changes "must be prepared to live with the consequences" (Connecticut General Assembly 1979, 3699). The problem, for Pier, was clear: either the legislature act by the court's deadline or the trial judge would take over the reform effort in some unknown fashion. The bill was a precarious house of cards; modify any element of it and the whole thing would come crashing down. The only way to keep the courts out of the matter was to pass the bill as it existed.

Some legislators resented the courts' influence and urged the legislature to pursue an independent course. Representative Yorke Allen (R-143rd, New Canaan), for example, complained that "The General Assembly has been dancing too long to the judge's minuet" (Connecticut General Assembly 1979, 3871). These objections, however, reveal that most Connecticut representatives felt pressure from the judiciary and were acting in the hopes of maintaining legislative control over the equalization effort.

At other times, state supreme court decisions function as more concrete proposals, rather than simply a vague or looming threat. In fact, court decisions on school finance can often become detailed policy blueprints or templates with which state legislatures begin their revamping of school financing structures. In Kentucky, the court specified seven characteristics of an adequate educational system and then imposed nine additional requirements for an "efficient" education.[2] The combination of these two sets of detailed policy instructions yielded a virtual checklist for the state legislature as it set about revamping Kentucky's educational system. Foremost among these issues was the Kentucky Supreme Court's bold declaration that the *entire* system of public education in Kentucky was unconstitutional. In order to rise to that complex policy challenge, the legislature could not help but respond to the court's detailed agenda. By simultaneously charging the state legislature with an enormous task and by defining the state constitutional requirements within the education arena in such a detailed fashion, the Kentucky Supreme Court acted more as a policy-making coordinator than simply the finder of a state constitutional right.[3]

At the same time, however, the Kentucky Supreme Court sought to preserve the illusion that it was not directly intervening in the legislative process. As the justices wrote:

We do not instruct the General Assembly to enact any specific legislation. We do not direct the members of the General Assembly to raise taxes. It is their decision how best to achieve efficiency. We only decide the nature of the constitutional mandate. We only determine the intent of the framers. Carrying out that intent is the duty of the General Assembly.[4]

This level of disingenuousness within school finance decisions may be a bit extreme, but it is not uncommon. As we will see, most courts do not want to be seen intervening in the central democratic functions of the legislature. In particular, they understand that their legitimacy is potentially compromised when they are seen interfering with taxation mechanisms and educational governance. But, of course, that level of intervention is precisely what courts must often engage in to address the larger regime issues that sustain and extend educational inequality within states.

Because of the important agenda-setting role that courts play within the policy process, the stakes for judges are quite high. Their understanding and articulations of the central issues to be resolved in the reform process structure the policy options for legislators. And although it may be loathe to admit it, a state supreme court can often make the policy-making process more complicated and convoluted than it need be. Because courts typically can only use judicial rulings to indicate to state legislators the policy options that would meet constitutional muster, the possibility of imprecision, or even error, is rather high. Indeed, the mistakes and misapprehensions that judges make within this rather technical arena are often replicated within the policy-making process of the legislature. If a state supreme court is imprecise, misstates it position, or contradicts itself, the policy-making process within the legislature will often reproduce those errors. If the court produces a legal blueprint of poor design, the policy structure that the legislature builds will be equally bad. Rarely will a legislature overcome the faults of a poor judicial decision. Instead, those errors will be compounded and multiplied due to the political pressures legislatures face. The Texas case is particularly illustrative of this.

The Texas Debacle: Beginning in October 1989 and extending over seven years, the Texas Supreme Court handed down no less than six decisions in the *Edgewood* case.[5] At the height of the conflict, the legislature and supreme court (with the district court caught in the middle) traded decisions and bills, with ultimatums and deadlines met and transgressed. The reasons for this seemingly unending crisis stemmed, in part, from the underlying nature of the conflict: forcing a legislature to do what its constituents deeply resisted doing. In such a conflict, any court would have had its hands full, but the struggle in Texas proved particularly nasty and confrontational. Part of the problem must also be attributed to the actions and decisions of the

Supreme Court itself. By attempting to influence very specific provisions of legislative policy-making and by handing down confusing, if not contradictory, decisions, the Texas Supreme Court badly handled its school financing decisions. The litigation and the entire series of decisions yielded a wearied legislature, as well as a distrustful public. In fact, the actions of the Texas Supreme Court delayed, even inhibited, a more equitable school financing system for Texas. Throughout its numerous *Edgewood* decisions, the Texas Supreme Court sought to actively shape specific programmatic details of the legislative remedy. In doing so, it severely hamstrung, even confused, the policy-making process, diminishing the Texas legislature's capacity to devise a solution.

To be sure, the fault does not entirely lie with the Texas Supreme Court. The Constitution of Texas is a notorious patchwork of provisions, running over 28,000 words and amended at least 326 times.[6] In the *Edgewood* litigation, the Texas Supreme Court was working with particularly difficult and cumbersome constitutional materials and texts. The Texas Constitution's provisions on education and on property taxation do not lie easily next to one another. In the words of one commentator, the section of the Texas Constitution concerning the taxation powers of Texas school districts (art. 7, sec. 3 of the Texas Constitution) illustrates "how not to write a constitution" (Braden 1977, 519). The text is, in short, a confused mishmash. That said, the Texas Supreme Court nonetheless exacerbated the disruptive impact of these conflicting constitutional texts and commitments. Instead of frankly acknowledging these difficulties, the Texas Supreme Court—at least a majority of the court—sought to advance a myth of constitutional coherence. The resulting logical contortions required to reconcile these contradictions would be amusing if they were not harmful in a very real sense: they were replicated in the public policies advanced by a legislature trying (at times) to comply with the state supreme court's decrees. Jurisprudence has consequences, and none are so apparent as those that find institutional form in public policy.

Two confusions stand out in the massive body of case law and legislative reforms that the *Edgewood* litigation produced. First, the Texas Supreme Court failed to specify clearly *who* should be made more equal by the reforms, students or taxpayers. If students are to be made more equal, then revenues or expenditures must be addressed. If taxpayers are the focus, then tax rates must be equalized. This distinction is important because the two forms of equality, in many instances, lie in deep tension. It is very difficult to achieve both forms of equity simultaneously, especially in places where property values diverge widely. The Texas Supreme Court repeatedly conflated taxpayer and student equity, at times declaring inequities among taxation rates to be the source of the constitutional harm and at other times identifying the unequal expenditures on children to be at fault. For example, in the first part of the *Edgewood I* decision, the court decried the ills of a financing system in which "spending per student varies widely, ranging from $2,112 to $19,333." This emphasis implies that unequal pupil expenditures rendered the educational system constitutionally infirm. But the court later bemoaned in *Edgewood I* that a taxpayer "owning a $80,000 home with no homestead exemption would pay $1,206 in taxes in the east Texas low-wealth district of Leveretts Chapel, but would pay only $59 in the west Texas high-wealth district of Iraan-Sheffield." The Texas Supreme Court never resolved this conflict among forms of inequality — although at the end of the decision it appeared to settle on taxpayer equity as the significant constitutional violation:

> Efficiency does not require a per capita distribution, but it also does not allow concentrations of resources in property-rich school districts that are taxing low when property-poor districts that are taxing high cannot generate sufficient revenues to meet even minimum standards. *There must be a direct and close correlation between a district's tax effort and the educational resources available to it*; in other words, districts must have substantially equal access to similar revenues per pupil at similar levels of tax effort.[7]

This suggests that the court hoped to equalize the capacity of districts to raise funds. This is, in effect, a focus on taxpayer equity: equal yields for equal efforts. The court altered this line of reasoning in later decisions and shifted to a pupil-based conception of equity, but only after the state legislature had devoted considerable time and energy to the question of taxpayer equity. The Texas high court's inability to make a key distinction in school finance analysis rendered the state legislature's task all the more complex, both politically and legally.

The second confusion in this long line of decisions emerged from the court's vacillation on the constitutionality of a proposed remedy to the financing crisis. In particular, the court failed to clarify whether an existing constitutional prohibition on a statewide property tax prevented the Texas legislature from imposing a *countywide* property tax. This county-level tax, known derisively throughout the state as the "Robin Hood" plan, was enacted partly because the Texas Supreme Court had hinted it would resolve the central constitutional problem with school financing in Texas. The tax was designed to equalize the revenues available to school districts within each county, but the court quickly struck it down after the legislature enacted it, claiming the Robin Hood tax violated a state constitutional ban on a statewide property tax. Its reversal dealt a serious blow to reformers.

The story of the Texas Supreme Court's conflicting advice to the state legislature begins in *Edgewood II*. After declaring SB1, the legislature's response to *Edgewood I*, constitutionally unacceptable, the court offered some guidelines for devising a new finance system that would provide greater "efficiency." "To be efficient," the court wrote, "a funding system that is so dependent on local ad valorem property taxes must draw revenue from all property at a substantially similar rate. The present system does not do so."[8] This suggestion was, perhaps, the most striking in this very energetic decision. By suggesting that the state set minimum taxation rates for *all* districts (including the most wealthy), and then using this windfall from wealthy districts for equalization, the court essentially argued for a "Robin Hood" proposal.

The existing system was flawed, the court added, because it "insulates concentrated areas of property wealth from being taxed to support the public schools. The result is that substantial revenue is lost to the system."[9] This loss thereby rendered the system less efficient than it ought to be. In writing these few words, the court tapped perhaps the most sensitive nerve in school finance battles: the capacity of wealthy districts to isolate themselves through their exclusive use of property tax revenues. The court sharply critiqued two institutional fixtures of school finance: local control of school districts and the property tax. The two in conjunction were inefficient, the court argued, for the educational system writ large. Although they ensured a few districts very high levels of funding at comparatively low levels of taxation, the combination of local control and property tax-based school financing also created the inequities and inefficiencies ruled unconstitutional in *Edgewood I.*

Other policy suggestions also emerged from *Edgewood II.* The court suggested that wholesale district consolidation might make the school system more efficient, indicating that 1,052 school districts (some with exceedingly small enrollments) was perhaps too many. The court also raised the possibility of tax base consolidation, suggesting that the district court judge who had declared tax base consolidation constitutionally impermissible had misread the precedents, in particular the sixty-year-old case of *Love v. Dallas.*[10] In fact, the court was rather dismissive of any obstacles that *Love* might present to tax base consolidation:

> The Constitution does not present a barrier to the general concept of tax base consolidation, and nothing in *Love* prevents creation of school districts along county or other lines for the purpose of collecting tax revenue and distributing it to other school districts within their boundaries.[11]

The response to *Edgewood II* was vociferous. Former Lieutenant Governor Bill Hobby called upon the electorate to defeat all nine justices at the next election (Elliott 1991a). Even supporters were a bit taken aback. Mark Yudof, dean of the University of Texas law school and a long-time advocate for school finance equalization called the decision "genuinely remarkable," adding that some would call it "radical." The result of the decision, he said, could be one of "the most sweeping school finance reforms in the country" (Elliott 1991a).

To the dismay of reformers, however, the Texas Supreme Court quickly changed its mind. The confusion over whether *Edgewood II* had implicitly overturned *Love*, prompted one set of plaintiffs to move for reconsideration, requesting that the court modify or clarify *Edgewood II* as to "the continued force and effect" of *Love*.[12] But rather than address that narrow issue, the court seized the opportunity to "clarify" the thorny issue of local enrichment, the capacity of local districts to supplement their educational revenues through additional taxation, not required by the state. The result, however, was a ruling almost wholly at odds with its decision handed down only four weeks earlier. The ruling in *Edgewood IIA* held — without a single citation to case law — that "Because the Constitution does permit such [local] enrichment, without equalization, local taxes cannot be considered 'state taxes subject to state-wide recapture.'"[13] In other words, "constitutional provisions mandate that local tax revenue is not subject to statewide recapture."[14] In a matter of four weeks, the Texas Supreme Court, most likely in response to negative press and legislative reaction,[15] changed its mind about a key element of the "Robin Hood" proposal.[16] In doing so, it squandered a rare opportunity to provide clear guidelines for a state legislature grappling with acute political pressures and a difficult policy issue.[17]

The Texas Supreme Court's failure to provide policy leadership, particularly its lack of analytical clarity and its inability to enunciate clear constitutional policy options for the state legislature, produced a protracted and bitter struggle that compounded an already difficult political situation. Clearly, state legislators did not want to enact costly reforms that drove up taxes, but they also needed clear signals from the Texas Supreme Court to navigate the politically dangerous waters of school finance reform. Instead, they received only inconsistent and conflicting opinions. According to press reports, the hostility toward the court was almost palpable among legislators. Mark Yudof and William Hobby, two veteran school finance analysts, wrote that the previous *Edgewood* decisions had produced a "politically unstable situation. A taxpayer revolt is a real threat." They added that many legislators and elected officials "are so traumatized by the first three rounds of Edgewood that they may refuse to enact any plan in response to an *Edgewood IV*" (Hobby and Yudoff 1991).[143] While it may be possible to cite the Texas legislature for intransigence and stonewalling in the face of the court's decisions, Yudof and Hobby's words capture a central fact of the Texas story of school finance reform: The mess of Texas school finance reform was as much the court's doing as it was the legislature's.

The Virtues and Perils of Advisory Opinions: Part of the problem facing the Texas Supreme Court was an institutional inability to advise the state legislature directly about the constitutionality of the reforms it was developing. That problem, of course, is endemic to judicial policy-making, but particularly acute under conditions of declaratory relief. Unlike injunctive relief, which allows a court to order direct remedies, declaratory relief simply acts as an agenda-setting device, rather than as a mechanism to substantially direct the course of public policy. As a result, the Texas Supreme Court felt the need, at times, to issue somewhat hasty opinions in the middle of the reform process. The result of decisions like *Edgewood IIA*, according to one state legislator, was not a better understanding, but more confusion. After that ruling, said the legislator, "we were like rats in a maze" (Bosworth 1997, 132).

Other state supreme courts, however, have used advisory opinions issued during the remedial phase more fruitfully. Of course, some state constitutions or statutes explicitly authorize the state supreme court (or the state's attorney general's office) to issue advisory opinions when requested by either the executive or legislative branches. This can be used to good effect in school finance cases. The New Hampshire Constitution, for example, allows both branches of the state legislature, as well as the governor, "to require the opinions of the justices of the supreme court upon important questions of law and upon solemn occasions."[18] New Hampshire's battle with school finance reform, while not as long running as Texas's, so far has been nearly as contentious. The New Hampshire Supreme Court struck down the existing financing scheme in 1993 and then declared the remedy adopted by the state legislature insufficient in 1997. In the subsequent legislative tussle over the reform package, the New Hampshire Senate asked the supreme court for an advisory opinion on its proposed legislation. The court advised the senate that its proposal was insufficient to meet the mandate of the previous two rulings.[19] While this did not alleviate tensions within the state legislature, it made its task clearer and shortened the remedial phase of the lawsuit.[20] Of course, there are significant dangers that a state supreme court could act as third legislative chamber in reform process, vetoing and stifling legislative initiatives before they have time to develop and evolve. Certainly, advisory opinions pose meaningful risks to the institutional boundaries between legislative and judicial bodies, boundaries of which state supreme courts, as we will see, are mindful. But an advisory opinion can be a useful foil for state legislators confronted with an unsavory choice between higher taxes or redistributed state aid to education. Also, when a state supreme court exercises caution, it can usefully eliminate legislative options or focus the attention of a state legislature on a limited range of policy choices. An advisory opinion can move the state legislature beyond superficial reforms without forcing the parties to renew their lengthy and costly litigation efforts. Since state supreme courts are clearly exercising a form of policy-making powers in the course of these school finance suits, it makes sense to use the few tools of legislative-judicial communication available to them, as the New Hampshire Supreme Court has done.[21] Being frank about the ways courts shape policy options in the school finance arena is, however, an essential first step to a successful advisory opinion, and it also requires that judges become astute political learners, understanding what motivates legislators and what they can and cannot stomach in a school finance reform package.

In some circumstances, plaintiffs seek judicial rulings in the midst of legislative reforms in an effort to compel or motivate lawmakers to pursue particular policy options. For example, in New Jersey, after the state supreme court had struck down a school financing structure for the third time in twenty-five years,[22] the attorneys from the Education Law Center sought a ruling from the New Jersey Supreme Court that the reforms being debated within the state legislature did not provide sufficient funding to meet the court mandate. David Sciarra, executive director of the Education Law Center, told a reporter "We think they [the state legislators] have to do substantially better this year, and we want the court to give them the nudge to get them to do it" (MacFarquhar 1996a). In effect, these filings become forms of extralegislative lobbying in which plaintiffs or other actors seek to deploy judicial influence over the legislative process. Rather than wait for the legislature to develop its reform bill and then relitigate the claim, the New Jersey plaintiffs hoped to shorten the "reform cycle" considerably by seeking a judicial ruling before the legislative reforms were signed into law. These midreform rulings can function, in effect, as advisory rulings, but they pose greater risks for state supreme courts than the advisory opinions that a state legislature might formally request. If the plaintiffs or the defendants seek the ruling, legislators may resent the intrusion into the legislative process, particularly if the court's ruling preempts the deal-making and negotiation that must transpire in all these reform efforts. In the New Jersey case, the court wisely dismissed the motion without prejudice, allowing the plaintiffs to refile their claims after the law had taken effect. Upon those renewed motions, the court ultimately agreed with the plaintiffs about the inadequacy of the reforms. Had the court come to that conclusion prior to legislative enactment, however, its reputation among lawmakers, already battered by its repeated rejections of reform legislation, would most likely have suffered even more.

Respect for Democratic Decision-Making

Part of the rationale for the New Jersey Supreme Court's deference to the legislature stems from a broader judicial commitment, expressed in virtually every state supreme court opinion on school finance, to respect the legislative process and the representative function of legislatures. School finance decisions are rife with statements about the centrality of education and taxation issues to democratic decision-making, declarations of respect for institutional autonomy, and utterances on the importance of negotiation and bargaining within legislatures. Indeed, in many of the lawsuits in which state supreme courts uphold the existing system, the court's reluctance to recognize the plaintiffs' claims stems precisely from its understanding of the appropriate role of the judiciary in educational policy-making. For example, as Chief Justice Henry McWade of the Idaho Supreme Court wrote in the mid-1970s:

> We reject the arguments advanced by the plaintiffs-respondents and the conclusions made by the trial court. To do otherwise would be an unwise and unwarranted entry into the controversial area of public school financing, whereby this Court would convene as a "super-legislature," legislating in a turbulent field of social, economic and political policy.[23]

This refusal to engage in judicial policy-making is, of course, itself a form of policy-making, one in which legislative majorities and democratic imperatives trump any legal or constitutional claims made about inequality or inadequacy in educational financing. Thus, even though the language of deference may express a sincere conviction about the appropriate judicial role in educational policy-making, it may also simply provide a cover under which a state supreme court can pass the school financing buck, as it were, back to the legislature.

But in cases in which state supreme courts *do* strike down existing financing systems, they still engage in this rhetoric of deference and strict separation of powers. Part of this rhetoric is simply that—an effort to ease the bitter pill of educational finance reform down the throats of reluctant legislators who would seize upon impolitic or overly expansive language as an abuse of judicial office. Still, a significant portion of these overtures to state legislatures on the part of state supreme courts are legitimate expressions of the respect for the difficulties that lawmakers face as they contend with powerful interests and sometimes severe fiscal constraints. For example, in a per curiam decision, the Vermont Supreme Court went out of its way to "acknowledge the conscientious and ongoing efforts of the Legislature to achieve equity in educational financing" and to make clear that the court "intend[s] no intrusion upon its prerogatives to define a system consistent with constitutional requirements." It added that "the Court's duty today is solely to define the impact of the State Constitution on educational funding, not to fashion and impose a solution. The remedy at this juncture properly lies with the Legislature."[24]

A court's deference may stem from the criticism, often made by justices on the court, that the judiciary ought not engage school financing issues or that state courts are even barred from undertaking these reforms. Justice

Richard Neely of the West Virginia Supreme Court in his dissent suggested that school financing issues fall under a classic political questions doctrine and are not amenable to judicial resolution. "Consequently," he wrote:

> [I]t is with reluctance that I must dissent from the opinion of my learned col-
> leagues, not because I am less outraged than they about the condition of West
> Virginia schools, but because I am neither Governor nor the entire Legislature.[25]

The rejoinder to this kind of criticism of judicial intervention typically argues that state constitutional obligations are serious commitments that the state government (and, hence, state legislature) must uphold. Arizona Chief Justice Stanley G. Feldman wrote in his concurring opinion in *Roosevelt Elementary School District Number 66 v. Bishop* that

> Parents, their children, and all citizens need to know what rights the constitu-
> tion gives our children, and the legislature needs to know the extent of its
> obligation in effectuating those rights. *This court exists primarily for the purpose
> of resolving such issues.*[26]

These commitments and obligations, so Feldman's rejoinder to Neely goes, must be defended by the state judiciary if they are to mean anything at all.[27] In making this argument, Feldman implicitly contends that state constitutional obligations are comparable to national constitutional commitments and that the state constitution represents, in some sense, a foundational document for the state. In contrast, the quote from Connecticut Supreme Court Associate Justice Alva P. Loiselle that introduces this chapter sees the dispute not as a constitutional issue, but simply as one of resource allocation in which courts are dragged through political struggles best left for state legislatures: "After you have brushed the foam off the beer, the plaintiffs' argument concerns only one item — money."[28] These competing views of both the binding quality of state constitutional commitments and the judiciary's role in defending those commitments form a major cleavage in rulings on educational opportunity. At this divide, some judges' respect for legislative responsibility and the democratic process subsides and their perceived obligations under the state constitution (for both themselves as justices and the state as a provider of education) become preeminent. Their task is no longer simply one of setting the legislature's agenda and urging it on through the difficult task of reform. Now, it is a project of translating, in Arizona Chief Justice Feldman's phrasing, "the dry words on paper" into an institutional reality reflecting the framers' constitutional vision of the state.

Nonetheless, state supreme courts are reluctant to battle head-to-head with state legislatures. Even when a state supreme court strikes down a financing scheme, it will almost invariably give the state legislature the benefit of the doubt and allow it to try again. As Chief Justice Brock of the New

Hampshire Supreme Court wrote in 1997, in the court's second declaration that the existing school financing system was constitutionally inadequate:

> Accordingly, we do not remand for consideration of remedies at this time, but instead stay all further proceedings until the end of the upcoming legislative session and further order of this court to permit the legislature to address the issues involved in this case.[29]

The patience of judges, however, has its limits, and legislatures can sometimes misinterpret kind words of judicial understanding for an inability to compel legislatures to reform the existing system. In those situations, judges have reacted sharply. In spring 1991, after the Texas Supreme Court struck down Senate Bill 1 as an inadequate legislative response to its 1989 ruling, District Court Judge Scott McCown was charged with enforcing a deadline on legislative action. Frustrated by the legislature's failure to adopt a plan, some state legislators turned their ire against the court. Texas Speaker of the House Gib Lewis even suggested that the state might do battle with the judiciary, saying, "I am not for schools shutting down, whatever the circumstances. . . . I would certainly encourage the comptroller or anybody else to take whatever measures necessary to prohibit that, even if it means defying the court order" (Donahue 1991).

McCown stood his ground, however, ordering Texas Education Agency deputy commissioner Lynn Moak to devise a plan for meeting the *Edgewood* mandate by April 15. That plan, he suggested, would go into effect if the legislature did not approve a plan of its own. Indicating his frustration with the legislature's request for more time, McCown stated in court, "We're not playing horseshoes, so close doesn't count. We don't yet have a bill." He also vividly portrayed the conflict tearing apart the legislature: "This debate is about equal resources, not about how we use those resources. . . . Local control [is] a code word for the rich spending money the poor don't have" (Racine 1991).

While Moak designed his own plan, the Texas legislature had a brief two-week reprieve to arrive at a compromise. A conference committee hammered out an agreement between senate and house members, and both houses approved the revised conference committee bill on 11 April 1991, only four days before Moak was to deliver his plan for restructuring Texas's school finance system to Judge McCown. At times, it seems, respect for democratic processes can only carry a judge so far. The willingness to unilaterally impose alternative reforms on state legislators is sometimes necessary to spur the democratic process forward. While some may argue that coercion reveals the imperial ambitions of judges, a more sensitive reading attributes judicial steadfastness to a commitment to constitutional interpretation and a respect for constitutional obligations.

Judges as Political Learners

One key to success in the policy-making arena is to understand what motivates your opponents. This is true of both legislative and judicial policymaking. The ability of a state supreme court justice to transform her immediate task of rendering a decision on school finance into an occasion to write a policy blueprint stems, in large part, from her capacity to understand the political importance of educational finance to state legislators. If they are to write effective policy blueprints, state judges, at both the trial court and appellate levels, need to understand why and how state legislators are made uneasy by efforts to reform the funding of public education. The financing of educational opportunity is linked to a host of state functions that are central to the task of representative governance. The judge who understands those connections and fuses her explication of state constitutional obligations to the political realities of state legislative process will be in a much better position to forge a policy blueprint that has a meaningful chance of actually expanding educational opportunity. There is a tremendous normative attraction behind the phrase "equal educational opportunity," and judges who can reduce or clarify obstacles facing state legislators as they strive to achieve it will be more likely to capitalize on that political support and less likely to be dragged through an endless forest of litigation. At the same time, this process of political learning shows the resilience of the economic and political forces that generate and sustain inequalities. Without political learning, courts would be much less effective, but the necessity of political learning reveals the complexity and influence of forces that undermine equitable access to education.

Two examples aptly illustrate this point. The first, from Connecticut, shows a somewhat timid court adroitly using principles gleaned from the reapportionment struggles of the 1960s and 1970s in an effort to set an agenda rather than impose particular outcomes on the legislative battles. The second example, from New Jersey, reveals a court partly redefining its goals in response to political tensions within the state legislature while simultaneously scaling back its ambition of restructuring the regime of educational inequality in New Jersey.

Connecticut and the lessons of reapportionment: In 1979 the Connecticut Assembly, in response to the state supreme court's 1977 decision in *Horton v. Meskill*, enacted a potentially transformative school finance bill. That reform bill put in place a guaranteed tax base formula, with provisions for phasing in state funding over a five-year period. The formula was, in many ways, a state-of-the-art financing plan that would have substantially equalized the tax bases of Connecticut's cities and towns, enabling property-poor jurisdictions to overcome through a guaranteed tax base program (GTB) the handicaps of low property wealth. Unfortunately, fiscal disaster hit the Northeast in the late 1970s and early 1980s. Inflation spiked in 1979 to over 13 percent annually, driving up real estate prices (and the cost of equalizing property tax bases), and then state revenues began to dry up in the recessionary climate of 1981–82. In the midst of this turmoil, the state legislature adjusted its newly enacted plan to restructure school financing, and between 1980 and 1984 passed no fewer than ten amendments to the 1979 legislation in an effort to reduce costs.[30]

Early on, attorney Wesley Horton (and father of plaintiff Barnaby) saw the trend of amendments emerging and returned to court to seek the reversal of these amendments, claiming they threatened the viability of the landmark *Horton I* decision. After a few years of procedural delays,[31] Judge Arthur L. Spada, the trial court judge, ruled in 1984 that the amendments violated the state's constitutional obligation to decrease the inequities in public school expenditures. Spada wrote: "The pattern is clear that the GTB formula is being systematically eviscerated for both budgetary and fiscal reasons."[32] Spada also found that because the Connecticut Supreme Court had declared education a fundamental right in Connecticut in the first *Horton v. Meskill* ruling,[33] he was obliged to invoke strict scrutiny when evaluating the amendments to the reform package. And "[s]trict judicial scrutiny," in Spada's view "requires that the state rather than the plaintiffs carry the heavy burden of justification for these legislative amendments which have retarded the goals of *Horton v. Meskill*."[34] Not surprisingly, Spada could find no compelling state interest that would justify the state's failure to meet its constitutional obligations. The amendments were, therefore, unconstitutional.

While Spada struck down the amendments, he found that the original reform instrument, the GTB formula, was a constitutionally sufficient distribution mechanism to address the funding inequalities in the state. It simply had never been funded adequately. The pipeline was in place, according to Spada, but the legislature's various amendments had diverted the flow of funds for political and budgetary reasons. The legislature simply had not provided enough money to reduce existing inequities.

As it confronted these issues on the state's appeal, the Connecticut Supreme Court was in a rather delicate position. The state had made it clear that it would not jeopardize its fiscal health for a newly found fundamental right to education in Connecticut. On the other hand, if the court sided with Spada, the state judiciary would be forced to monitor closely any and all legislative developments that affected educational revenues or expenditures. The Connecticut Supreme Court was thus left in an awkward position, especially with a deteriorating economy and a clearly implacable state legislature.

The resolution of this dilemma illustrates how a court can rather astutely

preserve a measure of influence over school finance reform without imposing particular outcomes. Rather than engage the state legislature and governor on the issue, the court chose to reinterpret the state legislature's obligation to comply with the court's mandate in *Horton I*. In doing so, the
court rejected a compliance framework based on strict scrutiny of the continued denial of a fundamental right. Instead, it argued that the litigation of
school finance inequalities did not fall neatly within the bounds of traditional equal protection analysis. In a unanimous decision, Chief Justice
Ellen Peters wrote:

> [T]he *sui generis* nature of litigation involving school financing legislation mili-
> tates against formalistic reliance on the usual standards of the law of equal
> protection, in particular against the requirement that the state must demonstrate
> a compelling state interest.

Rather than utilizing the traditional "compelling state interest" standard, the
court borrowed a framework that the U.S. Supreme Court developed to
evaluate the compliance of state legislatures in reapportionment cases. A
three-part test, this analytical framework requires that the plaintiffs first make a
prima facie case that the continuing disparities are, in fact, meaningful and
continue to jeopardize the plaintiff's fundamental right to an education. If
that showing is made, the burden then shifts to the state, which must show
how the continuing disparities advance a "legitimate state policy." Finally, if
the court accepts the state's explanation, the state must still show that the
financing plan, taken as a whole, "significantly equaliz[es] state support to
local education." Because Judge Spada used a "compelling state interest"
standard to evaluate the post-1979 amendments, the court overturned his
finding that the amendments were unconstitutional. The court directed him,
however, to reevaluate the amendments in light of the three-tiered standard
the court developed in its opinion. The court also admonished Spada for
simply compelling the state to spend in accordance with the 1979 plan and
for not holding new remedial hearings to determine a suitable rectification of
the constitutional harm. The remedial phase, the court asserted, must balance
three factors: "the nature and the scope of the constitutional violation, the
plaintiff's right to meaningful relief, and the interests of state and local authorities in managing their own affairs."[35] The court pointedly insisted that the trial
court must balance the rights of the plaintiff against the need to avoid "embarrassment to the operations of government."[36]

By providing the trial judge with a somewhat more deferential standard of
review and specifically instructing him to conduct extensive remedial hearings, and to take into account the potential "embarrassment" to other
branches, the court demonstrated an astute capacity for political learning.
This flexibility allowed the judiciary to exercise influence over school finance reform but in a more nuanced way. The new standard Judge Spada

was to employ would still center around the fundamental right of education, but it would not be as mechanistic and formulaic as strict scrutiny and the "compelling state interest" argument. It would, in other words, create a more accommodating procedure while still asserting the central constitutional value of equality.[37]

The Connecticut Supreme Court's use of a reapportionment standard to discern limits to the judicial role in school finance reform highlights an important similarity between the two bodies of law. Conflicts involving both reapportionment and school finance wind up in court largely because of the structural inability of the democratic process to remedy the existing inequalities. In reapportionment cases, voting inequalities are unlikely to be redressed via legislative means because those reforms would unsettle and undermine the existing power distribution within the legislature itself. Similarly, in school finance cases, electoral pressures often prevent legislators from reforming a system that materially benefits a majority of their constituents. The Connecticut Supreme Court's ready application of reapportionment standards to school finance reform shows the deep similarities between the two issues: the presence of electoral incentives make it exceptionally difficult to redress the problems of both school financing inequities and malaportionment. In both situations, legislators are unwilling to diminish their electoral fortunes — either by creating riskier seats or by materially harming the interests of their constituents. The Connecticut Supreme Court's willingness to recognize those similarities can perhaps be seen as sacrificing constitutional principle for political expedience, or it can be seen as an innovative and effective way to avoid a damaging institutional collision.

The political and legal developments in Connecticut between *Horton I* and *Horton III* illustrate an important dimension of court-ordered school finance reform. The Connecticut Supreme Court realized that its limited political and institutional capacities prevented it from imposing an outcome on a politically volatile issue. It had engendered reform, but it could not ensure the success of reform and thus chose to conserve its judicial energies. Whether the court could have summoned the resources to force a more ambitious reform on a reluctant and fiscally strapped state legislature is uncertain. What is certain is that the Connecticut Supreme Court relied on a rather innovative legal and political strategy to keep the issue on the legislative agenda without provoking an institutional showdown between the legislature and state judiciary.[38] The cost of that compromise, however, was an inability to rework meaningfully the institutional settings that produce these inequalities.

How Does a Court Know If It Has Won? New Jersey's Example

At first glance, it may be difficult to argue that the phrase "political learning" characterizes the legal and constitutional struggle over school financing that stretched on for over twenty-five years in New Jersey. Indeed, some may argue that the justices on the New Jersey Supreme Court learned little in their efforts to direct more resources to the poorest districts in the state, especially state legislators who had to contend with the wrath of angry voters and taxpayers. Nonetheless, there is a distinct development over the course of the three decades in which the court addressed the issue. The first effort, *Robinson I*, broke away from the U.S. Supreme Court's "fundamental rights" approach and provided an initial definition of the "thorough and efficient" clause within the New Jersey Constitution. Seventeen years later, the court revisited the matter in *Abbott II*. That decision focused the reform effort on a set of districts that were particularly disadvantaged within New Jersey. Finally, in the *Abbott IV, Abbott V,* and *Abbott VI* decisions, the court scaled back its judicial ambitions to restructure the regime of inequality that characterizes New Jersey school financing and contented itself with delivering particular resources to a few districts. Throughout each of these developments, we see the court trying to reconcile its constitutional commitment to greater educational opportunity with the political repercussions of its decisions. The result is a gradual erosion of judicial enthusiasm for the conflict and a dampening of judicial expectations of the state legislature. While the New Jersey Supreme Court may have been a slow political learner — or, conversely, particularly committed to the project of expanding educational opportunity — it did eventually realize its limitations.

The central analytical distinction of the 1973 *Robinson I* decision was its rejection of the fundamental rights approach of the U.S. Supreme Court and its heavy reliance on the "thorough and efficient" clause of the New Jersey Constitution.[39] Because education was not declared a fundamental right under the New Jersey Constitution, equal protection analysis became irrelevant to the issue of school financing. Instead, the court viewed the constitutional mandate that the legislature provide a "thorough and efficient" education as the central issue of the litigation. The court chose to interpret a "thorough and efficient" education not as one that requires the provision of precisely equal resources, but one in which the state provides an "equal opportunity" to obtain an education. As the court wrote in *Robinson I*:

> [I]t cannot be said the 1875 amendments were intended to insure statewide equality among taxpayers. But we do not doubt that an equal educational opportunity for children was precisely in mind. The mandate that there be maintained and supported "a thorough and efficient system of free public schools for the instruction of all the children in the State between the ages of five and eighteen years" can have no other import.[40]

According to the court, the New Jersey Constitution expressed a commitment to equal educational opportunity in its "thorough and efficient" phrasing, thereby requiring a particular level of educational offering throughout the state. The public education system must meet a minimum level of thoroughness and efficiency in its delivery of education. The problem, however, was that the constitution did not specify the precise level of educational offering that is required, and at the time of *Robinson I* neither the legislative nor executive branch had attempted to define a constitutionally appropriate public education. But in order for the court to determine whether the financing system provides such an education, it required a standard by which to judge educational opportunities. It settled on the following test:

> The Constitution's guarantee must be understood to embrace that educational opportunity which is needed in the contemporary setting to equip a child for his role as a citizen and as a competitor in the labor market.[41]

This standard requires the state to ensure that its educational system provides sufficient opportunities for *all* students to become suitably trained as informed citizens and employable workers. Thus, as a result of *Robinson I*, the constitutional requirement of "thorough and efficient" focused on the provision of a mandated minimum of educational opportunity, not equality per se.

In its 1990 *Abbott II* decision, the court revisited the *Robinson I* holding, stating that "[T]he clear import [of *Robinson I*] is not of a constitutional mandate governing expenditures per pupil, equal or otherwise, but a requirement of a specific substantive level of education." The court added a few lines later:

> The State's obligation to attain that minimum [level of education] is absolute — any district that fails must be compelled to comply. If, however, that level is reached, the constitutional mandate is fully satisfied regardless of the fact that some districts may exceed it. In other words, the Constitution does not mandate equal expenditures per pupil.[42]

This passage demonstrates clearly that the New Jersey Supreme Court was not concerned with educational financing disparities per se. Unequal expenditures were not the issue; the provision of a constitutional minimum was precisely the issue. The next logical step, then, would be to identify those districts where the minimum is not being provided. Those would be the districts in which the state had failed to meet its constitutional obligation.

Instead of pursuing this line of inquiry (by asking what a constitutional educational minimum looks like) the court returned to a notion it advanced in *Robinson I*: educational opportunity as equality in labor market competition and citizen development. Indeed, the court expanded that notion and required the state to ensure that students from poor, disadvantaged districts be placed on an equal competitive footing with students from advantaged areas. No longer content with ensuring *basic* labor and citizenship skills, the court sought to equalize not money, but achievement. Referring to an earlier decision, the court wrote:

> We said, in effect, that the requirement of a thorough and efficient education to provide "that educational opportunity which is needed in the contemporary setting to equip a child for his role as a citizen and as a competitor in the labor market," meant that poorer disadvantaged students must be given a chance to be able to compete with relatively advantaged students. The Act and its system of education have failed in that respect, and it is that failure that we address in this case.

It is important to note that this is a far more rigorous standard than the one articulated in *Robinson I*. Under the *Robinson* formulation, school districts (and the state) were obliged to equip students with the *basic* principles of citizenship and with employable skills. Now, the disadvantaged must be put in a position to effectively compete with the advantaged. Through the educational system, the children of losers in the socioeconomic struggle in New Jersey must be made able to compete with the children of the winners of that struggle. In the court's view, this would require a compensatory educational program that exceeds the offerings in districts of privilege:

> It is clear to us that in order to achieve the constitutional standard for the student from these poorer urban districts — the ability to function in that society entered by their relatively advantaged peers — the totality of the districts' educational offering must contain elements over and above those found in the affluent suburban district. If the educational fare of the seriously disadvantaged student is the same as the "regular education" given to the advantaged student, those serious disadvantages will not be addressed, and students in the poorer urban districts will simply not be able to compete.

In a twist, however, this equalization of the opportunity to compete does not apply to students in all districts in the state — but only to those who do not receive the constitutional minimum. And here is where the court makes a fateful move: It applies its decision only to a limited number of central city school districts, with high percentages of poor and minority students. Relying on a New Jersey Department of Education classification scheme that places districts in socioeconomic groupings, the court applied its ruling only to the twenty-eight districts in District Factor Groups A and B — the districts with the lowest socioeconomic score. These "poorer urban districts" were "the sole object of the remedy we impose. . . ."[43]

The result is a decision in which the court simultaneously rejected a strict equalization of funds as the constitutional goal and then required an equalization of educational accomplishment, which would mean additional funds for low-achieving districts. The court was trying not to bring low-funded districts up to the level of affluent districts — but beyond them:

> We find that in order to provide a thorough and efficient education in these
> poorer urban districts, the State must assure that their educational expenditures
> per pupil are substantially equivalent to those of the more affluent suburban
> districts, and that, in addition, their special disadvantages must be addressed.[44]

In *Abbott II*, the court handed down a ruling that tried to live up to the
promise of *Robinson I*, but it actually went beyond *Robinson I*. *Abbott II*
significantly expanded *Robinson*'s scope, but targeted its effects on far fewer
districts. The New Jersey Supreme Court in *Abbott II* tried to learn from the
experiences of the *Robinson* decisions and focused its attention on the worst
harms of the existing educational financing system in the Garden State.
Rather than trying to make educational opportunities for all New Jersey's
students more similar, the court narrowed its task, striving to make the educational opportunities of the worst off equivalent to the best off.

While that narrowing of the reform task may have made sense jurispru-
dentially, it was difficult to sell politically. To place the educational offerings
and achievement in some of the worst school districts in the country on par
with some of the best meant an enormous reallocation of resources. Moreover, residents in the districts excluded from the remedy, middle-class and
lower-middle-class schools throughout the state, were not inclined to contribute taxes to an educational distribution scheme that would benefit only a
few districts, especially when there was pronounced need and disparity in
their own school districts, as well. As we will see in chapter 7, Governor Jim
Florio felt the wrath of these voters when he attempted to comply with the
Abbott II mandate. The New Jersey taxpayer revolt of 1990 and the subsequent installation of a solid Republican majority in the legislature and a
Republican governor illustrate the widespread popular discontent with an
education finance reform plan that raised income taxes throughout the state
to deliver benefits to only a few districts. In many ways, Jim Florio's Quality
Education Act, despite its overtures to the middle class throughout the state,
never stood a chance because the jurisprudential logic of the *Abbott II*
could not be reconciled with the political logic of the regime of educational
inequality in New Jersey.[45]

In *Abbott IV*, the court shows some realization of the political and educational difficulties of implementing *Abbott II*'s mandate of equal achievement between the poorest and the most affluent districts in the state. Nonetheless, the decision struck down the plan adopted by Florio's successor
Christine Todd Whitman and continued to insist that it must vindicate the
constitutional rights of the plaintiffs:

> We consistently have recognized that no single remedy can assure the provision
> of a constitutionally thorough and efficient education to the children in the
> special needs districts. . . .
> The judicial remedy [we impose] is necessarily incomplete; at best it serves

only as a practical and incremental measure that can ameliorate but not solve such an enormous problem. It cannot substitute for the comprehensive remedy that can be effectuated only through legislative and executive efforts.

The finiteness of judicial power, however, does not diminish the judicial obligation to vindicate constitutional rights.[46]

Significantly, the *Abbott IV* decision did not strike down the basic framework of Whitman's plan, simply the funding level that had been approved. For the first time within the *Abbott* litigation, the court approved, in theory, the structure of a reform package enacted by the state legislature. As we shall see in chapter 7, that acceptance of a constitutionally required "core curriculum" marks a major shift in the court's willingness to attack the broader regime of inequality within New Jersey school finance. Although it required still more money from the state, *Abbott IV* signaled an important retreat from the lofty goals of *Abbott II*. What followed in *Abbott V* was simply an express acceptance of that retreat. *Abbott V* is in large part an administrative ruling doling out educational resources to particular districts, rather than a systematic evaluation of structural change in New Jersey school finance. That is, quite simply, because there was little structural change. Instead, Whitman's funding plan provided more resources to particular districts, but preserved the regime's basic design. The court admitted its inability to tackle this larger problem at the end of *Abbott V* when it urged all parties concerned with public education in New Jersey to commit to its own vision of educational opportunity:

> It is not enough, however, that the three branches of government, sometimes working together and sometimes at apparent odds, have each responded to the challenge to carry out the Constitution's command of a thorough and efficient education. We must reach the point where it is possible to say with confidence that the most disadvantaged school children in the State will not be left out or left behind in the fulfillment of that constitutional promise. Success for all will come only when the roots of the educational system — the local schools and districts, the teachers, the administrators, the parents and the children themselves — embrace the educational opportunity encompassed by these reforms.[47]

In effect, the court was saying that its job was done. It had secured more resources for these children in a decades-long battle with the state legislature and New Jersey taxpayers, and it was now up to parents, teachers, and children to make good use of these resources. As the court wrote: "[T]his decision should be the last major judicial involvement in the long and tortuous history of the State's extraordinary effort to bring a thorough and efficient education to the children in its poorest school districts."[48] This is not the voice of a court still determined to uproot the organization of educational finance, but is instead a court somewhat chastened by political resistance, somewhat proud of its accomplishments, and definitely wearied by the fight.

Perhaps not surprisingly, the court's pronouncement of the end of this litigation was a bit premature. In 2000 the New Jersey Supreme Court handed down two further decisions in the case, *Abbott VI* and Abbott VII, but both had all the hallmarks of a mop-up operation.[49] *Abbott VI* clarified the nature of the early education programs required in the special needs districts, while *Abbott VII* insisted that the state, not local districts, pay the full costs of new school construction required under *Abbott V*. Nevertheless, the court seems to have little enthusiasm for continued litigation. While the experiences of the New Jersey Supreme Court show that political learning may not come easily or quickly, and that some courts may be more willing to stand by their commitments than others, they do show that political learning is a necessary, but painful, consequence of judicial attempts to restructure the institutional features of education that foster continued inequality.

Higher Law Obligations of State Constitutions

One reason a state supreme court may be reluctant to accept the lessons of politics within the realm of school financing is its conviction that an important and substantial right is at stake, a right that is articulated within the state constitution and should be defended by judges. The view that state constitutional language should control the distribution of educational resources is not only a judicial assertion of power within the state context, but also a theory of constitutionalism. Within this theory of constitutionalism, state constitutions are national constitutions in miniature, a higher law controlling the rough and tumble of legislative and executive lawmaking. The ability of state constitutions to impose fundamental obligations on lawmakers and law enforcers is a relatively new view in American politics. Until the early 1970s, state constitutions were the forgotten documents of the American political order. Then, the "new judicial federalism" came into prominence as federal courts began to scale back the civil rights and civil liberties protections of the Warren era.[50] School finance reform, in fact, was one of the first areas in which this form of judicial policy-making took root. As the adherents of the new judicial federalism (judges and legal academics alike) developed a body of law based on state supreme court interpretations of state constitutions, they also applied, largely without question, the prevailing academic view of the U.S. Constitution to state charters. That view, still vigorously defended today, holds that the meaning and content of the U.S. Constitution is determined exclusively by the decisions of the U.S. Supreme Court.[51] But the advocates of the new judicial federalism did more than assign exclusive interpretative powers to state supreme courts when they pursued these decisions. They also signed on to a theory of higher law constitutionalism and applied that theory to state constitutional interpretation. This state-level higher law constitutionalism contends, simply, that a state constitution is a fundamental expression of both the powers of state government and the rights of citizens and that it ought to control the mere statutory language that state legislators codify in their pluralistic bargaining and negotiation.

Yet there are a number of potential problems with viewing state constitutions as mere replicas of the U.S. Constitution, allowing for cultural and regional differences. These problems present both interpretive and political difficulties for courts. In the course of ruling on school finance issues, state supreme courts have not been unmindful of the problems that their state charters pose. Indeed, we can attribute at least some of the reluctance of some state justices to striking down school finance systems to their misgivings about the fundamental nature of state constitutions and the higher law obligations they allegedly impose.[52] Perhaps the most apparent difficulty with state constitutions is their mutability — the ease and frequency with which they are amended, altered, or supplanted. The American states have had a total of 145 constitutions and have amended them nearly six thousand times.[53] In addition, state constitutions are amended at a rate nearly ten times that of the U.S. Constitution. Finally, proposed amendments have a very high success rate at the state level: between 1776 and 1979, nearly two-thirds of all proposed state constitutional amendments were adopted, via all forms of amendment processes (legislative, convention, and initiative).[54] The resulting picture is one in which the provisions of the "fundamental" state charter of a state are junked, scribbled on, and scratched out with dramatic regularity and remarkable ease. State constitutions are simply much more fluid documents than the U.S. Constitution, and open to much greater democratic expression. Another difficulty arises when judges consult the historical record to interpret provisions of state constitutions: Typically, it does not exist or is very thin. The statements of the "founders" at state constitutional conventions are generally not available or of poor quality. Ascertaining original intent in such situations is difficult, if not impossible, given such a scant record.[55] Finally, state constitutions typically blend mundane statutory provisions with fundamental protections. For example, the New York Constitution stipulates the width of cross-country ski trails, while the Oregon Constitution regulates the sale of alcohol by the glass. This mixing of higher law with common statutory enactments means some judges are less likely to view the higher law mandates as sufficiently compelling to overturn the legislative interpretation of the clause in question. This is especially true in light of the mutability of the state constitutions, which allows a sufficiently mobilized democratic majority to reverse a court decree at the next election. Certainly the electoral reversals that same-sex marriage activists have suffered in Hawaii and Alaska in the wake of court victories in those states give pause to a judge intent on imposing an unpopular structural reform on a democratic majority.[56]

Despite these difficulties of interpretation, the higher law vision of state constitutionalism generally holds sway within state supreme courts (at least within school finance law), most likely because such an orientation maximizes judicial power and is consonant with the traditional judicial ability to define the meaning of the U.S. Constitution. The following statement by the Vermont Supreme Court is an apt illustration:

> [I]n Vermont the right to education is so integral to our constitutional form of government, and its guarantees of political and civil rights, that any statutory framework that infringes upon the equal enjoyment of that right bears a commensurate heavy burden of justification. The State has not provided a persuasive rationale for the undisputed inequities in the current educational funding system. Accordingly, we conclude that the current system, which concededly denies equal educational opportunities, is constitutionally deficient.[57]

This passage sets out the basic structure of the higher law view of state constitutionalism: education is a fundamental right of Vermont's citizens and a statute that impairs that right cannot stand. Contrast this view with one articulated by Justice Sherman Horton in the neighboring state of New Hampshire, only ten months later:

> We have held that our constitution invests in the legislature and the magistrates of this State the duty to provide a constitutionally adequate education and to guarantee the funding thereof. . . . "Constitutional adequacy" is not "general adequacy." The former must be determined by a careful reading of our constitution. The latter may be important to the makers of policy, but it is clear that one man's adequacy is another's deficiency. Under our system of government, the elected representatives of the people must strike the balance.

Horton goes on to say that his "constitutional standard for adequacy would be satisfied if the education provided meets the minimum necessary to assure the preservation of a free government."[58] Although there are obviously two different constitutional texts at issue here, the contrasting views of the burdens imposed by the respective state constitutions are striking, and I suggest that they actually reveal two different understandings of state constitutionalism.[59] Horton may believe that the New Hampshire Constitution guarantees only the barest of educational rights, but such a minimal right does not rest easily with a higher law view of state constitutionalism. Instead, it suggests a state constitutional order in which legislative majorities hold greater sway over policy-making than countermajoritarian courts striking down statutory frameworks that impinge on fundamental rights. The contrast between a minimalist view of the educational obligations that a state owes its children and a fundamental rights perspective can be attributed simply to a judicial disagreement over the depth of a state's commitment to public education. But it also provides a glimpse into a realm of state constitutional adjudication where rights simply mean less and democratic majorities and localist concerns are better able to resist the judicial imperatives of higher-law constitutionalism.[60]

Conclusion

Providing some measure of coherence to the various threads of school finance jurisprudence and judicial policy-making is no easy task. The law touches on numerous issues: the theoretical and political dimensions of equality, separation of powers, democratic processes, sound educational policy, and even constitutional theory. My aim here has been to highlight the significant political and jurisprudential obstacles that state supreme courts must confront as they wrestle with the complex issues of educational opportunity and school financing. The survey has been by no means exhaustive, and undoubtedly important dimensions of important rulings have been neglected. But the primary aim — to reveal the necessary boundedness of judicial ambitions as courts enter and do battle within the constitutional arena of educational opportunity — emerges through the numerous accounts provided here. Part of the reason judicial ambitions are necessarily bounded is because other actors have their own visions of the educational opportunities and obligations the state constitution demands. The judicial project of ordering educational opportunity within a state, clarifying the state's obligations, and ensuring that sufficient revenues exist to meet those obligations is only one facet of the constitutional politics of educational opportunity that these cases evoke. Constitutional ordering of educational opportunity goes beyond courts and the limitations, obstacles, and frustrations they face. It touches on both the normative commitments of the citizenry and the institutional organization of education and educational politics. It is to those forms of constitutional ordering that I turn in the next two chapters.

6

THE PUBLIC'S OPINION:

UNDERSTANDING PUBLIC COMMITMENTS

TOWARD EDUCATIONAL OPPORTUNITY

CONSTITUTIONAL ORDERING of educational opportunity transcends the judicial opinions that establish the terms of conflict and reform. Like any good constitutional conflict, the struggle for educational opportunity necessarily mobilizes public sentiment and attitudes. Judicial opinions are one part of the process of constitutional ordering, but they cannot, in themselves, generate the political will and commitment needed to meaningfully change the distribution of educational resources. The success of school finance reform also depends, in part, on public support. Because school finance is centrally concerned with state taxation and state aid to education, keen public opposition on these issues will spell legislative defeat. Indeed, public opinion often forms a brake on reform efforts, inhibiting or restricting the scope of school finance changes.

This chapter explores the divisions in public attitudes toward funding schools equally and toward school finance reforms generally. The data analyzed here show strong support for equal educational opportunity, across states and across time. The language of equal educational opportunity clearly taps into a widely held American commitment, but it also implicitly threatens another cherished American value, the local control of schools. By analyzing surveys that question respondents about their attitudes toward school finance equalization and school reforms generally, we can map out the differences between those who support greater equality in educational opportunity and those who oppose it. Using state-level public opinion polls, this chapter examines the characteristics of those who support and oppose funding schools equally. Through the use of statewide polls, we can get a more nuanced picture of public sentiment toward school funding than is available at the national level. Moreover, since school finance reforms are exclusively the province of state legislatures, state-level polls are the only appropriate means for gauging the influence of opinion on state legislatures.

These state-level polls, however, are not ideal. Polling questions vary across states and across times, and sample sizes are often small. But all of the polls analyzed here are done by highly reputable public opinion institutes primarily affiliated with universities in each state. These organizations have no ideological axes to grind and consistently produce high-quality surveys of public opinion. And aggregating polls helps overcome the problems inherent in small sample sizes. Through these polls, it is possible to map out the reactions of the public at large to school finance decisions and to identify the determinants of support for and opposition to school finance reform. Moreover, we can turn the curse of different question phrasings into a blessing: the aggregation of polling data provides a test of the salience of different phrasings of equality questions, allowing us, in turn, to assess the relative strength of egalitarian commitments vis-à-vis other normative and political values.

In short, understanding these cleavages in public opinion over school financing can help us see where courts may underappreciate or overstate the nature of public opposition to this rather energetic intrusion into local democratic processes. Many court decisions in the school finance arena explicitly cite public opposition as either a legitimate concern of the state legislature or as irrelevant to the demands of the state constitution. These decisions, however, do not fully understand the nature of this opposition; they simply assume, typically, that opposition is governed by the array of interests that are harmed and benefited by the decision. If one's ox is being gored, judges reasonably conclude, then one is less likely to support the goring. While that may be a logical premise, this study of public attitudes toward school finance reform shows that this assumption is not always true. The question, "Who opposes school finance equalization?" may be a simple one, but the answer is complex, not neatly breaking down into winners and losers. Courts should be aware of this fact as they deal with recalcitrant legislatures and organized interests that seek to influence the reform effort.

The first section of this chapter will briefly introduce the argument of the chapter, and the second section will then discuss the evidence offered by analyses of state-level polls and election returns.[1] The collective picture shows us that overall levels of support for equality are high, but that support is eroded when the public perceives an attack on local control. Moreover, a number of background variables, most notably ideological and partisan differences among respondents, as well as class and age differences, are significantly related to opposition to equal educational opportunity. Some states also show evidence of a racial division among respondents. The constant concern of respondents, however, can be found in the local circumstances of schools — particularly school effectiveness, school fiscal responsibility, and local control of schools.

Comparing all these dimensions across multiple states, multiple polls, and multiple years can be a messy task, and it is not always easy to obtain comparable results. In general, I have minimized these problems by defining one basic model, applied in each of the states, which defines the relevant variables, as far as possible, in comparable terms. By pooling data across different surveys that ask similar questions, we can derive a thorough picture of attitudes toward educational opportunity, even if that picture at times looks like an impressionist's portrait rather than a sharply focused photograph.

The Argument

Americans like equality — at least the notion of it. Survey respondents in repeated statewide polls broadly endorse some form of egalitarian sentiment within educational opportunity, typically by margins of 70 to 80 percent. When asked whether school funding *ought* to be equal, most Americans say yes — at least until they are confronted with other conflicting values: localism and higher taxes to name the most prominent. In short, when pollsters frame the equality question in the context of competing values or cost, support for equality diminishes significantly. This fragmentation of support for equal educational opportunity is important because it reveals how political values fare when pitted against each other and it demonstrates the relative strength of the American commitment to equality. By analyzing the determinants of opposition to equality and school financing reform — and how the introduction of competing values erodes egalitarian sentiment — we can better understand the legitimacy and illegitimacy of state supreme courts efforts to restructure school financing, particularly when judges choose to ignore or discount public opposition to court-ordered reforms.

Despite the importance of public opinion to reform efforts (and despite the enormous size of state and local education budgets), attitudes toward school financing are not extensively studied.[2] Attitudes toward taxes–general taxation, income tax, and property taxes — are widely surveyed, but there has been little investigation of how attitudes toward education and taxes for education vary by income and potential exposure to taxes. The limited research that has been conducted generally shows that self-interest is not a central element of support for either school bond measures[3] or educational reform in general. The two groups most likely either to pay the costs of these initiatives or to reap their benefits — higher income taxpayers and parents of school-age children — have shown attitudes roughly comparable to the population at large. In short, researchers have not, thus far, shown that supporters and opponents of educational finance issues break down neatly into beneficiaries and bankrollers.

These findings, however, may stem from the nature of school finance itself. Let's face it: the nuts and bolts of school financing are boring. From the perspective of citizens who face increasing job and family demands, declining free time, and far better entertainment options, tracking the developments of school financing and bond issues is not a high priority. To make matters worse, school financing is both confusing and difficult to understand.[4] Although exceedingly important to policy-makers and educational officials, the issue of school finance is precisely the daily drone about budgets, finances, and taxes that most citizens and voters tune out — unless they are directly affected, either through pending tax increases that *they* will have to pay or looming budget cuts for schools that *their* children attend. In this context, the disconnection between respondents' lives and the policy issue means that their positions may not be terribly reflective or informed. Salience and focus, then, may sharpen one's understanding of the relationship between self-interest and a proposed policy. That is, if an issue strikes close to home and one clearly perceives the impact of the policy, chances are one's perception of one's self-interest will generally prevail.[5]

In general, we can imagine three or four competing explanations as to why someone might oppose equal educational opportunity, given the relatively high rates of support in general. One possible explanation is premised on material self-interest. There are, of course, costs (both direct financial outlays and policy trade-offs) that accompany any effort to increase educational opportunity for some students. Money must be obtained from somewhere, and pursuing one policy option often prevents the pursuit of another. From this perspective, then, it might be reasonable to expect older residents, parents in middle-class or affluent districts, and those with high incomes (three groups most exposed to any potential increased costs accompanying a more equitable education and less likely to reap direct benefits from the reforms) will be opposed to the notion. Another possible explanation is more symbolic, rooted in ideology and party politics. The Democratic and Republican parties have differing views on the social goods that should be pursued in public education, and individual respondents may reflect those positions. In addition, political conservatives may wish the state were less involved in the pursuit of social policy through education and oppose greater educational opportunity on those grounds. These are two dimensions of an ideological or partisan explanation, which emphasize the more symbolic bases of conflicts over school finance. Finally, we might expect a racial and/or geographic division among respondents based on the perception of which groups and which places would most benefit from greater educational opportunity. That is, if racial minorities are seen as the typical beneficiaries, white respondents may be less likely to endorse the initiative. Similarly, if increased state aid is targeted to rural areas or urban centers (the two most visible forms of geographically concentrated poverty), then respondents who live in the suburbs may be more likely to oppose the educational reforms. Finally, respondents' attitudes may be influenced less by their demographic or individual characteristics and more by their perceptions of the harms and benefits these reforms may visit upon their local school districts. If, as Tip O'Neill reminded us, all politics is local, then the impact of these reforms on the local bottom line may be a strong determinant of support or opposition to the reforms. None of these four possible explanations precludes another, and it is, of course, possible that all of these explanations may be in play at once.

In the analysis below, I test each of these propositions. Not surprisingly, since the world is a complex place, many factors influence individual attitude towards educational opportunity, and each explanation surfaces at different points in the analysis. That said, I have found that when respondents perceive reforms as a threat to local control of their district, they typically react most negatively. In addition, I found that income and age are robust predictors of opposition as are the symbolic, ideological, and partisan differences among respondents. Finally, it seems that race and place considerations influence public attitudes less frequently, but they nonetheless have a statistically meaningful impact. It may be useful to think of these rival accounts of public attitudes toward educational opportunity as concentric circles or parallel levels of explanation, none of them precluding the other, but all of them meaningfully shaping the complex array of attitudes and opinions that Americans hold on educational opportunity.

The central role of local impact on school districts highlights a particularly sharp political difficulty for courts that engage in this kind of reform. The localism of school financing — and the politics that arises from that localism — is precisely what fuels the racial and geographic disparities of educational opportunity, and it this close nexus that state supreme courts have been directly challenging. Thus, the very thing Americans fear most in education reform, a retreat from localism, is the primary means by which courts and legislatures have attacked the sources of inequality and inadequacy in school finance. This clash, although not conclusively demonstrated in the polling results, becomes much more apparent when we look at political activity and political mobilization around the issue of school financing reform, the subject of chapter 7.

The remainder of this chapter is devoted to stepping through this argument. First, I will show that expressions of support for equality are quite high across the board, with nonwhites even more enthusiastic than whites. Second, I provide analyses of public opinion and election returns from five states (Connecticut, New Jersey, Kentucky, Tennessee, and Texas) I examined in chapter 2, highlighting the relevant differences among these states, and suggesting possible explanations for those differences. The chapter will conclude with a summary of the primary lessons to be learned from public attitudes toward educational finance reform.

The Evidence

A. How Much Do We Love Equality? Let Us Count the Polls

In poll after poll, respondents indicate that they favor a norm of equality in school financing. Although poll questions vary, sometimes significantly, we can nonetheless safely conclude that a strong majority of those surveyed expressed support for the notion that educational resources ought to be distributed equitably. Table 6.1 summarizes the findings for four of the five states I examine in this book.[6] In New Jersey, for example, 71.0 percent of 2,120 respondents indicated that they approved of the New Jersey Supreme Court's decision. In Tennessee, in polls taken in 1991 and 1992, nearly 81 percent of the 1,452 respondents said they approved of the Tennessee Supreme Court's decision. In Kentucky, when pollsters asked respondents to choose between equal educational opportunity and high academic achievement, 72.6 percent chose equality over achievement. In Connecticut, over 61 percent of respondents supported equality of funding for schools. The pattern of these polling results indicates that equality enjoys a high measure of support among respondents — at least when there are few countervailing norms to dampen the enthusiasm. As Table 6.1 shows, virtually all groups strongly support the notion of equality in educational opportunity. These polling results illustrate both the durability and geographic extent of public support for equality, as these state-level polls were taken across four states, over a fifteen year period. Support for equality garners a strong majority of respondents in all states shown, and in some places runs exceptionally high.

Some groups, of course, endorse equality more strongly than others. In particular, racial minorities favor equal funding for schools at higher rates than whites. In New Jersey 68.1 percent of whites supported the New Jersey Supreme Court's decision in *Abbott II*, while 82.6 percent of nonwhites supported the decision. In Kentucky 71.5 percent of whites chose equal educational opportunity over high educational achievement as their preferred single goal in the educational system. Nonwhites in Kentucky favored equal educational opportunity over high achievement by an even higher margin: 86.0 percent. In only one state examined here, Tennessee, did white support for equality in educational opportunity exceed nonwhite support. In Tennessee, white support was exceptionally high, the highest of all the states examined here: 81.7 percent. And nonwhite support almost matched that level at nearly 77 percent. In general, however, while whites strongly favor equality in educational opportunity, nonwhites favor it at even higher rates. The historical denial of equal educational opportunity to blacks, particularly within education, probably accounts for this large divergence of opinion, but the results are striking nonetheless.

Other trends also emerge within categories across these states. In general, these changes reflect prevailing cleavages within American politics. For example, low-income respondents generally favored equal educational opportunity at higher rates than middle- or high-income respondents, with the exception of Connecticut. Also, liberals (except in Tennessee) favored it more than moderates and conservatives, and Democrats more than Independents and Republicans (except in Connecticut). Along the geographic dimension, we see that suburban respondents were typically the least sup-

TABLE 6.1
Support for Equality in Educational Opportunity, by State and Demographic Group

	Connecticut (1979, 1980)	New Jersey (1990, 1993, 1996)	Kentucky (1992)	Tennessee (1991, 1992)
	(N = 962)	(N = 2120)	(N = 609)	(N = 1452)
All Respondents	61.1	71.0	72.6	80.9
Race				
Whites	60.2	68.1	71.5	81.7
Nonwhites	74.6	82.6	86.0	76.7
Income[1]				
Low Income	58.8	84.5	77.4	83.1
Middle Income	65.9	77.6	72.8	81.7
High Income	55.2	68.0	59.1	75.7
Ideology				
Liberal	67.9	77.1	76.7	76.3
Moderate	61.8	76.9	73.1	80.9
Conservative	55.3	65.5	63.6	82.2
Party Affiliation				
Democrat	65.4	78.8	74.0	83.1
Independent	65.5	68.2	72.4	79.4
Republican	47.0	63.0	69.9	80.7
Residence				
Central/Large City	—	83.0	74.0	77.5
Suburban/Town	—	69.6	67.1	80.5
Rural/Small Town	—	71.2	80.0	85.4

Sources and dates: Connecticut, Roper Survey Center, University of Connecticut, ConnPoll #1 (May 1979), ConnPoll #7, June 1980; New Jersey, the Center for Public Interest Polling, Eagleton Institute of Politics, Rutgers University: EP-79, 2–10 July 1990, EP-94, 10–15 September 1993, EP-106, 22–29 February 1996; Kentucky, Survey Research Center, University of Kentucky, Kentucky Spring Poll Survey 1992, 20 April–12 May 1992; Tennessee, Social Science Research Center, University of Tennessee, Tennessee Survey, Fall 1991, 20–25 October 1991, Tennessee Survey, Spring 1992, 22 February–2 March 1992. With the exception of the Connecticut data, all data are available in original form from University of North Carolina's Institute for Research in Social Science Data Archive (http://www.irss.unc.edu/data_archive/). In all cases, "don't know" responses were treated as missing data. N reported is valid only for all respondents.

[1]Because different polls used different income groupings over the fifteen-year span that these polls were taken, income levels were broken into low, middle, and high categories according to the brackets used at the time. In Connecticut low income was $0–$10,000, middle income was $10,000–$30,000, and high income was greater than $30,000. In Kentucky and New Jersey, low income was defined as less than $20,000, middle income was $20,000–$50,000, high income was $50,000 and up. In Tennessee, low income was defined as less than $25,000, middle income was $25,000–$50,000, and high income was greater than $50,000.

portive, while central/large cities, along with rural areas and small towns, were more in favor of equality in educational opportunity.

These results are not terribly surprising; other than the high aggregate level of support for equal educational opportunity and the width of the racial cleavage on this issue, little stands out as shocking or perplexing. These levels of support for educational opportunity seem a bit like supporting Mom and apple pie. Equality has, from America's founding, proven to be a powerful claim in American politics, perhaps not as powerful as the claim of liberty, but certainly a cornerstone faith in the American civil religion. The interesting question, then, is what separates us from our commitment to equality? Along what lines do we divide when we go our separate ways on the issue of equal educational opportunity? In order to assess this, we need to see which factors predominate and in what settings. Thus, in order to understand the relative weights of these possible determinants of opposition to equal educational opportunity, we need to control for the independent effects of class, race, ideology, and even geography on these attitudes. Regression analysis can help us determine the relative strength of each of these independent variables (race, class, ideology, and geography) to predict the dependent variable, in this case opposition to equality.[7] The remainder of this chapter will present regression analyses (both logistic regressions and multiple linear regressions) of public opinion in four states (New Jersey, Connecticut, Kentucky, and Tennessee) and election returns from Texas. These regression analyses will help us better understand those factors that reduce respondents' support for funding schools equally and will better explain the cleavages within the electorates of these states over this issue.

New Jersey

New Jersey's battles with school financing date to the early 1970s, when the state supreme court declared the inequalities in New Jersey in violation of the state constitution, only thirteen days after the U.S. Supreme Court's decision in *Rodriguez*. Since then, litigators, judges, and lawmakers have wrangled for nearly thirty years to produce a school finance scheme compatible with the state's constitutional obligation to provide a "thorough and efficient" system of public education. In 1989 the battle flared up yet again, as the state supreme court ruled in the *Abbott II* decision that the then-existing method of financing education was still constitutionally unacceptable. As I will discuss in the next chapter, Governor Jim Florio used the *Abbott II* decision as an opportunity to substantially overhaul the state's aid to local districts. His initiative, known as the Quality Education Act, not only sought to increase funding for the twenty-eight poorest districts in the state that the state supreme court had singled out, but also to increase funding to some two hundred lower- and middle-class districts across the state. His logic, that increased aid to middle-class districts would ensure political support for the costly educational assistance plan, proved to be wide of the mark—very wide. The plan sparked intense outrage among New Jersey's voters—who were also angry about a $2 billion tax increase to eliminate the state budget deficit and to pay for the school finance equalization plan. So angry, in fact, that they eventually swept Florio and the Democratic state assembly out of office, replacing both with Republicans.

A symbol for the moderate wing of the Republican party, Christine Todd Whitman immediate announced a three-year plan to reduce the state's income tax by 30 percent. Whitman, however, still confronted a difficult school funding problem. Eventually, Whitman and the state legislature ponied up more money for the twenty-eight poorest districts in the state, those that the New Jersey Supreme Court had singled out as the appropriate beneficiaries of the constitutional remedy. Pacified partly by Whitman's income tax cuts and partly by a rising economy within the state, the New Jersey electorate gave Whitman and the state legislature the political space to increase the aid to these twenty-eight "special-needs" districts. The state supreme court, however, continued to apply pressure throughout this ongoing political saga, repeatedly holding that the state must provide more resources to the poorest districts in the state in order to meet its constitutional obligation.

Amid these political developments, the Eagleton Center at Rutgers University conducted numerous polls on the mood of the New Jersey electorate. Many of their polls touched on educational issues, particularly the *Abbott II* decision and other, more specific reforms. Although not all questions related to school finance reform were asked in each poll, in three polls between 1990 and 1996, the Eagleton Center pollsters asked essentially the same question: "In general, do you agree or disagree that spending for education must be equal in all of New Jersey's school districts? Do you (agree/disagree) mildly or strongly?"[8] In aggregate, over 2,100 respondents answered this question, with 71 percent endorsing equal funding for schools. But what about the opposition? Is it possible to predict opposition to the *Abbott II* decision based on the characteristics of respondents? Table 6.2 presents regression analyses of attitudes toward the court case that seek to do precisely that.[9] These findings illustrate some of the basic themes of this chapter: the importance of the local effects of reform; the salience of self-interest, age, ideology, and party affiliation; as well as the significance of income and race to attitudes toward school finance reform. The table presents the standardized coefficients of the regression equations as well as the t-scores. For the sake of full presentation, both the pooled regression results (All Dates) and the regression results for each individual poll are presented in the tables. The comments presented here, however, will focus on the pooled results.

TABLE 6.2

Regression Analysis of Opposition to the *Abbott II* Decision in New Jersey, 1990–96

	All Dates (pooled analysis)	7/90	10/93	3/96	7/90 with Local Effects Variables
Common Variables					
Age	0.102*	0.067	0.163*	0.061	0.026
	(3.912)	(1.150)	(3.905)	(1.370)	(0.416)
Community Type	0.027	0.007	0.055	0.023	−0.059
	(1.077)	(0.119)	(1.335)	(0.520)	(−1.039)
Education Level	0.109*	−0.037	0.126*	0.184*	−0.022
	(4.132)	(−0.633)	(2.937)	(4.182)	(−0.365)
Ideology	0.067*	0.156*	0.045	0.020	0.134*
	(2.781)	(2.896)	(1.132)	(0.513)	(2.397)
Income	0.141*	0.151*	0.183*	0.104*	0.105
	(5.207)	(2.584)	(4.117)	(2.298)	(1.734)
Parents of School-Age Children	−0.019	0.010	−0.031	−0.025	0.048
	(−0.792)	(0.180)	(−0.805)	(−0.602)	(0.864)
Party Affiliation	0.093*	0.103	0.104*	0.079	0.068
	(3.695)	(1.764)	(2.525)	(1.935)	(1.138)
Race	−0.053*	−0.095	−0.017	−0.069	−0.053
	(−2.031)	(−1.688)	(−0.393)	(−1.527)	(−0.902)
Poll-Specific Variables					
Perceived effect of tax package on "people like you"	—	—	—	—	0.195*
					(3.623)
Perceived effect of reform on state aid to local District	—	—	—	—	0.184*
					(3.210)
Perceived effect of reform on local property taxes	—	—	—	—	0.094
					(1.665)
Poll Date Control Variables					
July 1990	0.277*	—	—	—	—
	(10.586)				
October 1993	0.051*	—	—	—	—
	(1.980)				

TABLE 6.2 (*continued*)

	All Dates (pooled analysis)	7/90	10/93	3/96	7/90 with Local Effects Variables
Model Summary Statistics					
Constant (unstandardized)	0.223	1.011*	0.044	0.540	−1.047
	(1.064)	(2.084)	(0.150)	(1.562)	(−1.642)
R^2	0.140	0.085	0.118	0.088	0.175
Adj. R^2	0.135	0.065	0.107	0.076	0.145
N	1602	363	627	612	318

Data Source: Center for Public Interest Polling, Eagleton Institute of Politics, Rutgers University, Polls EP-79, EP-94, and EP-106.
Standard coefficient reported, *t*-scores in parentheses; *$p < 0.05$

ANALYSIS OF THE POOLED DATA

The first column in table 6.2, All Dates, shows the regression results of the entire pooled data set from all three Eagleton polls taken between 1990 and 1996 that surveyed respondents about the *Abbott II* decision. The next three columns present the results for each individual survey, while the final column applies the same basic model to the July 1990 poll, but adds three additional variables that were asked only in that survey.

The All Dates analysis shows eight significant variables: Age, Education Level, Ideology, Income, Party Affiliation, Race, a dummy variable for the July 1990 poll, and a dummy variable for the October 1993 variable. By far, the dummy variable for the July 1990 poll is the single largest coefficient within the regression analysis. This suggests that the nature of opposition in July 1990 was significantly different from the opposition registered in the other polls. In short, respondents surveyed in July 1990 supported the *Abbott II* decision at far lower rates than the respondents in the September 1993 or the February 1996 poll, even those with similar incomes, educational levels, racial identification, age, residence, and so forth. The July 1990 opponents were motivated, it appears, by different factors than the respondents in the other two polls.

Why the difference between July 1990 and the other dates? Part of the answer may lie in a general decline in opposition over time. The decreasing size and significance of the coefficients of the poll date control variables suggest that the initial reaction to the *Abbott II* decision was one of outright hostility, which then faded as time went by. Certainly the events of the New Jersey tax revolt — which peaked in the late summer and early fall of 1990, resulting in the ouster of a Democratic majority from the New Jersey state house and the near-defeat of Senator Bill Bradley to political newcomer Christine Todd Whitman—suggest that the New Jersey electorate in the summer of 1990 did not support equalization because it translated, in their eyes, into tax hikes and possible cuts in state aid to middle-class and affluent school districts.

But even when we control for these poll date differences, the All Dates analysis reveals some striking results. For example, income is the second largest predictor of opposition to the court decision. Party affiliation also exerts a modest influence on attitudes, as do the age and educational level of the respondents, with ideology and race showing less sizable, but still significant relationships. Thus, the pooled analysis column of table 6.2 reveals a meaningful class educational cleavage among New Jerseyans on the *Abbott II* decision. The class and education variables exhibit significant, if not sizable, relationships to the respondents' views on the court decree. It appears, then, that respondents with higher incomes were less favorable to equalization while more educated respondents were less favorable. In New Jersey, at least, part of the opposition within the electorate to the court decisions and the subsequent legislation designed to remedy the constitutional injury was clearly rooted in class, as well as age, ideology, and race. Here, the typical tensions one associates between rich and poor, white and nonwhite are evident in the public attitudes toward school finance. Equally salient, the respondent's educational level is a useful predictor of support; that is, the more education one has, the less likely one is to support funding schools equally—at least within New Jersey in the 1990s.

In sum, the pooled analysis tells us that the attitudes of respondents toward equality (as represented by the *Abbott II* decision) are influenced by a complex mix of variables, in which the expected clusters of interests (age, class, and race) are compounded by more symbolic cleavages of party affiliation and ideology. In this sense, we can regard the divisions within New Jersey's electorate over school finance equalization as one defined both by concrete interests and by ideological and partisan disagreements over the appropriate role of the state in educational financing. Material interests intersect with symbolic ones, resulting in a public opinion in which some respondents align along racial and class lines, while others view the issue more ideologically.

CONTROLLING FOR LOCAL EFFECTS IN NEW JERSEY

Let us consider the July 1990 poll again. In that poll, the Eagleton Center asked respondents questions that allow us to assess the salience of self-interest and local control concerns in school financing disputes. Unfortunately, these questions were not repeated in later polls, making direct comparisons across polls impossible. The final column of table 6.2 shows the results of the regression model for the July 1990 responses only, including three additional variables—the perceived effect of Florio's tax package on "people like you," the perceived effects of the proposed reforms on state aid to local districts, and their perceived effects on local property taxes. The results are remarkable: The perceived effects of the tax package and of reforms on state aid to local districts substantially exceed the effects of ideology—the only other statistically significant variable.

Of the six demographic variables that were significant in the first column in table 6.2, only ideology remains salient to respondents' support for the *Abbott II* decision in the final column. In addition, perceived loss of aid to one's school district (local control) and the perceived effects of the Florio tax plan on people "like you" (self-interest) show highly significant and large relationships to opposing the *Abbott II* decision. In other words, respondents were highly attuned to both the personal and local impact of Florio's tax and educational spending plans, and those concerns substantially outweighed the effects of their age, education, and income on their attitudes toward the court decision, effects that were prominent in column one of table 6.2.

So, what does all this mean? First, it is reasonable to conclude that something different was going on in July 1990. Those effects show up in both the size and significance of the control variable for July 1990 in the pooled data set and in the different results obtained in the July 1990 local effects analysis. In July 1990 a sharp sensitivity to both economic self-interest and the local effects of the reform package seemed to drive the conflict, along with ideology and income differences.

Also interesting in table 6.2 are the factors that are not reliable predictors of support for equalization. The residents of New Jersey's central cities—the most prominent beneficiaries of New Jersey's equalization reforms—do not exhibit any greater support for equalization than the nonresidents of central cities, when we control for race, class, ideology, income, and so on. The mere fact of being a central city resident, in itself, does not make one more likely to support equalization. Similarly, whether one has children enrolled in public schools does not appear to be reliably related to support or opposition to funding schools equally. In short, this means that the attitudes of those who are most likely to benefit from the *Abbott II* decision—inner-city parents—are not distinguishable in a statistical sense from those who are not inner-city parents.[10]

Three lessons stand out from this series of New Jersey polls. First, we can expect opposition to a court decision to decline over time, as either the salience of the issue fades or the political response diminishes the redistributive threat of the court decree. Second, these findings suggest that local control issues are stronger predictors of opposition than other demographic variables, and they persist even when one controls for economic self-interest.

The evidence indicates that localism transcends the economic self-interest of respondents. More than just the financial costs of reform bother some respondents; the prospects of diminished local control are also troubling. Third, these findings also highlight the importance of symbolic and ideological concerns in attitude towards school funding. In the big picture, then, localism is a persistent and durable dimension of conflicts over educational opportunity, one that is on a par with both symbolic values and self-interest as a motivation for opposing greater educational opportunity.

Connecticut

In 1974 young Barnaby Horton was about to enter kindergarten in Canton, Connecticut. Most parents of kindergartners are fussing over school supplies, new school clothes, and tears at the classroom door. Not Barnaby's dad. He was preparing for Barnaby's trial against the State of Connecticut. His father, an attorney and Canton school-board member, had decided to sue the state on Barnaby's behalf, arguing that the school financing system violated the equality provisions of the state constitution (Horton 1992b). By the time the Connecticut Supreme Court had issued its final ruling in the *Horton v. Meskill* case in 1985, Barnaby was a junior in high school and the state of Connecticut had redesigned its system of funding public schools. In the midst of the contested and difficult legislative reform efforts, pollsters at the University of Connecticut surveyed Connecticut voters about public education, including some questions on how schools ought to be funded. Two polls, Connecticut Poll 1 and Connecticut Poll 7, conducted in May 1979 and June 1980, respectively, explicitly asked about respondents' attitudes toward funding schools equally. In this section, I analyze that polling data to understand the cleavages over equal school funding in Connecticut. In this analysis, these two data sets are merged and analyzed using logistic regression to discern the influences on respondents' attitudes toward funding schools equally. The findings, presented in table 6.3, highlight the salience of local control of public education to school funding as well as the more symbolic dimensions of school financing struggles.

As we look down the left-hand side of table 6.3, we see that a number of variables are closely associated with an opposition to equality in school spending. Among the demographic variables in the basic model, we see that party affiliation, age, ideology, and income (in decreasing magnitude) all contribute significantly to the likelihood that a respondent will oppose equal funding. Thus, when other variables are held constant, Democrats, liberals, the young, and the poor are more likely to favor equal funding, while Republicans, conservatives, older residents, and the wealthy are less likely to favor it. This sounds reasonable, given the historical commitments of the two major parties, the interests of the elderly, and class divisions in the

TABLE 6.3
Logistic Regression and Probability Analysis of Opposition to Funding Schools Equally in Connecticut, 1979–80

	Model Characteristics			Probability Analysis of Significant Variables	
	Parameter Estimate (B)	S.E.	Sig.	Change in this variable	. . . changes the probability that R opposed funding schools equally by this much . . .
Common Variables					
Age	0.3064* (4.26)	0.0720	0.0000	from "< 30 yrs. old" to "46–59 yrs. old" (1,3)	+2.25%
Community Type	—	—	—		
Education Level	0.0834 (1.16)	0.0719	0.2460		
Ideology	0.2640* (2.36)	0.1118	0.0182	from "liberal" to "conservative" (1,3)	+1.68%
Income	0.1683* (2.16)	0.0780	0.0310	from "10k to 20K" to ">50K" (2,5)	+1.36%
Parents of Children <18	—	—	—		
Party Affiliation	0.3112* (2.77)	0.1125	0.0057	from "Democrat" to "Republican" (1,3)	+1.90%
Race	0.0864 (0.27)	0.3233	0.7892		
Poll Date Control Variable					
Local Control Phrasing	1.3627* (8.23)	0.1656	0.0000	from "No mention" to "Local control stressed" (0,1)	+4.53%
Model Summary Statistics					
N	800				
−2 Log Likelihood	941.278				
Percent predicted correctly	68.78				
Distribution of dependent variable	1 (favor) = 68.1 2 (oppose) = 38.9				

Data Source: Connecticut Poll 1 (March 1979) and Connecticut Poll 7 (June 1980), University of Connecticut Social Science Data Center, Storrs, Connecticut.

Betas reported; beta/S.E. in parentheses.

*$p < 0.05$

'Change in probability calculated using the "first differences" formula described in Gary King's Unifying Political Methodology: The Likelihood Theory of Statistical Inference (Cambridge: Cambridge University Press, 1989), 107–108. All independent variables are held constant at their means, and two distinct values (derived from the variable coding) are entered into the formula to obtain the probability change.

United States. All these variables, however, pale in comparison to the largest predictor of opposition to equal funding: the issue of local control.

The final variable in table 6.3 is Local Control Phrasing, and it simply indicates whether the equal funding question mentioned local control. Although these two polls were taken a year apart, for our purposes, the primary difference between them lies in the way they describe the stakes of equal school funding. This phrasing, it turns out, is highly significant because it taps into a strongly held tenet of American education: the notion that schools ought to be locally controlled, both financially and politically. In short, the significance of this phrasing—and the size of its impact on attitudes—shows quite convincingly that a respondent's commitment to equality can be eroded if achieving equality is translated into a loss of local control of public schools.

In the first poll, the question focused on a trade-off some argue is inevitable in school finance equalization. Pollsters asked, "Some people feel that the same amount ought to be spent for the public schools throughout Connecticut. Others think that the citizens of each town should be able to decide how much they want to spend on education. Which do you think is more important, (1) to fund schools equally or (2) to let towns decide how much to spend on their schools?" This phrasing pits equality directly against local control; it suggest that equality can only be achieved by reducing the influence of each town over its level of educational spending. In contrast, the second poll simply asked, "Some people say that the state should see to it that rich communities and poor communities have the same amount of money per student to spend on their schools. In general, do you favor this, or oppose it?"[11] When pollsters framed the question this way, support for equality rose dramatically. In the first statewide Connecticut Poll ever conducted by the Roper Center at the University of Connecticut, in the spring of 1979, only 49 percent of respondents supported equality (when it was linked to local control). In a poll conducted by the same organization a year later, nearly 74 percent of respondents indicated support for equality.

Table 6.3 shows that the salience of local control is robust; those differences hold up even when we control for party affiliation, ideology, age, income, and other variables. But in order to determine the magnitude of these influences we need to look at the right-hand side of Table 6.3. There we find the change in probability that a respondent will oppose funding schools equally, holding all other variables constant at their means. What we find is that when pollsters suggest that equal funding might reduce local control, the probability of opposing equality increases by nearly five percentage points. This impact is twice the size of the impact of the age variable and over twice the size of the party affiliation impact. Local control phrasing is by far the largest and most significant determinant of opposition to equal funding in Connecticut.

In short, the five significant variables in this analysis—local control phrasing, party affiliation, ideology, age, and income—illustrate a basic argument of this chapter: Opposition to school finance equalization emerges out of a combined fear of diminished local autonomy and a charged symbolic and ideological environment in which one's class position is simply one relevant interest among many. Attitudes toward equality in public school funding involve a complex mix of ideology and attitudes toward school governance that transcends a battle of the haves versus the have-nots. Indeed, in Connecticut the strongest contributor to opposition to funding schools equally stemmed from fears of a loss of local control. That concern, when combined with a familiar distributional politics premised on liberal-conservative, Democratic-Republican, young-old cleavages, transforms the public opinion battles over funding schools equally into symbolic fights that are organized around predominantly *local* issues. Respondents in the Connecticut surveys warmed much more readily to the notion of equality when pollsters did not suggest to them that equality would reduce local control. This sensitivity to questions of control and governance is one that policy-makers would do well to heed as they design mechanisms of reform to comply with court decisions.

Despite the strong showing of intuitively important cleavages, others, seemingly equally relevant, do not appear to be relevant. Most surprisingly, education levels and race are *not* related to one's support for funding schools equally. This is somewhat counterintuitive, given the demographic characteristics of Connecticut. Long the most affluent state in the nation, Connecticut has also a long history of concentrated urban, African American, and Hispanic poverty. Throughout the 1980s, the three largest cities in Connecticut (Hartford, Bridgeport, and New Haven) consistently ranked among the ten poorest cities in the United States. The tensions between affluent suburban populations (until recently almost exclusively white) and poor, inner-city black and Hispanic residents constitute one of the major, if not *the* major, political and social cleavage within the state. In many ways, this finding that racial cleavages do not explain attitudes runs counter to both the New Jersey experience and the conventional wisdom on Connecticut politics. But before we write off race as a factor, we should remember the inherent limitations to public opinion surveys. They necessarily treat complex social issues as sound bites, reducing subtle positions to broad, unequivocal statements. The method of survey research, then, may flatten the racial dimensions of this dispute. Also, it is important to remember that it is not only affluent communities that seek to maintain, or even maximize, local control over the schools within their borders. The desire to assert local control can influence the attitudes of inner-city minority residents, as well — particularly when the state educational establishment is seen as a distant force, dominated by white bureaucrats who may not understand the needs of a predominantly black or Hispanic community. Unfortunately, the polls conducted in Connecticut did not gather information on the type of communities the respondents lived in, making it impossible to test this claim. But it seems at least plausible that localism may find support in both affluent, white suburbs and poor inner cities with large minority populations.

But the primary lesson of public opinion surveys in Connecticut on school finance reforms is that we cannot merely assume that race and class division alone undergird the fights over educational equality. Other factors such as concern for local control, ideology, partisan differences, and intergenerational conflict—factors perhaps not as obvious but certainly powerful—can sharply influence public opinion on these matters. The question that needs to be explored further is whether that pattern holds up across other states, especially those in which rural poverty predominates. I analyze those factors in the treatment of Kentucky and Tennessee.

Kentucky

In the Kentucky version of the school financing saga, the question of funding schools equally is a bit player in a larger drama about the nature of educational reform in general. The Kentucky Supreme Court's decision in *Rose v. Council for Better Education* sought not only the reform of the financing system within Kentucky education, but an overhaul of the entire *system* of public education, ranging from curriculum, to governance, to finance, to teacher training, even to the instruction of math and reading. The Kentucky educational system was so deficient, the state supreme court ruled, that only a massive overhaul of the entire system of education could meet the requirements of the state constitution. The *Rose* decision targeted more than unequal funding, seeking a systemic reform of Kentucky public education from the state legislature. The resulting legislation, the Kentucky Education Reform Act of 1990 (KERA), enacted sweeping changes in educational policy. Some of these, such as revamping the system of local educational governance, were long overdue and remedied widespread corruption in educational contracting. Others, such as the collapsing of grades one, two, and three during the first three years of primary education were more controversial. Throughout the course of reforms, the Kentucky Poll, conducted by the Survey Research Center at the University of Kentucky, queried state residents on a number of the features of the reform legislation. A few of these questions addressed equal funding, but because of the broad sweep of the KERA, other features received more prominent attention. In this analysis, I look predominantly at support for the KERA, but I also explore the extent to which Kentuckians favored equal educational opportunity over other values in public education. Pollsters asked respondents about their support for the KERA four times over two years. The results of regressions of the pooled poll responses appear in column one of table 6.4.

The analysis reveals a number of significant variables that predict opposition to the bill. Most prominent is the confidence one has in the ability of local schools to make good use of the new money. With a coefficient of 0.246, that variable is the largest and most clearly significant of all those

TABLE 6.4
Regression Analysis of Opposition to the Kentucky Education Reform Act (KERA) in Kentucky,
1992–94

	All Dates (pooled analysis)	4/92	11/93	5/94	11/94
Common Variables					
Age	0.097*	0.118	0.117*	0.102	0.088
	(3.072)	(1.709)	(2.083)	(1.477)	(1.308)
Community Type	−0.050	0.000	−0.097	−0.010	−0.136*
	(−1.696)	(−0.007)	(−1.826)	(−0.164)	(−2.079)
Education Level	0.049	0.028	0.152*	−0.059	0.088
	(1.558)	(0.412)	(2.639)	(−0.910)	(1.268)
Ideology	0.108*	0.081	0.053	0.107	0.217*
	(3.507)	(1.268)	(0.952)	(1.602)	(3.115)
Income	0.026	0.028	−0.036	0.138*	0.004
	(0.816)	(0.403)	(−0.639)	(2.092)	(0.060)
Parents of Children	0.089*	0.017	0.105	0.166*	0.073
< 18 yrs.	(2.797)	(0.248)	(1.872)	(2.443)	(1.111)
Party Affiliation	0.082*	0.065	0.007	0.163*	0.112
	(2.633)	(0.994)	(0.129)	(2.521)	(1.588)
Race	0.010	0.102	−0.093	−0.001	0.038
	(0.333)	(1.548)	(−1.765)	(−0.012)	(0.613)
Poll-Specific Variables					
Good Use of Local Funds	0.246*	0.230*	0.321*	0.190*	0.258*
	(8.655)	(3.772)	(6.195)	(3.148)	(4.125)
Poll Date Control Variables					
April 1992	−0.188*	—	—	—	—
	(−5.127)				
November 1993	−0.099*	—	—	—	—
	(−2.636)				
May 1994	−0.023	—	—	—	—
	(−0.622)				
Model Summary Statistics					
Constant	1.140*	0.895*	1.012*	0.804	0.859*
(unstandardized)	(6.212)	(2.704)	(3.523)	(1.884)	(2.262)
R^2	0.136	0.077	0.160	0.121	0.185
Adj. R^2	0.127	0.045	0.137	0.089	0.152
N	1094	266	336	264	228

Data Source: Survey Research Center, University of Kentucky, Kentucky Spring Poll Survey 1992, 20 April–12 May; Kentucky Fall Poll Survey, 1993, 18 November–22 December, 1993; Kentucky Spring Poll Survey, Part I, 1994, 12 May–2 June, 1994; Kentucky Fall Poll Survey, 1994, November 1994.
    Standard coefficients reported; t-scores in parentheses.
    *$p < 0.05$.

analyzed here. The other significant variables include two of the poll date control variables, ideology, age, parental status, and party affiliation. The overall picture, then, suggests that Kentuckians who were confident that their local schools could spend money wisely strongly supported the reform efforts. Also, it seems that Kentuckians were more enthusiastic about the KERA during the initial flush of reform and that their enthusiasm diminished over time, as evidenced by the statistical significance of two of the poll date control variables. Finally, we see that the divide over educational reform in Kentucky is partly attributable to the usual ideological, age, and partisan divisions that other states have shown. Liberals supported the measure more than conservatives, the young more than the old, and Democrats more than Republicans. Surprisingly, parents of children under the age of eighteen were less supportive of the KERA, all else equal. While the relationship is not a terribly strong one, it still is statistically significant.[209]

Table 6.4 also shows that attitudes toward the KERA are not linked to income. Class, as measured by income, does not have much to do with attitudes toward educational reforms, at least in Kentucky in the early 1990s. Also, it should be noted that race does not figure prominently in the split over the KERA. With essentially a zero beta and no statistical significance, race has no independent effect on respondents' KERA opinions. However, as we shall see, race plays a larger role in the negotiation over equal opportunity and high educational attainment. In general, however, the central division in Kentucky was whether one thought local schools could make good use of the funds that the KERA would generate. Those who had little confidence in their district's ability to use the funds wisely were less supportive of the KERA. Confidence in local schools, in contrast, boosted support for the KERA. Although this variable is not a direct measure of support for local control, it shows that local concerns in Kentucky, as in Connecticut and New Jersey, dominate ideological or class-based cleavages. The picture that emerges across states, regions, and forms of poverty is a localist referent to school issues. This referent is typically more important than income, party affiliation, ideology, and age. It seems that we perceive school reforms through a locally focused lens. In chapter 7, we will see how that localist orientation structures the mobilization of groups in the policy process.

One problem with the Kentucky surveys, for the present purposes, is that they examine support for a broad package of reforms rather than equal educational opportunity more specifically. In their earliest polling on the KERA, however, pollsters at the University of Kentucky focused directly on the issue of equality. Shortly after the legislature enacted the KERA, pollsters asked respondents to select one goal for Kentucky's educational system. After first querying whether respondents thought it was possible to achieve both high educational achievement and equal educational opportunity,[13] they then asked respondents, in effect, to pick sides: "If only one of these goals had to be chosen, which one would you consider more important?" As table 6.1 showed, a sizable majority of respondents opted for equal educational opportunity, nearly 73 percent. When these responses are further analyzed with logistic regression, we can see more clearly the independent effects of various factors on respondents' attitudes toward equality. Those results are summarized in table 6.5.

The results are important for two reasons. First, they reveal a significant racial difference between whites and nonwhites in Kentucky. Second, they suggest a parental and suburban divide over the goals of reform. The right-hand side of table 6.5 shows us that nonwhites are 21 percent more likely to support equal educational opportunity than whites in Kentucky. This large difference in support for equal opportunity requires careful analysis, but its significance can be summed up as follows: Although all respondents strongly support equal educational opportunity over high educational achievement, nonwhites support it even more, controlling for ideology, party affiliation, income, age, and community type. In this sense, race trumps these other possible influences rather resoundingly. Also important, at a lower level of statistical significance, are community type and parental status, with parents nearly 7 percent more likely to favor high achievement over equality and suburbanites over 5 percent more likely. Thus, even in a setting where the poverty cleavages are not urban-suburban, we see a suburban hesitation to pursue norms of equality. Surprisingly, the confidence in local schools to make good use of new educational revenues mattered little to the equality/achievement issue.

In sum, the Kentucky story is in many ways similar to Connecticut's: reforms are viewed through the localist lens, but a complex mix of ideological, age, and other interest-based cleavages exist on the issue of educational reform. Strikingly, however, when the issue is cast as one of equal educational opportunity versus high educational achievement, race is the predominate variable. Localism drops away, as does ideology, age, and party. Instead, we see a racial divide compounded by a mild suburban/rural split and a parental/non-parental divide.

Tennessee

Tennessee's foray into school financing reform began in 1991 when a superior court judge ordered the state to restructure its method of funding public education. Two years later, the Tennessee Supreme Court affirmed the lower court decision. In a relatively swift compliance, the Tennessee legislature endorsed a modest redistributional scheme. The results of that policy reform were seen in chapter 2, where the equality of Tennessee's system showed meaningful, but not dramatic, improvement between 1993 and 1997. But what of public opinion on the issue? Relying on surveys from the

TABLE 6.5
Logistic Regression and Probability Analysis of Support for High Academic Performance over Equal Educational Opportunity in Kentucky, 1992

	Model Characteristics			*Probability Analysis of Significant Variables*	
	Parameter Estimate (B)	*S.E.*	*Sig.*	*Change in this variable from this to this . . .*	*. . . changes the probability that R favored high performance over equal educational opportunity by this much . . .*
Common Variables					
Age	0.0622 (0.42)	0.1472	0.6728		
Community Type	0.2064* (1.69)	0.1224	0.0918	from "rural" to "suburb" (1,3)	+5.57%
Education Level	0.1482 (1.23)	0.1206	0.2192		
Ideology	0.0686 (0.91)	0.0755	0.3637		
Income	0.0173 (0.30)	0.0573	0.7632		
Parents of Children <18	0.5171* (1.73)	0.2984	0.0831	from "No children <18" to "Has children <18" (0,1)	+6.67%
Party Affiliation	0.0285 (0.45)	0.0639	0.6559		
Race	−1.2998** (−1.95)	0.1371	0.0511	from "white" to "nonwhite" (0,1)	−20.96%
Poll-Specific Variables					
Good Use of Local Money	0.1465 (1.07)	0.1371	0.2854		
Model Summary Statistics					
N	311				
−2 Log Likelihood	362.619				
Percent predicted correctly	69.13				
Distribution of dependent variable	1 (equal opportunity) = 72.6 2 (high performance) = 27.4				

Data Source: Kentucky Spring Poll Survey, April–May 1992; University of Kentucky Survey Research Center, Lexington, KY.

Betas reported; Beta/S.E. in parentheses.

**$p \leq 0.05$, *$p < 0.10$.

[1]Change in probability calculated using the "first differences" formula described in Gary King's *Unifying Political Methodology: The Likelihood Theory of Statistical Inference* (Cambridge: Cambridge University Press, 1989), 107–108. All independent variables are held constant at their means, and two distinct values (derived from the variable coding) are entered into the formula to obtain the probability change.

Social Science Research Institute at the University of Tennessee, conducted in the fall of 1991 and again in the spring of 1992, we can see the extent to which the politics of Tennessee's reform process mirrors or differs from those in other states. Clearly, one of the most remarkable aspects of the court decisions was their popular support. As noted in table 6.1, over 80 percent of Tennesseans approved of the lower court decision in the two surveys. Although most states studied here had substantial majorities in favor of some form of equality rhetoric, the support in Tennessee is staggering. Also, surprisingly, white support outpaced nonwhite support, bucking a trend we have seen in all other states studied here. As always, the interesting problem is to explain the variation in support, although little variation can be accounted for in this instance. Because the pollsters asked respondents simply whether they agreed with the court decision or disagreed, we need to use logistic regression analysis to uncover patterns in support or opposition to the court decision.[14] Those results, found in table 6.6, show a pattern that is substantially different from that of the other states. In all other states, ideology and party affiliation bear at least some relationship to attitudes toward equalization or education reform, more generally. In Tennessee, however, only one variable shows a statistically significant relationship: community type.[15] The right-hand side of table 6.6 shows that a respondent from a rural farm area was over 13 percent more likely to favor the court decision than a respondent from a large city. (It should be remembered, though, that the court decision had exceptionally high levels of support across the entire state and spectrum of political opinion.) This geographic divide in Tennessee is important because it reveals the continuing importance of public perception of the beneficiaries of the reform package. The rural areas of Tennessee were the clear beneficiaries of school finance reform, and those areas enjoyed substantial political support in both the legislature and public opinion. Given this support, it is remarkable that school finance reform even required a court decision in order to be enacted. Such broad support of reforms would typically be picked up by an entrepreneurial candidate seeking an issue. But as we shall see in the next chapter, the institutional regimes of school finance sometimes makes the translation of public attitudes into policy reforms a complex endeavor. Other obstacles besides a lack of public support may prevent their realization. In any event, the lesson of Tennessee appears to be that across ideology, class, race, and educational levels, geography matters. This finding, of course, will provide a useful starting point in chapter 7 when we address the ways that locality and local concerns—the very idea of community, in fact—structure the notion of what is politically permissible when a court intervenes into the funding of public education. In that light, Tennessee's lesson may be that court-ordered reforms that reinforce some idealized notion of community—particularly,

TABLE 6.6

Logistic Regression and Probability Analysis of Support for the *McWherter* Decision in Tennessee, 1991–92

	Model Characteristics			Probability Analysis of Significant Variables	
	Estimate (B)	S.E.	Sig.	Change in this variable from this to this . . .	. . .changes the probability that R supported the court decision by this much . . .
Variables					
Age	0.0977 (1.18)	0.0829	0.2386		
Community Type	0.1096* (1.97)	0.0555	0.0484	from "large city" to "rural farm" (1,6)	+13.36%
Education Level	−0.0774 (−1.09)	0.0711	0.2759		
Ideology	0.0497 (0.98)	0.0508	0.3282		
Income	−0.0325 (0.50)	0.0652	0.6182		
Parents of Children <18	—	—	—		
Party Affiliation	−0.0563 (−1.21)	0.0465	0.2262		
Race	−0.1873 (−0.87)	0.2160	0.3859		
Poll-Specific Variables					
Quality of TN Schools	−0.0321 (−0.40)	0.0807	0.1586		
Poll Date Control Variables					
February 1992	0.2322 (1.47)	0.1578	0.1412		
Model Summary Statistics					
N	1066				
−2 Log Likelihood	1036.997				
Percent predicted correctly	80.39				
Distribution of dependent variable	1 (Disagree w/ decision)=19.1% 2 (Agree w/ decision)=80.8%				

Data Source: Social Science Research Institute, Univ. of Tenn., TN Survey, Spring 1992; TN Survey, Fall 1991.

Betas reported; Beta/S.E. in parentheses.

*$p < 0.05$.

¹Change in probability calculated using the "first differences" formula described in Gary King's *Unifying Political Methodology: The Likelihood Theory of Statistical Inference* (Cambridge: Cambridge University Press, 1989), 107–108. All independent variables are held constant at their means, and two distinct values (derived from the variable coding) are entered into the formula to obtain the probability change.

small-town America — enjoy greater support than those that erode local control for the sake of equality and uniformity.

Texas

School finance politics in Texas is as contentious as in any place in the country. The sheer size and diversity of the system make simple declarations of fact difficult, and the fashion in which school finance politics is conducted only adds to the turmoil. In short, both the rhetoric and the sums of money involved are often staggering. The Texas legislature struggled mightily in the early 1990s to comply with numerous state supreme court decisions, often engaging in political brinkmanship with the courts. Public opinion clearly played a part in this drama, as legislators continually referred to the public's refusal to tolerate increased taxes. Unfortunately, large-scale public opinion surveys measuring support for the court decision or the notion of equal educational opportunity in Texas are not available. What we do have, however, is something no other state (to date) has yet produced in the course of school finance reforms: a constitutional referendum on the issue of school finance equality. By analyzing the election returns on Proposition 1, the proposed state constitutional amendment that Texas voters defeated in May 1993, we can better understand some of the cleavages within Texas over this issue.

The Texas legislature placed Proposition 1 on the May 1993 ballot in the wake of the Texas Supreme Court decision that struck down the remedy the legislature had adopted in response to an earlier ruling declaring the financing system invalid.[16] The remedy adopted by the state legislature and governor created consolidated education districts (CEDs) that would tax real estate within the district, pool the revenues, and then distribute that money to constituent school districts with low property tax bases. These CEDs existed only as taxing entities; they had no responsibility for education or educational policy within their boundaries. The Texas Supreme Court struck down these CEDs on the grounds that they constituted a statewide property tax, which the Texas Constitution does not permit. The legislature, in reaction, sought to constitutionalize the CEDs by asking voters to amend the Texas Constitution, allowing their continued existence. This, then, was the subject of Proposition 1: should the CEDs be made constitutional and continue to pool property tax receipts for school districts within their boundaries?

Most legal and political observers thought that the campaign for the amendment would be a difficult, but not impossible task. A poll conducted by the University of Houston Center for Public Policy a month before the 1 May 1993 referendum showed that 37 percent of survey respondents opposed Proposition 1, 29 percent supported it, and 34 percent were undecided.[17] Another poll, conducted by Mason-Dixon Political-Media Research, Inc. for the *El Paso Times* showed that 53 percent favored the amendment and only 27 percent were opposed. The remaining 20 percent were undecided.[18] Clearly, the numbers were not promising for supporters of Proposition 1, but no one anticipated the blowout that took place on 1 May 1993. On that date, Proposition 1 suffered a sizeable defeat, losing 63 percent to 27 percent. Voter turnout was low — with only 25 percent of eligible voters going to the polls. In fact, three times as many Texans wagered on May 1 for a $50 million state lottery jackpot as voted in the May 1 election (Verhovek 1993, Yearwood and Scott 1993).

Proposition 1 detractors contended before the election that Proposition 1 would simply increase taxes and do little to change Texas's educational system. Indeed, Tom Pauken, leader of the major opposition group Texans Against Robin Hood Taxes, explicitly played on taxation fears in his campaign efforts. Proposition 1 is "a backdoor tax increase, it has nothing to do with education," Pauken told a Houston Chronicle reporter. Distributing campaign newsletters that insisted "Governor Ann Richards Seeks $1 Billion Tax Hike in May 1 Election," Pauken's group drove home the perceived tax threat in its effort to defeat Proposition 1. As Pauken stated, "If we make this a tax issue, then we win. If Ann Richards is able to make it an education issue, she wins" (Rugeley and Markley 1993).

Answering this question of what determined the outcome of the Proposition 1 election is essential to an understanding of how courts can be effective in the realm of school finance reform. As we try to locate the sources of popular opposition to court-ordered school finance reform, it would be useful to examine the reasons why large numbers of Texans voted against Proposition 1. Ideally, we would examine statewide exit polls to determine explicit or implicit reasons voters had for casting their ballots. Unfortunately, no such exit polls exist. As a result, there are no individual-level voter surveys that can precisely identify the sources of opposition to Proposition 1 on 1 May 1993.[19]

What does exist, however, are demographic data and election returns from 150 state representative districts. These data can help determine some of the demographic characteristics of districts that voted against Proposition 1.[20] To be sure, uncovering the demographic characteristics of those regions that voted no on Proposition 1 is not the same as determining the *reasons* why people who live in those regions voted no, but in the absence of statewide individual-level exit polls, an analysis of demographic data is the only means to uncover patterns in the opposition to the school finance equalization referendum.

The findings of this analysis of Proposition 1 returns are shown in table 6.7. The regressions are identical, except for their treatment of the party variable. In Model 1, the party affiliation of the district is inferred from party

TABLE 6.7

Regression Analysis of Percentage of No Votes on Proposition 1 in 150 Texas
House Districts, 1993

	Model 1	Model 2
Independent Variables		
Per Capita Income	0.202*	0.068
	(2.479)	(1.000)
Party of House Representative	−0.124	—
	(−1.700)	
Percent Vote for Hutchison	—	0.692*
		(8.572)
Percent Non-Hispanic Blacks	−0.286*	0.056
	(−3.912)	(0.790)
Percent Hispanics	−0.590*	−0.273*
	(−6.726)	(−3.424)
Percent Housing Owner-Occupied	−0.001	−0.109
	(−0.020)	(−1.924)
Percent Urban Residents	−0.044	−0.013
	(−0.542)	(−0.210)
Model Summary Statistics		
Constant	0.699	0.235
(unstandardized)	(7.547)	(2.766)
R^2	0.648	0.763
Adj. R^2	0.633	0.753
SE	0.093	0.076
N	150	150

Data Source: Texas Legislative Council, May 1994.
Standard coefficients reported; *t*-scores in parentheses.
*$p < 0.05$.

of the representative elected to the Texas statehouse. In Model 2, party
affiliation is inferred from the percentage of the vote Republican Kay Bailey
Hutchison received in each district in the U.S. Senate runoff election just a
month after the Proposition 1 election. This second treatment of party affiliation can also be seen as a measure of conservative ideology, especially in a
state like Texas, which has, until recently, been a virtually one-party state.

In Model 1, we see that per capita income, percentage of non-Hispanic
blacks, and percentage of Hispanics all have a significant and fairly sizeable
relationship to the percentage of no votes on Proposition 1, with higher
incomes related to a higher percentage of no votes and higher percentages
of blacks and Hispanics related to lower percentages of no votes. Of these
three, the two racial categories show the strongest contributions to the percentage of no votes in a district. Surprisingly, the party of the district repre-

sentative (a rough measure of the party leanings of the district) is not a significant predictor of no votes, if we rely on the conventional 0.05 threshold. Also, the percentage of home ownership in a district and the percentage of urban residents in the district do not show a statistically significant relationship to the dependent variable.

There are, however, some shortcomings to this analysis. First, the measure of party identification is a bit crude. As a dichotomous variable (zero or one for Democrat or Republican statehouse representative), it does not capture the degree of party identification that a continuous variable would. To provide a more nuanced sense of party strength, and to generate a proxy for the ideological leanings of each state representative district, the data were reanalyzed, this time omitting the dummy party variable and replacing it with the percentage of votes received by U.S. Senate Candidate Kay Bailey Hutchison in the special runoff election against Robert Krueger, held a month after the Proposition 1 election. A continuous variable, this measure captures the degree of party strength in a way that is impossible with the dichotomous state representative party identification.[21] The results of this second regression are shown in the second column of table 6.7.

Three significant changes emerge from this change in the party identification variable. First, the degree of support for Kay Bailey Hutchison is a much stronger predictor of opposition to Proposition 1 than the party identification of the state district representative. Part of this is due, no doubt, to the fact that support for Hutchison is a continuous variable, not dichotomous, and thus more reliably tracks opposition to Proposition 1 than the Republican/Democrat distinction of the first party identification variable. Nonetheless, it is clear that support for Hutchison is a better predictor of opposition to school finance equalization than the party ID of the district representative. That fact begs the question, however, of why Hutchison supporters oppose school finance equalization. To answer this, it may be more instructive to view the percentage of votes Hutchison received less as a strength of party identification and more as an indicator of the ideological leanings of the district. In this light, Hutchison's candidacy registers a cluster of conservative ideological values more than it registers partisanship. From the regression, it is clear that those values are very salient to the school finance equalization debate.

Second, class, as measured by per capita income, no longer has a significant relationship to the question of school finance equalization, when we consider the degree of support within the district for Hutchison. Although there is some degree of collinearity between income and support for Hutchison (the simple r between the two is 0.591), it is clear that ideological/party support for Hutchison is more important than income in determining opposition to Proposition 1. The 1993 referendum on Proposition 1 was not a clash of the affluent versus the poor, per se, but of conservatives versus liberals. This interpretation is reinforced when we look at the near significance of percentage of owner-occupied housing in the district in Model 2. When the percentage of vote for Hutchison is introduced, that variable changes, but in an unexpected direction. In Model 2, districts with higher percentages of owner-occupied housing are *less opposed* to Proposition 1 than those with lower percentages. Again, this indicates that exposure to property taxes is of less concern when we control for the ideological opposition registered by support for Hutchison.

The third significant change produced by the change in the party affiliation variable is a change in the relative importance of race and ethnicity. The percentage of non-Hispanic blacks within a district is no longer a sizeable or significant predictor of opposition to or support of Proposition 1. In addition, the percentage of Hispanics within the district slips from being the largest to the second-largest factor in predicting support for Proposition 1. It is unclear why the importance of the percentage of non-Hispanic blacks would diminish so dramatically with the substitution of Hutchison's vote percentage for the party affiliation of the state representative. Perhaps the best explanation for the reduced salience of race is that the Hutchison vote percentage is such a good predictor of opposition to Proposition 1 that there is little variance "left over" for the remaining variables to absorb. Nevertheless, the percentage of Hispanic residents within a district is still a very strong and reliable predictor of support for Proposition 1. Thus, even though the class and party variables are more fickle, the ethnic cleavage of Hispanics versus non-Hispanics is an enduring one. With both regressions, racial or ethnic variables are always better and more significant predictors of opposition or support of Proposition 1 than is income.

The story of Texas public opinion on school finance equalization is one of ideological and racial and sometimes class cleavages that divide the supporters and detractors. The class and ideological divisions are to be expected, but the strength of the racial division is quite striking. In fact, of all the states studied, this analysis provides the strongest evidence of a persistent racial divide within the electorate over this issue. New Jersey saw a modest racial dimension in respondents' opposition to the *Abbott II* decision, but it was not as strong or as robust as the Texas cleavage. And in Kentucky, where whites and nonwhites divided over the goals of education reform, the division was not as strong as in Texas. The racial split in Texas was not directly presented in the local media, with newspapers usually depicting the issue in terms of burdensome taxes on the middle class, or a wasteful, inefficient educational establishment. While those issues may be have been salient and persuasive to a number of individuals, voters in predominantly black and Hispanic districts in Texas clearly saw this issue much differently from those in largely white districts — even taking into account their respective economic and ideological positions. In short, table 6.7 show that the racial composition of a district is more important to determining support for Proposition 1 than the presumed financial impact on that district—as measured by income and rates of home ownership.[22]

More important still, however, is the degree of ideological conservativism within a district. Although the redistribution of educational resources is a class-based issue, the cleavages it generates are not in themselves class based, but are ideological and racial. In Texas, ideological and racial divides are more important divides than class when an explicitly redistributive policy is submitted to the electorate for approval. The Texas vision of educational equality is filtered through ideologically and racially tinted glasses.

Conclusion: How Do We Interpret Public Attitudes about Equal Educational Opportunity?

What, then, can we infer from this polling and electoral data from these five states? Are there any broad patterns in public opinion that surprise us or confound us? Looking over these results, four primary lessons emerge. First, the importance of local educational issues is paramount. Second, opposition to educational opportunity is often ideological, rather than interest based. Third, one's race can significantly condition one's view of the importance of educational opportunity. Finally, these results show that the public's opinion is not rigidly fixed; attitudes toward school financing can and do shift over time and it may be possible for courts to function as educative institutions, using decisions to influence those shifts.

Public schools, parochial views: In every analysis presented here, whenever a measure tapped some sentiment of local control—whether it be the effects of reform on funding, the ability of local schools to use resources wisely, or the loss of local control due to equalization—that measure showed the largest and most significant relationship toward educational opportunity. Localism is paramount in American attitudes toward public education. Reforms that seek to diminish local control are much less likely to meet approval than those that do not. Importantly for judges and policy, the rhetoric of reforms matters considerably, too. As the surveys from Connecticut show, when the goal of broadened educational opportunity comes with a price tag of diminished local control, there is a substantial drop in public support for the reforms. This lesson is central to judicial effectiveness and legislative capacity to mobilize support for reforms. If concerns about diminished local control are raised, judicial or legislative coercion will do little to persuade the public. As the next chapter will show, it is terribly difficult to propose a reform to unequal educational opportunity without some effects on localism; localism is the very engine of educational inequality. In the next chapter, we will see how that conundrum played out in the policy process in New Jersey.

Ideological elements of educational opportunity: With the exception of Tennessee, in every state examined here, the ideology of respondents — typically measured along a liberal, moderate, conservative spectrum — bore a statistically significant relationship to their attitudes toward equal funding of schools or the desirability of educational reform. Often these relationships were the largest or second largest determinant among those explored here. Although support for equality ran high in the aggregate, the politics of educational opportunity nonetheless cleaved along ideological lines; respondents who identify themselves as conservatives are less interested in equality than are self-professed liberals. While class-based interests, such as exposure to increased taxes and higher personal incomes, also often drove opposition, in many cases ideology was a better and stronger predictor of opposition than was class. Educational issues are intimately related to economic prospects; the more education one has, the better one's economic fortunes. At the same time, the issue of equal educational opportunity is highly ideological. Education, and our views of how it should be distributed, are closely bound to our understandings of work, opportunity, and merit. The values of the American dream — that talented individuals who work hard can overcome virtually any obstacles — are played out in the ideological politics of educational opportunity. Americans simply hold a wide range of views on whether schools can or should help us overcome environmental obstacles to achievement and riches, and often those views are not closely related to our own achievement levels or our own individual riches. Precisely because it is both a substantive governmental benefit and a hugely symbolic statement about the value of work and talent, educational opportunity becomes a sharply contested ideological terrain.

How race matters: Another less reliable, but nonetheless persistent, dimension to public rifts over educational opportunity is the question of race. In these surveys, there was substantial evidence that the color of one's skin influences one's views toward the desirability of increased educational opportunity. In Kentucky, New Jersey, and Texas, those relationships existed, albeit to differing degrees. They did not exist in Connecticut and Tennessee. These results, of course, simply document the racial divide, telling us that whites and nonwhites, in a number of places with significant geographic diversity, hold substantially different views on the value of educational opportunity. While important, that assessment cannot tell us more, cannot highlight either the symbolic or the encoded racial meanings of educational opportunities. It is simply one clear measure that as a nation we are divided on this issue, as we are on many others. The racial divide stretches across a number of policy concerns: welfare, affirmative action, the death penalty, drug policy. Educational policy can now be registered among those issues that whites and nonwhites view differently.

What we cannot infer from this analysis are the political lessons whites and nonwhites draw from their own perceptions of that very difference. When educational opportunity takes on a racial hue, it may become "a black thing" that consequently has less significance within largely white halls of power where representatives can, politically, dismiss these concerns without repercussion. In the conclusion to this book, the themes of racial division and the connections between race and class components of the fight for educational opportunity will be reprised and we will see the symbolic and cultural resonance of the language of these court decisions. While many survey respondents would not place the *Abbott* litigation or Proposition 1 or the Kentucky Education Reform Act within the trajectory of the civil rights movement, that is precisely the symbolic and cultural significance of these political developments for many Hispanic and African Americans, particularly activists within those communities. For now, it is sufficient to say that these public surveys show that there is a racial divide on educational opportunity, even though it may be fickle and not as significant as other cleavages.

Public commitments to educational opportunity and constitutional ordering: Constitutional theorists rarely, if ever, rely on public opinion surveys to gauge the depth of constitutional commitments. After all, many surveys have shown that many Americans do not support activities protected by the Bill of Rights. How can these quick questionnaires provide us with a meaningful understanding of American sentiments toward the constitutional meaning of educational opportunity? By themselves, they cannot, but in conjunction with an understanding of the jurisprudence of these decisions and the political structure of the conflicts, public surveys can provide another dimension to the ways educational opportunity is ordered through constitutional norms. Opinion polls provide a needed empirical referent to highly theoretical discussions of American faith in equality. Its admittedly crude empiricism can show us how our egalitarian faith dims when held in the bright light of competing norms and conflicts, like localism, ideological differences, and racial divides.

Educational opportunity is a constitutive value in American politics; views toward education undergird a vast array of resource distributions, from property tax assessments to lunch programs to spending levels in schools. But it also undergirds sentiments about community, home, work, and merit—all rich veins of politics. One argument of this book is that constitutional ordering is not strictly text bound and that it is not entirely encompassed by the terms of the U.S. Constitution. If that is so, then the process of constitutional ordering must have some relevance to these highly charged issues of political conflict and accommodation. Constitutional ordering is, in other words, the means by which we organize our public and personal beliefs into public policy. In no other field does that process of reconciling normative commitments to institutional organization happen with such richness and controversy as in public education. The conflicts in public education are so sharp because they are so *constitutional*. In looking to public opinion polls, we can uncover the terms on which that reconciliation between normative commitment and institutional organization proceeds. While the results may not always be encouraging (it certainly is dispiriting to see racial divisions over educational opportunity), they are informative. They are, simultaneously, necessarily incomplete. Only by turning to the institutional contexts in which education is organized and delivered can we understand fully the constitutional politics of educational opportunity.

7

REGIMES OF INEQUALITY:

THE ORGANIZATION OF EDUCATIONAL POLITICS

Our Constitution demands that every child be given an equal
opportunity to meet his or her promise.
—*New Jersey Supreme Court Associate Justice Alan B. Handler,*
Abbott v. Burke

It's become part of the discussion in public life that there are
winners and losers. But we don't like to think that there will be
children that are winners and children that are losers.
—*James H. Murphy, President of the New Jersey Association of*
School Administrators

[The bill] still has to go to the legislators and the first thing a
legislator does is to look at his districts, to say, "Am I
winning or losing?"
—*John Rocco, Chair of the New Jersey Assembly*
Education Committee

THE RHETORIC OF EDUCATIONAL POLITICS in the United
States strives to place the child at the center of public concerns.
"We need to do more for our children." "We can no longer short-
change our kids." "A child only gets one education." The child-focused
language of actors in our educational politics plays, of course, to the inno-
cence and desert of all children; in a moral sense, the youth of children
makes them equal. When young, a child has not had time to "earn" the
label of undeserving. A child is promise embodied.

The discourse of educational opportunity seeks to release that promise
held within every child. While it acknowledges that every child has different
talents and capacities, educational opportunity anchors us to the notion that
whatever our children's abilities, the educational system should be organized so that they can fully realize their potential. This view of the aims of
education holds political power because it reinforces and focuses the American vision of equality. We espouse not an equality of results or an equality of
talents, but an equality of chances to develop. In this way, Americans can
reconcile the tensions between our ethos of individualism and our commitment to equality.

Of course, the rhetoric of educational politics and its organization are vastly different things. The varied social and home experiences children bring to kindergarten are compounded by enormously stratified educational settings. As I have tried to draw out in the preceding chapters of this book, judicial efforts to redress those educational differences meet resistance at a variety of levels. First, judges must overcome myriad obstacles to judicial policy-making within a state constitutional context. Second, the public attitudes toward improving educational opportunities become increasingly hostile as judges' reform proposals touch on local control of school districts and resources. Those are not the only difficulties, though. In this chapter I want to focus on the organization of interests in educational politics and how the geographic nature of educational inequalities entrenches and advances particular interests in the legislative arena and the policy process. In short, the organization of public education by geography heightens the salience of local control, creates incentives for particular groups to fight changes that would expand educational opportunity, and, as a result, makes legislators less likely to pursue policies that advance educational opportunity for middle- and lower-income districts. Thus, judges who engage the issue of making geography irrelevant to children's education immediately confront those interests that are linked to the preservation of precisely that relevance.

A Jules Feiffer cartoon from the *New York Times* concisely illustrates this point (Feiffer 1999). A teacher leading a class discussion asks her students what high test scores mean. They respond in unison, "*Good schools!*" "And good schools equal—?" she asks. "*A desirable area for our parents to buy a home!*" comes the reply. And that equals: "*A thriving community with growing service needs and business opportunities!*" And she asks again, "And that equals?" The students respond: "*A strong real estate market!*" Finally, the teacher asks "So, this year by cutting down on our teaching hours to test you more, we are accomplishing what?" "*Expanding new housing starts and resale values!*" In a wry comment on the sophistication of grade-schoolers, Feiffer closes the cartoon with the teacher's observation, "You are amazingly well educated for the third grade." While there is no better way to kill a joke than to explain why it is funny, let me suggest that Feiffer's Op-Art is more than simply a lighthearted jab at the test-happy educational establishment.

The connections between public education, property taxes, real estate values, and the stratification of communities along socioeconomic lines are clear, strong, and robust. This chapter aims to explore some of those connections and to understand how they are made manifest among interest groups and within political institutions, particularly state legislatures. There exists a network of reinforcing interests that are readily mobilized and highly effective at reducing the egalitarian aspirations of the court decisions studied here. These interests emerge and are mobilized, in significant part, because of the connection between geography and education. That connection—

FIGURE 7.1. Jules Feiffer on test scores and property values. Used by permission of the artist.

particularly within fragmented metropolitan areas — is, in many ways, the fulfillment of a particular form of the American dream: rising mobility; a move to a safe, perhaps more expensive, neighborhood; the liberty to purchase through one's residence a quality education in a neighborhood school; the accompanying associational and community ties that emerge from personal involvement in local schools and community. All of these things are simultaneously held out as an aspirational ideal for parents and children, and many do find a high quality of life within that framework. At the same time, threats to that reinforcing network of concerns (safety, home values, quality of schools, community ties) are taken seriously — often because these values seem increasingly endangered in atomized American life, where lives and communities are fragmented and divided. These court decisions pose credible threats to this organization of public education, this system by which resources are delivered to children according to a regime of property taxes, home values, and local district control of revenues. As the New Jersey Supreme Court wrote in its *Abbott II* decision:

> All of the money that supports education is public money, local money no less than state money. It is authorized and controlled, in terms of source, amount, distribution, and use, by the State. The students of Newark and Trenton are no less citizens than their friends in Millburn and Princeton. They are entitled to be treated equally, to begin at the same starting line.[1]

This notion of the public character of educational expenditures directly challenges the conviction that local tax dollars ought to be restricted to local residents. Similarly, in New Hampshire, the state supreme court argued that the state-level public benefits of education ought to outweigh parochial (and individual) concerns about costs and benefits:

> It should not be forgotten that New Hampshire is not a random collection of isolated cities and towns. Indeed, all of us live in a single State. The benefits of adequately educated children are shared statewide and are not limited to a particular town or district. We live in a highly mobile society such that a child may be educated in Pittsfield and, as an adult, reside in Moultonborough. . . . The benefits of that citizen's public education and contributions to community may be felt far beyond the boundaries of the educating town or district. Therefore, it is basic to our collective well-being that all citizens of the State share in the common burden of educating our children.[2]

While many court decisions in favor of greater adequacy and equity have expressly held that local control need not be disrupted by legislative efforts to comply with these court decisions, the rulings nonetheless create the potential of disruption or harm to districts at the high end of the spending scale.[3] One fear is that state aid to affluent districts will be reduced (in order to pay for increased aid to property-poor districts), while another, often worse, concern is that local property tax revenues will be shunted away from local districts, toward those with lower tax bases and lower revenue potential. Under either scenario, these court decisions represent a potential or real threat to the fiscal autonomy of local school districts. Moreover, they challenge the increasingly insular and withdrawn quality of residential life in the United States. As enclave suburbs seek to distance themselves from crime (either perceived or real), poverty, and general decline in central cities, they also feel less inclined to share the benefits of locally produced tax dollars. The salience of local control issues to public attitudes toward educational opportunity illustrates the linkage in the public mind between local schools and local tax revenues. School districts in states where courts are intervening in school finance have had good reason to worry about losing influence in the direction of local education.

There has been a general trend away from local control in many facets of public education. As a result, changes over the past forty years in educational governance have altered significantly the capacity of local school districts to remain outside the orbit of state and federal influence. Beginning in the late 1950s, the federal government made increasing amounts of money available to local school districts, but established conditions and terms under which those funds could be used.[4] Moreover, with mounting legal challenges to school financing beginning in the 1970s, many state legislators increased the state share of educational financing to boost funds dedicated to equalization among school districts.[5] State legislators began to assert control over other areas of educational policy as well. Spurred in the mid-1980s by A *Nation at Risk* report, which warned of a "rising tide of mediocrity" in public education,[6] many state governments boosted money for education, but also asserted greater control over testing of students, added curriculum requirements, lengthened the school day and year, and toughened teacher certification requirements. In general, over the 1980s, states became much more willing to intrude on areas that had previously been the exclusive province of local school boards, parents, and local superintendents. One study claimed that the 1983–88 period "saw a level of state policy activity in education unprecedented since the formation of the common school system" (Firestone et al. 1991, 235).

Other actors as well began to chip away at the sanctity of local rule. Most prominently, federal courts asserted power over many school districts when school integration did not happen quickly enough, or even assumed control when school boards balked at implementing court decrees. Between 1963 and 1999, in the Fifth and Eleventh Circuit Courts of Appeal alone, at least 189 school districts operated under a court order to integrate their schools.[7] This profound shift in power in educational policy represented perhaps the clearest loss of local autonomy but not the only one. Teachers' unions also became increasingly visible in the 1960s and 1970s, mobilizing effectively for better pay and working conditions. Their collective bargaining agreements, however, restricted the autonomy of school boards, especially when those contracts indirectly established educational policy by stipulating classroom size, course offerings, teacher school assignments, and layoff criteria.[8] School boards also had to contend with taxpayer revolts in the late 1970s and early 1980s, as measures such as California's Proposition 13 sharply constrained the ability of local school boards to boost revenues through increases in local property taxes. While essentially a form of local rule, these property tax restrictions had an unanticipated effect of forcing local school districts to seek increased state aid to maintain educational offerings in the face of inflation. These funds, when they were made available, often came with strings attached. The upshot of these changes at the federal, state, and local levels was a decreasing sense of local school district autonomy, not only over revenue and expenditure matters, but also over broader policy considerations such as pupil assignments, curricular issues, staffing levels, testing programs, and teacher training.

Throughout this sea change in educational governance, however, one constant remained: local revenues raised by local property taxes would remain within local jurisdictions.[9] Those funds may no longer have been sufficient to meet the educational needs of the community or they may have to be supplemented by increasing state and federal funds, but the principle of local control of local resources seemed safe — at least until state supreme courts began to disrupt those expectations with their rulings on school finance. In this climate, the slow erosion of local control took on a new meaning and has often resulted in some rather robust political mobilization of local actors seeking to both preserve their exclusive access to local resources and to fight off any limitations on their capacity to spend above state-level norms.

The chapter is organized into three parts. The first part explores how power is deployed within the educational arena and also advances a theory of educational politics that asserts the primacy of place within the contests over control of educational resources. The second part illustrates the geopolitics of education through a case study of a local school district and interest group mobilizations in New Jersey. This state has seen the longest-running and one of the fiercest political battles over educational financing. The New Jersey experience, while perhaps extreme, aptly illustrates the geopolitical tensions over educational finance and judicial efforts of reform. The final section of the chapter returns to the theme of constitutional ordering by examining how these court decisions seek to reorder the institutional features of public education within these states.

What Is Educational Politics?

Political scientists rarely examine systematically the politics of education. Part of the problem, of course, is that educational politics takes place on so many levels and in so many ways. On the federal level, congressional fights over educational policy differ substantially from the contests that erupt within the Department of Education. These fights, in turn, are dramatically different from the rather ideological (even religious) conflicts that take place in school board elections and within local schoolboards. Simultaneously, state legislatures — which generate and appropriate nearly half of all public school educational expenditures in the country — see an altogether different kind of conflict over both resources and educational organization. And state boards of education, which have their own internal politics, must engage sometimes independent-minded school districts on a host of issues and exhibit a wide range of organizational strength and institutional capacities to develop educational policy. Schools themselves are sites of incredibly intense political activity, ranging from skirmishes over First Amendment rights of students to a broader normative project of inculcating the democratic values of citizenship within their students. Finally, the interest groups that emerge from the delivery and consumption of education — teachers' unions, superintendent organizations, parent-teacher organizations, taxpayers' groups, business-school alliances, publishing company interests, granting organizations — all exercise some measure of influence over the organization and provision of public education in the United States.

In sum, public education is a macroinstitution, one that touches on and transcends an incredible array of social settings, political institutions, economic relationships, religious faiths, and forms of bureaucratic organization. As a result, to speak of a single politics of education is clearly misleading. The profusion of forms and relationships and conflicts that make up the universe of actors in public education makes it impossible to speak in a single voice about such a rich and complex institution. Of necessity then, we must limit the scope of our inquiry. In this chapter educational politics refers to issues surrounding governance — the ability to decide who controls policy and resources within schools, school districts, and state educational programs. In many ways, this leaves the federal government out of the equation. Although the federal government is now again emerging as a central actor in education reform (particularly surrounding such issues as testing, standards, and the formation of charter schools), the federal relationship to public education ensures that its innovations will, most likely, never be compulsory. Instead, the federal government, in its usual fashion, will offer incentives and inducements for participation in a federal program. While this may become an indirect form of governance, it is always messy and often unreliable. The federal government may limit — through categorical grants — the ways some funds are used, but there is also increasing pressure to provide resources as block grants.[10] In addition, the extent of control will always be at the margins, particularly when the federal government provides only roughly 7 percent of educational revenues to schools. Unless that figure jumps substantially, the federal government's role in issues of governance will be to set agendas and provide incentives, but rarely, if ever, to act as a decision-maker.

Thus, the question of governance is reduced to six or seven sets of actors: state legislators and their aides, state-level executive branch officials, including the governor and administrators in state departments of education; state courts; local school boards; state-level educational interest groups; local community leaders, including business organizations; and, finally, parents. By limiting our discussions here to questions of governance, we maintain a focus on things political scientists are well suited to examine: the pursuit, distribution, deployment, and maintenance of power, in this case power over resources and substantive policy issues. Of course, in federal systems, power will always be shared, but by paring down the number of actors and the objectives of the political fights, we can begin to see patterns in that power-sharing arrangement. Political scientists who have examined the politics of educational governance have advanced two competing explanations for those patterns. A number of studies employ, either implicitly or explicitly, a model of competitive pluralism,[11] while others rely on rational actor models.[12] The next section offers another theoretical perspective on educational politics, one based on the central institutional fact of public education in the United States, its geographic organization.

The Geopolitics of Public Education

A clue to untying the knot of educational politics may be found in the results of the polling analysis in chapter 6. There we found that poll questions touching on the local control of schools struck a nerve in the public. Efforts to equalize or simply increase revenue for poorer districts were less favored if they diminished local control. In this section I want carry that insight a bit further and examine the broader structure of local control and how it intersects with public attitudes. My contention here is that we cannot separate public attitudes toward educational opportunity from those institutions that structure and deliver educational services. Thus, attitudes toward educational opportunity give us a window onto the political salience of the institutional design of public education, particularly the local rule of municipalities and school districts and local control of local property tax receipts. These two institutions implicitly structure our beliefs about the proper way to organize education, and, indirectly, they inform a good deal of our democratic politics surrounding education. In order to understand the importance of these features of the educational system, we need to examine the nature of local politics in the United States.

The governmental landscape of the American polity is a patchwork of multiple governmental entities and subdivisions. One scholar has noted that there were 82,341 units of government in the United States, as of 1983 (Weiher 1991, 1). This enormous array of political jurisdictions and localities serves a wide variety of needs and demands, but one particular consequence of this governing arrangement is especially noteworthy: our metropolitan areas are deeply fragmented in a political sense. These multiple jurisdictions both create an environment of competition among local government actors, (with coordination of policies often the casualty), and also provide convenient informational cues to local residents about goods, services, and quality of life in metropolitan areas. Thus, our urban landscapes do not consist of cores and peripheries, but complex, overlapping, intersecting, and often autonomously controlled units of governance. One consequence of this fragmentation is the stratification of residents by income and race. Part of this segregation has emerged due to conscious policies of some localities, while other parts appear to be the product of more indirect, but tremendously powerful forces. In many places, localities can organize their population through a variety of mechanisms—strict building codes, exclusionary zoning, minimum lot sizes, refusal to allow public or subsidized housing, banning apartment buildings, and so on. In some states, small, homogeneous suburb communities can effectively determine the income level of any new resident (Danielson 1976, 50–78). Not all suburbs do this, but the institutional and legal framework of local control enables some communities to become enclaves of affluence while others become collection nodes of lower-income families (Frug 1999).

The result is profoundly segmented metropolitan areas, in which residents are clustered into highly homogeneous income and racial groups. Moreover, these activities allow some suburbs to shunt socially and economically undesirable activities and individuals into the urban core and, increasingly, poorer old suburbs. As Kenneth Jackson writes about the post–World War II suburban boom,

> While zoning provided a way for suburban areas to become secure enclaves for the well-to-do, it forced the city to provide economic facilities for the whole area and homes for people the suburbs refused to admit. . . . Instead of becoming a useful tool for the rational ordering of land in metropolitan areas, zoning became a way for suburbs to pirate from the city only its desirable functions and residents. Suburban governments became like so many residential hotels, fighting for the upper-income trade while trying to force the deadbeats to go elsewhere. (Jackson 1985, 242)

Clearly, not all suburbanites fit the traditional conception of upper-middle-class, home-owning residents who commute to jobs in the city. Suburbs have changed dramatically over the past thirty years. There is tremendous variation in the size, population density, and class of suburban towns and cities. Older suburbs face different problems than the newest boomtowns. Working-class suburbs view economic trends differently than exclusive, upper-class enclaves. But suburbs, by and large, share at least two things: political fragmentation and racial homogeneity. One scholar explicitly includes fragmentation in his definition of suburbia: "The suburban area is characterized by political and economic fragmentation. No municipality serves as the main focus for work or commercial activities. Also, many independent local governments operate with little coordination" (Baldassare 1986, 5). This emphasis on "local autonomy" is seen as a point of pride among suburban residents and advocates: home rule provides local residents a greater sense of control over their lives and a mechanism by which they can fight off threats — perceived or real — to their quality of life and personal values. This decentralized, locally controlled decision-making process, in the opinion of two scholars, "propagates democratic processes in which people create, without being forced to, new self-governing entities and decide for themselves (subject to state and federal mandates) what services those entities will offer and what rules they will abide by." The result, from their viewpoint, is that suburban fragmentation creates "expanded opportunities for democratic self-government" (Hawkins and Percy 1991, 482).

In many ways, this line of argument makes sense. Because civic life, at its best, relies on face-to-face exchanges between individuals — involving meetings, public speaking, group interactions — the smaller scale of administration and governance within localities helps foster the kind of involvement and participation that bolsters civic equality. It is simply easier to participate in a direct way at local school board meetings than it is at state-level hearings on educational policy. Moreover, there is a good deal of academic literature that shows parental involvement contributes to academic achievement among students. Thus, to the extent that local control induces more parents to take part in educational decision-making and policy-making it contributes to the formation of better schools.

There is, however, a cost to this autonomy of local districts and the general principle of home rule. To the extent that schools (and more broadly school districts) reflect the racial and economic stratification of their settings, contests over local control are cast as exclusionary battles in which whites and upper-middle-class residents seek to preserve advantages secured through the sorting mechanisms of political and school-district boundaries. Moreover, because political involvement and political efficacy are closely related to socioeconomic status, those school districts, towns, and suburbs that contain a high proportion of upper-middle-class residents will, in general, be more successful (and motivated) in their mobilization efforts. Economists contend that the varying levels of public services offered within metropolitan areas actually contribute to greater efficiency in the provision of public services because residents can "vote with their feet" and relocate to those areas that provide the level of taxation and public services (like parks, education, trash collection, libraries, etc.) that match their preferences.[13] The unacknowledged dimension of this variation, however, is that the income sorting mechanisms of political and jurisdictional boundaries (which some economists might see as contributing to metropolitan efficiency) produce communities with different levels of political capital that can then be deployed to secure aid from higher levels of government to preserve their relative advantage. Or, at a minimum, the political capital that accompanies economic sorting enables those communities to fight off attempts to diminish services and state aid. When these sorting mechanisms also produce stratification that even economists would argue is undesirable (such as racial isolation and exclusivity), the political salience of the divisions among communities becomes even sharper, because their class differences are overlaid with racial divides (either explicit or implicit) that rank communities by the relative desert of their members. Thus, entire districts or communities can be seen as undeserving of greater aid because of the low incomes and racial characteristics of their residents.[14]

The final piece in this puzzle is representation within state legislatures. Because state aid constitutes an increasingly larger share of public education revenues, the resource battles in public education are no longer limited to local bond issues and securing community approval for the local school budget. More and more, the important political struggles in public education occur in state legislatures as members seek to produce financing formulas that direct aid to particular communities, or at least prevent the reduction of aid. Because state house districts are geographically defined, the electoral fortunes of state senators and state representatives are tied to securing aid for those school districts within their respective boundaries. This issue becomes particularly acute when state supreme courts threaten to disrupt existing political equilibrium over the distribution of state aid for public education. As state supreme courts insist that either additional money be provided to low wealth districts or that district revenues be made more equal, the question of who wins and who loses in the educational apportionment game is up for grabs. Many state legislators find it politically exceptionally difficult to vote for a reform package that either produces less state aid for their home school districts or that provides greater state aid for neighboring districts. Either way, the geographic nature of property taxes and home rule intersects with the geographic nature of state electoral representation, yielding a political logic that can produce intense opposition to court decisions that seek the reform of school financing.

This logic also spills over to interest groups that are not directly geographically organized. For example, some states pay the contribution to teachers' retirement funds. This form of state aid reduces the incentives of local districts to keep teacher costs down, especially in affluent districts that can afford to pay higher teacher salaries to attract and retain the best instructors. Thus, teachers' unions have an incentive for the state to pick up the retirement costs of teachers. But when New Jersey sought to force local districts to pay their share of teacher retirement benefits, the New Jersey Education Association rallied around the cause of affluent districts that protested the move. The interests of some groups, then, are formed indirectly by the advantages that accrue to particular districts through the geopolitics of education. The geographic inequalities in public education shape even those dimensions of educational politics that are not directly geographically based.

This point brings us back to the models of educational politics that political scientists and others have used to study these conflicts. My contention here is not that pluralist competition among groups does not exist or that individuals act irrationally in politics, but that a broader institutional context structures both the competition among groups and the calculation of individual rationales. And without an awareness of those institutional contexts, we will fail to see how certain rationalities, interests, and groups are advantaged within the processes that dominate educational politics. Thus, the geographical facts of local property taxes, home rule, and geographic representation in state legislatures provide much of the structure for interest-group mobilization and the strategic calculation of political incentives and advantages. They are the foundation of educational politics at the local level and they indirectly control the outcomes of political fights over educational governance, especially the fights over the distribution of educational resources. The remainder of this chapter is devoted to illustrating these claims by exploring episodes of executive, legislative, and interest group responses to the court decisions in New Jersey, the site of perhaps the longest and most divisive conflict over school finance. New Jersey is, at the same time, the clearest illustration of educational geopolitics. Finally, at the end of the chapter I will return to the theme of constitutional ordering, and explore whether it is possible for state supreme courts to restructure the geopolitics of education and build new institutions of educational finance and governance that truly constitute greater equality and adequacy in education.

The New Jersey Case Study of the Geo-Politics of Public Education

It is, of course, impossible to summarize quickly the political responses to a litigation reform effort that has stretched across three decades, at least fourteen state supreme court decisions, three governors, and hundreds, if not thousands of community meetings, planning sessions, and legislative hearings.[15] Entire books have been written on New Jersey's battles with school finance reform, and even those do not convey the full scope of the conflict.[16] That said, we can identify distinct stages in the political and legal struggles over school finance reform in New Jersey and identify consistent patterns in the ability of some groups to achieve advantage through that process. In short, there have been three phases to the political response to the *Abbott II* decision. The first phase began when Governor Jim Florio proposed a school finance reform package known as the Quality Education Act (QEA) shortly before the New Jersey Supreme Court handed down its decision in early June 1990. The second phase began when the court declared the QEA, as amended, unconstitutional and gave the state legislature two years to come up with a solution. The third phase began when the court ruled on the constitutionality of the Comprehensive Educational Improvement and Financing Act (CEIFA), the Whitman administration's reform package enacted shortly before yet another judicial deadline. The first two phases are marked by executive efforts to restrict or otherwise limit state aid to wealthy districts and generally successful countermobilizations by those districts and the groups whose interests are tied to the high spending of those districts, particularly the teachers' unions. In the third stage, we see that the court is no longer aiming at comprehensive or ambitious institutional restructuring of school finance in New Jersey, but is instead focusing on the administration of particular programs that deliver particular resources to poor inner-city schools. From the court's perspective, the shift comes as a result of repeated failures to reorder the regime of inequality that undergirds public education in New Jersey. The more modest aims of the latest *Abbott* decisions show that the constitutional ordering aimed at structural and institutional reforms has been far less successful than the efforts simply to direct more money to property-poor districts.

Jim Florio and the Battles over the QEA

Governor James Florio rode into Drumthwacket, the New Jersey governor's mansion, in 1989 with the third largest margin of victory in a New Jersey gubernatorial race (Salmore and Salmore 1993b, 68). He quickly put that political capital to work, advancing gun control and raising income and sales taxes to erase the state budget deficit and to fund a school finance equalization program. Within two years, his approval rating had eroded to 26 percent (Newman 1991) and his Democratic majority within the statehouse was turned out by a veto-proof Republican majority that vowed to rollback virtually every Democratic legislative achievement of the previous two years. Clearly, Jim Florio was no longer a popular man. What had so provoked the ire of New Jerseyans within those two years?

The fiscal consequences of Florio's aggressive efforts to equalize school financing and eliminate the state deficit were enormous. To accomplish both, he had to increase taxes by $2.8 billion when New Jersey was beginning a recessionary downturn. These fiscal consequences, in turn, had enormous political consequences: the disastrous results for Democrats in the 1991 statehouse elections and the loss of the governorship in 1993. Indirectly, then, the issue of school finance reform — and more important, Florio's handling of the issue — directly influenced the political control and direction of the Garden State.

But what were the specifics of the QEA that elicited such outrage? The following list details the important elements of the school finance package passed by the legislature less than three weeks after the New Jersey Supreme Court's decision in *Abbott II*.[17]

- The existing guaranteed tax base formula was replaced with a foundation formula, setting the basic foundation aid at $6,835 per pupil.[18] Each district would receive a proportion of that aid, depending on its wealth (measured in both property and income) and local tax revenues.
- State aid to education was increased by $1.15 billion, boosting aid to some 360 districts statewide.
- Thirty "special needs" districts received an additional payment of 5 percent of their foundation aid. These are almost exclusively poor urban districts.
- The minimum foundation aid to 151 so-called wealthy districts was phased out over four years, by 25 percent per year. Minimum aid to an additional 77 districts was to be reduced over this period.
- Teacher pension fund payments and social security costs were shifted back to school districts. This meant that school districts now had to pay the employer's share of pension payments and social security taxes. In the past, the state had assumed these costs.
- An important categorical aid program was revamped, transforming it from a "compensatory education" program (based on the number of students in a district with failing test scores) into one for "at-risk" students (based on the number of economically disadvantaged students in a district).
- Each district had to assess a minimum local property tax, dubbed a local "fair share" in order to be eligible for state foundation aid.

The Quality Education Act was billed not only as providing greater equity in New Jersey's school finance, but also as a tax break for the middle class. Upon legislative approval of the plan, Governor Florio declared, "Something historically significant is happening here." . . . "This is a day we bring fairness to the children of New Jersey and the beleaguered and besieged middle class" (Kerr 1990c).

The heart of the appeal to the middle classes was a property tax rebate, passed in conjunction with the QEA. Florio and his advisors thought they could reduce property taxes on the middle class in two ways: first, provide a progressive property tax rebate of up to $500; second, pick up the tab for local costs of welfare, AFDC, and psychiatric hospitals, thereby allowing local governments to lower their tax rates (Kerr 1990a). By increasing the amount of state educational aid to a majority of the state's districts, and by sweetening the pot with a property tax rebate, Florio and his advisors hoped to secure middle-class support for school finance equalization.

Unfortunately for the middle class, Florio did not stop there. At the same time, he sought to raise income taxes by $1.4 billion to pay for both the

QEA and the property tax rebates. In addition, he called for an increase and expansion of the sales tax to erase the state's $1 billion deficit and create a $275 million surplus to guard against future shortfalls (Bogart et al. 1992, 372). Thus, the news of the property tax rebate was lost on an electorate that saw only a dramatic increase in the income and sales taxes. Moreover, in districts where state education aid would be reduced or eliminated (approximately 220), school officials indicated they would have to either increase property taxes or slash school offerings (Hanley 1990a, Hanley 1990b, Hanley 1990d). Thus, for many residents the prospect of a tax rebate paled in comparison to the prospect of boosted local property taxes. Statewide, the Eagleton Poll indicated in July 1990 that 69 percent of the New Jersey population thought their property taxes would go *up* in the wake of the QEA, precisely the *opposite* of what Florio said the proposal would do.

But the QEA and Florio's tax changes did more than pit public opinion against him. Various elements of the QEA directly assaulted the interests of organized groups, thereby ensuring that they would not only oppose the original passage of the QEA, but actively work for its reversal. The key elements that turned traditional (or potential) friends into enemies were: (1) the shift of teachers' pensions and social security payments to districts; (2) local districts' "fair share" requirement for state aid eligibility; (3) the elimination of minimum foundation aid to so-called wealthy districts; and to a lesser extent (4) the reformulation of compensatory education (based on failing test scores) into an aid program for "at-risk" students (based on family income of students). Each of these components of the QEA helped forge a broad alliance dedicated to revising the QEA. The New Jersey Education Association, financially strapped cities, and wealthy districts each lobbied hard for revisions and, simultaneously, rode the public outrage that peaked in the late summer and fall of 1990. Combined, these organized interests and intense public pressure forced Florio to accept in March 1991 revisions to the newly enacted QEA that struck at both the original intent of Florio's plan and the New Jersey Supreme Court's objectives as articulated in *Abbott II*. This dual-edged democratic backlash, from pressure groups and mobilized public opinion,[19] reversed major elements of QEA I in the spring of 1991 and placed the legislature and the executive on yet another collision course with the New Jersey Supreme Court.

In political terms, perhaps the most costly of the QEA's changes was the shift of teachers' pension payments and social security taxes back to the districts. The rationale for the change was simple: because districts negotiate retirement packages and wages with teachers, but do not pay either the pension costs or social security taxes that accompany those contracts, they have no incentive to keep those costs down. They can, in effect, spend the state's money without first obtaining the state's approval. Moreover, these payments amount to indirect subsidies to affluent districts since they generally pay their teachers better than poor districts. The result is that pension payments and social security taxes paid by the state increase inequality rather than improve it.

By attacking these payments, however, Florio and the legislature incurred the wrath of the New Jersey Teacher's Association, a group consistently ranked as the strongest interest group in New Jersey (Salmore and Salmore 1993a, 235–36). With a half dozen full-time lobbyists, the state's largest PAC fund,[20] nineteen field offices throughout the state, and thirty-seven field representatives, the NJEA's capacity to mobilize pressure is virtually unmatched among New Jersey's interest groups (Salmore and Salmore 1993a, 236, 240, 246). The NJEA opposed the pension and social security shift because it would mean, in effect, lower wages or benefits if districts could not raise taxes to offset the new burden. And the stakes were huge: newspaper reports at the time indicated that the state would save $800 million with the local assumption of pension and social security obligations (Kerr 1990b). In June 1990 Florio and his aides muscled the bill past a legislature heavily lobbied by the NJEA by labeling the organization a special interest that was holding New Jersey's children hostage for financial gain (Kerr 1990b). But this name-calling stung the NJEA, which had endorsed Florio enthusiastically in his 1989 gubernatorial bid.[21] Dolores Corona, NJEA's director of Governmental Relations, told a *New York Times* reporter that the organization felt betrayed by the Florio administration and that it had been treated like "an enemy" (Kerr 1991c). Later, this loss of a key potential ally hurt Florio significantly when the legislature — terrified by the tax revolt of 1990 — turned to the QEA as a source of funds for tax relief in the winter and spring of 1991.[22] Moreover, without the educational establishment behind him, it was difficult for Florio to claim that the enormous changes wrought by the QEA would improve New Jersey's educational system.

Another group that had reason to oppose particular elements of the QEA consisted of, strangely enough, some of New Jersey's financially strapped cities. Although the thirty poorest urban areas were slated to receive approximately 40 percent of the $1.15 billion dollar infusion of state aid,[23] they would also have to raise their local tax rates in order to qualify for foundation aid — the bulk of the state's contribution. Estimates in the fall of 1990 indicated that eight of the thirty districts would have to raise taxes in order to qualify for full foundation aid.[24] Given the vehement anti-tax sentiment raging throughout New Jersey at this time, tax increases in these urban areas would prove no more popular than in the suburbs, especially tax increases virtually mandated by the state.[25] This dilemma, combined with the local assumption of pension and social security payments, meant the QEA was not a godsend for many urban localities. In fact, local assumption of pension and social security payments would offset the projected increase in state aid these special needs districts were projected to receive. Although unwilling to directly criticize the QEA because it provided them with a large infusion of resources, these districts were not opposed in early 1991 to some tinkering with the recently enacted, but not yet implemented QEA—especially concerning the pension and social security payments and the local "fair share requirement." Thus, if districts that gained the most from the QEA were willing to see it amended, then virtually no one would be opposed to some modification of the plan. In this regard, the urban districts' objections to the QEA removed the brakes from the amendment process in early 1991—barely seven months after the original QEA was signed into law.

Another group was understandably dismayed by the effects of the QEA: administrators and parents in the relatively affluent districts that were to be weaned from state aid over a four-year period. Some 151 districts would see their foundation aid eliminated over that time period, while an additional 77 would see their foundation aid diminished in proportion to their property and income levels. The 151 districts that would lose all foundation aid would now operate entirely on the basis of local revenues, state categorical aid (such as aid for special education), and compensatory education aid, slated in the QEA for replacement by aid for "at-risk" pupils. Thus, in order to balance their budgets, these districts would have to either cut existing programs or raise local taxes.[26] Neither of these options were seen as desirable.

On 31 October 1990, only four months after the QEA's passage, hostile superintendents and school administrators heatedly expressed their opposition to Education Commissioner John Ellis and Thomas Corcoran, Florio's top education advisor and chief architect of the QEA, at the annual conventions of the New Jersey School Board Association and the New Jersey Association of School Administrators. As the *New York Times* reporter wrote: "Today's conference became a forum for confronting Dr. Ellis and Mr. Corcoran." When Ellis asked for a show of hands from those who supported the law, detractors outvoted supporters by a ratio of nine to one among the approximately four hundred people in the room (Hanley 1990d).

The next day, chief administrative officers of twenty-five wealthy suburban school districts met with Ellis for two hours to persuade him of the necessity of changes to the QEA. One subject raised at that meeting was the topic of compensatory educational aid. Because "at-risk" aid was now to be allocated on the basis of a student's poverty rather than on the basis of her or his test scores, affluent districts stood to lose a tremendous amount of aid. Affluent districts are more likely to have students who are performing poorly on achievement tests than they are to have students from poor families. Indeed, this change irked some superintendents more than the elimination of minimum aid. The New Jersey Supreme Court had explicitly ruled, after all, minimum aid unconstitutional in *Abbott II*, but Florio's revamping of compensatory education in order to direct more aid to poor (and typically urban) districts went beyond the court's mandate, in the critics' view. Under the old compensatory education plan, the thirty poorest districts enrolled about 53 percent of the kids eligible statewide for compensatory aid. Correspondingly, they received about 53 percent of total compensatory aid. Under the new plan (according to projections in the fall of 1990), these thirty districts would enroll about 69 percent of the students eligible for "at-risk" aid, and receive about 70 percent of the total "at-risk" funding.[27]

Stung already by the loss of minimum aid, affluent districts were particularly angered by the additional cut in compensatory aid. Also, they viewed the shift as poor educational philosophy: "There's not a one-to-one correlation between kids who have academic problems and kids who can't afford lunch," Robert S. Kish, superintendent of Livingston school district, told a *New York Times* reporter. Alan Sugarman, superintendent of Fort Lee schools, put it more strongly: "I think the concept is ridiculous. . . . For somebody to come to the conclusion a student is at risk because he qualifies for free lunch is crazy" (Hanley 1990c). The bifurcation of compensatory aid and academic performance struck many suburban administrators as not only damaging to their districts' financial interests, but to their academic interests as well. As they stated in a position paper developed after the passage of the QEA, "the Quality Education Act goes beyond the mandate of the court . . . and includes provisions which will fundamentally weaken the most successful and highest-achieving public school districts in the state. . . . Weak schools should not be made strong by making strong schools weak" (Goertz 1992, 13).

It is worth noting at this point that these interest groups were objecting to policies that were not necessarily products of the Florio administration alone. Many of the complaints — laid directly upon Florio's doorstep — were in fact disagreements about the content of the *Abbott II* decision. In its policy response to *Abbott II*, the Florio administration — while going beyond the decision in some respects — largely accepted the validity of the court's demands. Thus, the political abuse suffered by the Florio administration stemmed in large part not from its own proposals, but from the policy implications of the *Abbott II* decision. For example, the Florio plan to phase out minimum aid emerged from the court's direct ruling that minimum aid was unconstitutional. In addition, the QEA's overall aim to pump additional aid into New Jersey's cities — through both the at-risk aid program and the substantial infusion of foundation aid — can be directly linked to the court's insistence in *Abbott II* that the funding of inner-city school districts be "substantially equal" to that of affluent suburbs and that the funding level cannot rest upon the taxation and budgetary decisions of local school boards.[28]

On one issue the Florio administration went beyond the court's ruling:

the shift of teachers' Social Security and pension payments back to local districts. On this matter, the court respected a prior decision that upheld the state's assumption of these payments on administrative grounds, but it explicitly stated that the payments may be "constitutionally infirm" and left its jurisprudential options open for a future ruling. The Florio administration seized upon the court's cue, and included local assumption of pension and Social Security payments in the QEA, only to stir up a political hornet's nest. Because Florio aggressively undertook the reforms, his administration bore the brunt of the political outrage over them.

In sum, however, many of the problems with the QEA that organized interests cited were not wholly of Florio's making. His administration — although perhaps overeager and lacking political foresight — formulated a response to *Abbott II* that specifically and meaningfully addressed the constitutional violations found by the New Jersey Supreme Court. The political costs of doing so were exceptionally high. But to say the goal and aim of the reforms were Florio's alone is to understate the policy implications of the New Jersey Supreme Court's actions.

Whether the QEA was a result of judicial or executive policy-making, the opposition among organized interest groups was intense. Moreover, the NJEA, the superintendents' associations, and the urban districts were instrumental in the movement to amend the QEA. Confronted with mounting public pressure — taking the form of a tax revolt — legislators saw that few would actively defend the QEA, beyond members of Florio's administration. Moreover, Democratic legislators saw that they would suffer at the hands of voters if they did not repair their image as proponents of increased taxes. The expert opinion that the QEA needed amending — as represented by these three groups — provided legislators with the legitimate cover they needed to rework the QEA dramatically in early 1991.

It should be noted, however, that neither the urban leaders nor the NJEA were at all happy with the revisions that the legislature ultimately enacted.[29] But their support for the *process* of modification was necessary for the outrage felt by voters to result in substantial changes to the QEA. The fact that the NJEA and New Jersey's cities could not control the outcome of that revision process shows the strength and breadth of the tax revolt in New Jersey. Their urging was necessary to begin the amendment process, but it was not nearly sufficient to control it. And once initiated, the rush to amend the QEA took on the form of a political panic among legislators seeking cover from the surging tax revolt.

The organized opposition to QEA I (as expressed vocally by affluent districts and the New Jersey Education Association, and more quietly by New Jersey's urban areas) ensured that there would be some modification to the plan in the winter and spring of 1991.[30] But the sweeping changes to the QEA far exceeded those anticipated by these groups. Indeed, the NJEA wound up opposing the reform bill passed into law by a Democratic majority. Having prodded for significant revisions, these groups helped initiate revisions that soon exceeded their own goals — or fears. The calls for reform initiated a new round of policy-making, but under a completely changed political climate. The near defeat of U.S. Senator Bill Bradley to political neophyte Christine Todd Whitman in November 1990 showed both Florio and New Jersey state legislators that voters were willing to punish legislators for raising taxes in a recessionary economy. Florio himself stated that voters had sent him a "humbling message" in the November 1990 election. He added that the electoral results "were really directed at me and the policies of my administration" (Kerr 1990d).

The massive public opposition to the sales and income tax increases created legislative and electoral incentives to rescind the benefits of Florio's original fiscal priorities. The hostility and animosity generated by Florio's tax package created a legislative rush to reform the QEA and to replace aid to inner-city districts with middle class property tax relief. Legislators, fearful of the wrath of New Jersey's voters in the upcoming November 1991 elections, sought to present a more tax-friendly face to the voters who held the reins on their destiny: the suburban voters, pinched by both tax increases and looming cuts in state aid to school districts. The legislative result — QEA II, enacted in March 1991 — produced a significant shift in the distribution of school aid, *from* urban districts *to* suburban districts, both middle class and affluent. These modifications did not, however, eliminate increases to the special needs districts, but they did reduce the size of the increases, primarily to grant property tax relief to homeowners in the suburbs.

In early January 1991, Senate President John Lynch and Senate Majority Leader Daniel Dalton introduced a plan to cut back the QEA's $1.1 billion price tag by $450 million and apply the funds to property tax relief. The thirty special needs districts would lose, under the Lynch-Dalton plan, $170 million of the total $450 million cut. Florio administration officials claimed they were surprised by the size of the proposed cutbacks and hoped to reduce the figure to around $150 to $200 million (Hanley 1991).

In an attempt to forestall huge cuts to the QEA, Florio signed onto a proposal put forth in mid-February by Speaker of the Assembly Joseph Doria (D-Bayonne, 31st). The Doria plan would have provided only $244 million in property tax relief (instead of Lynch-Dalton's $395 million) and would have obtained the funds from the transition aid suburban districts were scheduled to receive under the QEA (Kerr 1991a). It also would have protected most of the aid to the state's thirty special needs districts. In response to the proposal Senator Lynch stated, "The plan appears to be strongly weighted in favor of the urban centers at the expense of the suburbs. . . . I must say the plan leaves me disappointed" (Kerr 1991a).

After Doria put forward his proposal, negotiations between the Florio administration and the legislative leadership soon drew to a close, with Florio conceding much ground. On March 4, state legislative leaders announced a compromise on QEA II. The total amount of aid shifted from the QEA to property tax relief was to be $355 million. Other objections to the QEA were also resolved: the local assumption of Social Security and pension payments was deferred for two years, and the minimum tax effort for property poor districts was relaxed (Kerr 1991b). Within a week the plan passed both houses and Florio signed the bill on March 14. At the bill-signing ceremony, Senator Lynch stated that "The people who pay property taxes in this state . . . made us do the type of reform that we arrived at here, and made us put in place a system that will work for the short-term and for the long-term for property tax relief" (Bird 1991).

The QEA II reduced the state's infusion of new money into education by $355 million, but that reduction was not evenly spread among all districts in the state. The thirty special needs districts lost $238 million, accounting for approximately 67 percent of the cutback (Goertz 1992, 25, table 4A). Although the QEA II represented a $750 million increase in state spending for education over the 1990–91 school year (Goertz 1992, 27, table 5), it basically restored the status quo ante distribution of those educational resources. The QEA I had tried to enlarge the slice of the educational pie allocated to inner-city schools, but the QEA II—although it increased the overall size of the pie—actually shrank or kept constant the slice of the pie for New Jersey's special needs districts. For example, before the QEA was passed (the 1990–91 school year), the thirty special needs districts received 36.9 percent of the Total Maximum School Aid fund.[31] If QEA I had been implemented, they would have received about 39.4 percent of the Maximum School Aid fund. Under QEA II, they received 37.2 percent, only 0.3 percentage points more than prior to the QEA (Goertz 1992, 26, table 4B). Within certain categories of funding those percentages declined *below* pre-QEA levels. For example, in 1990–91, the thirty special needs districts received 52.1 percent of all foundation aid; under QEA I this would have grown to 53.8 percent, but under QEA II they received only 47.7 percent of the state's foundation aid (Goertz 1992, 26, table 4B).[32] At best, the QEA II left, in aggregate, the thirty special needs districts in roughly the same position vis-à-vis the other districts in the state as they had been prior to the *Abbott II* decision.

The QEA II, then, harmed the special needs districts in New Jersey in two ways. First, the tax relief measure aided largely suburban homeowners, and, second, the QEA II's redistribution of educational funds primarily benefited the *non*–special needs districts. Although the overall spending went up under QEA II, that aid did not directly increase the slice of the pie allocated to the special needs districts. The practical result, then, was that the raised income taxes used to pay for QEA I were applied in QEA II not for school finance equalization, but to middle-class property tax relief and to further state subsidization of middle-class and affluent school districts.

Because legislators responded sharply to the vocal demands of both organized interests and popular pressure, the redistribution scheduled under the original QEA became politically untenable. After Bill Bradley's near defeat, legislators saw that the popular outrage over the QEA and its attendant tax increases had potentially disastrous electoral results. But their efforts to appease an angry electorate appear to have failed. In the November 1991 state legislative elections — eight months after the passage of the QEA II and its property tax rebates — voters replaced Democratic control in the New Jersey legislature with a veto-proof Republican majority. The Democrats lost ten seats in the Senate and twenty-one seats in the Assembly, putting the Republicans in absolute control of both houses for the first time in twenty years.[33] The legislative changes to the QEA were for naught — in an electoral sense.[34]

Despite their ascendence to legislative dominance in New Jersey, the Republicans contributed surprisingly little to the school finance reform effort in 1992 and on into 1993. They promised much, but delivered little. With strong rhetoric, they vowed the complete reversal of the QEA, even though the act had been essentially converted into a property tax rebate measure by the Democrats prior to the 1991 elections. Even more boldly, the Republicans held hearings in the summer of 1992 on a state constitutional amendment that would have redefined the "thorough and efficient" language in an effort to diminish the state's obligation to provide educational opportunities. Both episodes in chest thumping, however, soon met with a united front of resistance from educational interest groups. The hearings on the state constitutional amendment, in particular, soon degenerated into opportunities for Republican critics to scold the legislative leadership for abandoning even the ideals of educational opportunity and locking urban districts into an expressly inferior funding structure. With no organized group supporting the state constitutional amendment, the hearings soon collapsed; although the measure was reported out of committee, neither house in the New Jersey legislature ever voted on it (Paris 1998, 364–68).

Part of the Republican inability to advance the debate on educational financing can be attributed to a vigorous united front put forward by educational interest groups and the Education Law Center, the group that had organized the *Abbott* litigation. This united front, however, did not emerge spontaneously. Indeed, the coalitions formed as groups sought advantage within the legislative process, and the concessions educational litigators made, highlight the central claim here: the regime of geographically based educational interests presents formidable obstacles to the kinds of structural reforms sought by the New Jersey Supreme Court in *Abbott II*. In his rich account of the school financing battles in New Jersey, Michael Paris details a fascinating episode that took place in the community of educational activists and interests groups during the summer of 1992, an episode that shows the depth of suburban power in New Jersey educational politics. As Paris describes it, Marilyn Morheuser, the dogged and passionate legal reformer who brought the *Abbott* suit, was worried about two things in the summer of 1992: her group's inability to influence the legislative reform process and the NJEA's willingness to trade equity between urban and suburban districts for their pet concern, state funding of teachers' pensions. The NJEA's focus on the pension issue stemmed from Florio's efforts to shift the pension contributions back to the local districts under the QEA. That provoked, as described above, a fierce howling from the teachers' unions because of the downward pressure it would exert on salaries in the affluent, suburban districts. The Florio administration had underestimated the influence of suburban interests in the NJEA when it developed the original QEA legislation, but Morheuser was not about to make the same mistake (Paris 1998, 374–76).[35]

After the state rolled back funding to urban districts in QEA II, Morheuser refiled her suit against the state. One of her claims focused on the continued state funding of pension contributions. In *Abbott II*, the New Jersey Supreme Court had suggested that the pension arrangement was unconstitutional because it was, in effect, regressive state aid (giving more money to affluent districts), but the court reserved judgment for the time being. In her renewed litigation, Morheuser asked the court to rule directly on this matter. While the supreme court remanded the matter back to a lower court in July 1991, Morheuser's claim against the pension aid remained a viable threat to the interests of the NJEA. In the summer of 1992 Morheuser decided to use the claim as a bargaining chip (Paris 1998, 327–30, 375–76).

The deal was simple: Morheuser would withdraw her legal argument against the state's pension aid, and, in return, the education groups in New Jersey would agree to support the aims of *Abbott II*. As Morheuser said at a joint press conference with NJEA Executive Director Robert Bonazzi, "We need their support, plus a widespread understanding of the *Abbott* decree." She added that "We must have unity in the ranks."[36] The cost of that unity was not cheap, however. The state's contribution to pension costs was, at the time, nearly $700 million annually. By removing that pot of money from the negotiating table, Morheuser reduced the resources available for redistribution of aid from wealthy districts to poorer central-city districts. Her options, however, were limited. If NJEA had cut a deal with Republicans to save pension costs in exchange for a revamped funding formula that sliced aid to the urban districts even further, Morheuser would have been left with an even smaller aid package, little political clout, and only holding a paper court decree that, quite obviously, could not alter the distribution of educational opportunity based on geography and affluence. By trading the pension costs for support for *Abbott II* and increased political visibility, Morheuser was making a calculated political concession to the power of suburban districts and their ability to combat court-ordered redistribution of resources. The consequence of her decision was that new aid to the central-city districts had to come out of new money to education, not a redistribution of existing aid to affluent districts.[37] In short, the solution to New Jersey's school financing troubles would be new money pumped through the existing system rather than a structural shift in the provision of educational resources.

A year later, however, the political influence of this united front on education dimmed substantially when Christine Todd Whitman narrowly defeated a resurgent Jim Florio for the governorship of New Jersey. The Republicans now held both legislative houses as well as the governor's office, dramatically transforming the character of fiscal policy in the state. In his last two years in office, Florio had quietly held his own against the Republicans, reducing his own rhetoric of reform and checking the Republican zeal for wholesale reductions in aid to the cities. Instead, he worked out a one-year stopgap measure in 1992 called the Public School Reform Act of 1992. This compromise measure increased aid to the special needs districts by $115 million, preserved the state assumption of pension costs, preserved funding levels for all school districts at 1992–93 levels, and created a bipartisan Education Funding Review Commission to propose a new financing plan (Paris 1998, 380).

But with the arrival of Whitman, promises of tax cuts — and a political need to fulfill those cuts — soon superseded further talk of increased aid to central cities to meet the mandate of *Abbott II*. Instead, Whitman chose to bide her time on the school financing issue, while vigorously pushing forward on her promised 30 percent reduction in the state income tax. Political and judicial events allowed her to wait. Dueling school finance commission reports arrived on the scene in the spring of 1994, and the newly inaugurated Whitman administration took the opportunity to rethink the fundamentals of financing public education in the Garden State.[38] In the summer of 1994 that opportunity became a constitutional obligation. On 12 July 1994 the New Jersey Supreme Court struck down the QEA II, saying the legislation "fails to assure substantial equivalence between the special needs districts and the richer districts in expenditures per pupil for regular education."[39] The final nail now pounded into the QEA's coffin, Whitman and the Republicans could reassess the obligations that the *Abbott* decision imposed on the state. Their reassessment, compounded with Republican notions of pursuing "accountability" of school districts and "standards" for students, transformed not only the legislative educational agenda in New

Jersey, but also the judicial ambition of the *Abbott* litigation. By refocusing the debate onto the nature of the constitutional language at issue, Whitman sought to simultaneously minimize costs and transform *Abbott II* from a decision requiring equity between urban and suburban school districts to one committed to a notion of educational adequacy. That feat — combined with more money pumped through the existing framework — appears to have halted, at least temporarily, the upheavals in New Jersey educational politics. In the next section, I recount how Whitman accomplished that difficult task.

Christine Todd Whitman and the Politics of "Thorough and Efficient"

In the midst of the legislative wrangling and the political tempests over the course of the 1990s, the constitutional provision that sustained these conflicts remained unchanged. Article 8, sec. 4 of the New Jersey Constitution reads: "The Legislature shall provide for the maintenance and support of a thorough and efficient system of free public schools for the instruction of all the children in the State between the ages of five and eighteen years." That phrase also provided an opportunity to the Whitman administration to settle the issue of school financing reform once and for all. Previous efforts to restructure New Jersey's school financing scheme had never specifically defined the characteristics of a "thorough and efficient" education. Faced with the rising costs of assuring that education in New Jersey's central cities kept pace with their wealthy suburbs, and politically committed to a 30 percent reduction in New Jersey's income tax over three years, Whitman and the state department of education looked to the "thorough and efficient" clause as a means to overcome the judicial-legislative impasse on financing inner-city schools and to minimize the costs of that effort.

The logic behind her scheme was simple: if the state is obligated to ensure that children receive a "thorough and efficient" education, then it needs to define what is meant by that requirement and to establish a funding level necessary to provide that level of education. Since the initial *Robinson* decision back in 1973, the state had never fully defined what it considered a "thorough and efficient" education. As explained in chapter 5, the court had for its purposes defined "thorough and efficient" as substantial equivalence in spending between affluent suburbs and the poorest school districts in the state — all urban and largely African American and Hispanic.

This definition was unpalatable to the Whitman administration for several reasons. First, the court's view of "thorough and efficient" placed no meaningful limits on the state obligations. As spending rose in the affluent districts, the state had to make up that gulf in the special needs districts.

With meaningful spending caps on affluent districts politically difficult to impose, the state faced rising costs in its aid to special needs districts for the foreseeable future. Moreover, the court's definition did not respond to Whitman's political desire for greater "accountability" within urban school districts. Citizens and political actors across the state perceived central-city schools as plagued by corruption, mismanagement, and excessive administrative costs. State takeovers of the Jersey City and Paterson school districts only confirmed those assumptions for many political observers.[40] By refocusing the reform agenda onto the meaning of "thorough and efficient" Whitman could rein in "wasteful" educational spending — not only in central-city districts but in the multitude of small school districts that also had high administrative overhead on a per pupil basis. During their efforts to restructure the state's plan Whitman and her education commissioner repeatedly cited a statistic that New Jersey was first in the nation in school spending, but "49th in the nation in the amount of money actually going to instruction."[41] Finally, by turning to the definition of "thorough and efficient," Whitman was following a national trend in education policy that demanded clear and meaningful standards of academic achievement for students. By clearly specifying what students were expected to learn, and holding districts accountable for that learning, Whitman felt she could impose some discipline on an educational system in which overall spending was growing dramatically, but academic performance was not noticeably improved, at least as measured by test scores.[42]

In early 1995 Whitman announced her intention to redefine the scope of the state's funding of education. The court had imposed a September 30, 1996 deadline, and Whitman and her education commissioner, Leo Klagholz, planned to spend the next year and a half putting together a proposal that would both increase accountability, reduce the rate of growth in education spending, and still comply with the court's mandate. The process began with a vague, preliminary sketch of a funding scheme released in February 1995. That twenty-eight-page report, entitled a "Comprehensive Plan for Educational Improvement and Financing: An Interim Report," laid out the reasons why the state needed to define a "thorough and efficient" education.[43] In doing so, the plan implicitly attacked the supreme court's reasoning in *Abbott II* and its cash-based definition of "thorough and efficient." The report states, "There may be an apparent logic in attempting to achieve fiscal equity and educational equality through a primary reliance on the established spending practices of districts in wealthier communities. . . . However, all such assumptions [supporting that logic] are at least debatable and probably false."[44]

Having disposed of the basic framework of *Abbott II*, the report then goes on to describe the ad hoc nature of determining the content of New Jersey's public education: "[T]hrough a piecemeal accumulation of laws and practices, a 'thorough and efficient system of education' has been defined as whatever the state requires plus whatever each local school board determines to be 'necessary.'" Still, the sloppiness and imprecision of defining "thorough and efficient" in this way was not the central problem with the current scheme, according to this document. The real problem was that

> [T]he state must routinely direct communities to spend money through their schools on a range of purposes and at levels that are virtually unlimited.
>
> Under such a non-system which lacks substantive criteria, educational equity must be defined primarily in fiscal terms. Further its achievement ultimately requires, in effect, that all expenditures for all purposes be made everywhere until an undefined substantive purpose is accomplished.[45]

It was essential, therefore, that the state define the components of a thorough and efficient education program before it defined its funding scheme. This approach put local districts and educational interest groups on notice that the state would strive for a new level of rigor in the funding process. Not only would the state define a core set of educational topics and lessons, but it would ensure that each district had sufficient resources to convey this curriculum to its students. Klagholz assured districts that the state would meet the costs of the core curriculum, but he would not attach any dollar figure to the state's contribution until much later in the process. It was essential, he insisted, that the components of the curriculum be established first, and a price tag attached later. In Whitman's more memorable phrasing, the slogan was "Put the textbook before the checkbook" (Thompson 1995). The catch, of course, was that the state would fund *only* this core curriculum, and any extras would have to be paid out of local property tax receipts. In some instances, there would be no state funding available for a number of wealthy districts because the state-mandated minimum local property tax would generate sufficient funding to meet the cost of the core curriculum. Moreover, the plan asserted that if local school districts wanted to continue these "excess expenditures" they would have to seek voter approval.

Whitman and Klagholz sought to reconcile a number of disparate fiscal, political, and policy objectives with this proposal. First, for fiscal reasons, they hoped to rein in state costs for education, especially the growth of funds being expended in the special needs districts. In order to do that, they needed to check the growth of educational expenses in affluent districts, because of the supreme court's linkage of the two. Second, for political reasons, they wanted to check "administrative waste" in public education. Cutting the income tax back 30 percent gave Whitman an aura of a cost cutting fiscal conservative at a time when that was politically desirable. This proposal enhanced that image, but forced the cost-cutting onto other political actors. Third, the proposal was linked to a broader, standards-based movement in educational policy circles. Goals 2000 was a prominent educational initiative of both the Bush and Clinton Administrations, and Whitman's plan to give New Jersey's educational system a core of high standards meshed nicely with that national objective. In fact, U.S. Secretary of Education Richard Riley appeared with Whitman and Klagholz in a televised town hall meeting to kick off the series of public hearings aimed at defining the core standards, and he praised her efforts to set high expectations for New Jersey students (Reilly 1995a). In general, the plan was sufficiently developed to give school districts some idea of the state's new role under the proposal, but was also sufficiently vague to allow for the prospect of modification. School districts and educational interest groups quickly went to work blasting particular components of the plan. As we shall see, the changes they forced inflated the total cost of the plan and preserved their existing advantages in the regime of inequality.

It quickly became clear that the central stakes lay in the definition of the core curriculum and the method by which that curriculum would be "costed out." During the meetings held across the state in the spring and summer of 1995, various teaching interests testified to the essential nature of their programs, including nutritional advising, computer and technology instruction, music and art instruction. Another important concern was the role of special education in the state aid package. District administrators also worried about the tag of "excessive spending" that the report used to describe district spending to promote programs above the state-mandated core curriculum. That phrasing, they said, would make voters more likely to vote down the school budgets. Moreover, the proposal's requirement that voters approve any budget increases beyond 3 percent would jeopardize the ability of schools to promote high achievement. In the central cities, the largest complaint was that Klagholz's road show did not stop in their town. No hearing was scheduled or held in any of New Jersey's large cities, and only one special needs district made the hearing list. Instead, the hearings heard only suburban interests and needs and neglected central city concerns, especially aid for at-risk youth. In general, however, the vagueness of the plan and the still distant September 1996 deadline led most observers, politicians and educational interests alike, to take a wait-and-see attitude.

In November 1995 Klagholz and the Department of Education released a much more specific reform plan, detailing the core curriculum by using "model school" definitions for elementary, middle, and high schools. The state payments for the core curriculum were based on these ideal types. This approach irked a number of districts that saw their circumstances as unique: "They seem to be trying to develop a one-size-fits-all model of education for all districts despite their individual circumstances," said Hackensack superintendent Joseph Monetsano (MacFarquhar 1995b). The Education Law Center, the legal organization coordinating the *Abbott* litigation, attacked the plan for failing to respond to the court's mandate and labeled parts of the plan "fantasy, pure and simple." ELC board member and Rutgers Law School professor Paul Tractenberg, the litigator in the *Robinson v. Cahill* case, testified before the state senate that "[t]he plan as presented appears to be unconstitutional and it's not a close call" (Young 1995). Others worried that the local taxpayers would balk at picking up the tab for programs above the state-mandated minimums. Said Lynne Strickland, the spokesperson for the Garden State Coalition, the association of roughly one hundred affluent suburban districts in the state, "It appears that the property taxpayer in the higher wealth districts is going to be required to cover the costs of programs that they didn't have to before" (MacFarquhar 1995a). For his part, Klagholz defended the plan, indicating that his proposal was caught on the horns of a difficult dilemma: How do you reconcile a court order mandating equality with an existing system of financing that virtually guarantees inequality. "At one level," he said, "we have a court saying no fiscal disparity per student. The other extreme is you have a system that says all differences are allowable, whether it's $5,000 or $16,000" per student (Glovin 1995). One assembly member even went so far as to raise the issue of amending the constitution again, saying "The Legislature is tired of it [the issue], the people are tired of it, and if we went the constitutional route I think the public would support it" (Peterson 1995). At a minimum, it was clear that the legislature would substantially modify the proposal. State Senator John Ewing responded to a journalist's query: "Who says we're going to use that plan?" He conceded only that the Klagholz plan "could maybe serve as a skeleton and we [will] fill in the rest." He also indicated that the primary obstacle would be the responsiveness of each legislator to the bottom line in his or her district: "People say 'I'm not going to support something if my district doesn't get more.' . . . But we can't look at it like that any more. You have to take into account these growing needs. The needs of the cities have to be taken into account" (Chiles 1995). The question remained, however, whether legislators could be induced to take the broader view.

Despite criticism of the plan, both Whitman and Klagholz stood by it. Whitman devoted her entire 1996 State of the State address to the funding proposal, and in early February, Klagholz submitted specific curricular standards for approval by the State Board of Education. Pressure continued to mount on all sides, however. The Garden State Coalition mobilized over one thousand supporters from across Bergen and Passaic counties on a cold February night to rally at Livingston High School to protest the voter approval requirements for "excessive spending." Even ten state legislators attended the event (McLaughlin 1996a). In April the Education Law Center (ELC) returned to the supreme court in an effort to force the Whitman administration to earmark more money in the funding proposal for the special needs districts.[46] The ELC was not the only one concerned about the spending levels, however. In the continued absence of hard figures from the administration, various groups grew increasingly worried. In particular, the NJEA fretted that the state minimums would become the norm, thus placing downward pressures on teachers' salaries throughout the state, because it would force local districts to pick up the difference. Michael Johnson, vice president of the NJEA, told a reporter, "When you compare the standards being proposed to the curricula being offered in many school districts of New Jersey, this is less than many of them do" (MacFarquhar 1996a). The implication, of course, was that the Whitman administration was proposing a dumbing down of elite suburban schools. The NJEA's practical concern was that this reduction in state aid could cost some teachers their jobs. In any event, the political pressure exerted by major educational interest groups focused on preserving the norms of educational quality — and staffing levels — prevalent within the wealthy suburbs.

Finally, in mid-May 1996, the Department of Education released its cost estimates for the core curriculum: $8,285 per pupil. That figure, $132 less than the state average of $8,417, would have reduced state aid in 146 school districts, held aid constant in 68, and boosted aid in 381 districts. More troubling for equity activists, however, was the impact of the plan on the special needs districts. Three of them, according to state estimates were slated for *reduction* in state aid. Newark, the most hard hit, was scheduled to lose over $30.5 million or 5.6 percent of its budget (MacFarquhar 1996b, Schwaneberg 1996).

Reactions to the plan illustrate that the alliance between the central-city schools and the suburbs forged only a few years earlier was now under strain. Paul Tractenberg contended that the state was "trying to find some way for the wealthy districts to keep spending more on their advantaged students and still get out of the court order (MacFarquhar 1996b). Lawrence Feinsod, president of the Garden State Coalition and superintendent of Madison schools, on the other hand claimed that the plan was aimed at harming the wealthy districts. He insisted that the state's "numbers do not reflect the actual cost of running a school district today. . . . [The impact] would be dreadful. A lot of kids would be hurt. It is poor public policy to level down achieving school districts. No child should be made a loser" (Chiles 1996). While the notion of a child attending an affluent suburban district school being tagged a loser in society strains credulity, Feinsod's comments reveal the enormous gulf between attitudes about spending in the central city and spending in the suburbs. Contrast Feinsod's comments with Whitman's reaction to a question about cuts to Newark: "Newark is a prime example of why dollars alone are not the answer. There has to be accountability" (Chiles 1996). For Feinsod, the reduction transforms his students into academic losers and renders the district less able to compete. For

Whitman, the reduction in Newark gives the district discipline and does no harm to children. Their views toward the institutional contexts of educational spending reinforce prevailing attitudes toward the "deservedness" of the children in Newark and in Madison. Not coincidentally, those views also reinforce the racial divisions between the two groups of students and towns — which are only fourteen miles apart.

While particular interests opposed elements of the proposal, others were more sanguine about its overall political prospects. Assemblyman John A. Rocco, chair of the Assembly Education Committee and a Republican from Camden County, stated that "Each legislator is going to look at his district and decide how they are going to go. But some 75 percent got the same or better, so I would assume that most legislators would be pretty positive in regard to the proposal" (MacFarquhar 1996b). Nonetheless, affluent districts continued to work against elements of the proposal that harmed their interests. The Garden State Coalition organized a letter-writing campaign against the proposed voter approval of excessive spending and delivered more than ten thousand letters to the statehouse in early June (Pristin 1996). Perhaps the central development over the summer of 1996 was the sudden resignation and subsequent death of Chief Justice Robert Wilentz due to cancer. Wilentz had been the author of the *Abbott II* decision and had hoped to resolve the litigation before his scheduled mandatory resignation in February 1997.[47] Despite the strong language of *Abbott II* and *Abbott III*, Wilentz's departure from the court nonetheless created some uncertainty among observers about the direction of the *Abbott* litigation. Governor Whitman appointed her attorney general, Deborah Poritz, to replace Wilentz, but Poritz quickly recused herself from the *Abbott* proceedings because she had worked on the state's case in the latest round of litigation. Then, in September, the court denied the Education Law Center's motion to force the state legislature to spend more money on the special needs districts, but it allowed the group to refile its claim after the legislature passed a new funding law. At the same time, the court extended the legislature's deadline to 31 December 1996.

With a politically realistic funding amount now on the table and with a somewhat looser timetable, it became apparent that the serious bargaining could begin. Between July and December 20, 1996, when Whitman signed the Comprehensive Educational Improvement and Funding Act into law, state legislators and Whitman reached a number of compromises designed to preserve the high level of educational offerings within affluent districts. In the course of presenting its demands, the Garden State Coalition patched over the differences between poor and affluent districts and focused on boosting the overall level of educational support. Molly R. Emiliani, the Coalition's parent coordinator from Livingston, New Jersey, told a reporter that "When this whole thing started, they were just trying to pit the urban against the suburban school districts." But, she said, "[t]hat is not the case at all. . . . The urban and suburban districts have joined hands and said that this does not help any of the districts. We are not going to stop until we close the gap and it is equal for all the kids" (Preston 1996). The political cleavages now became a little dicier for Republican lawmakers. With suburban educational interest groups making an alliance with central-city advocates, and both demanding more money, Democrats found a useful way to criticize Whitman's plan. Democrat Gordon A. MacInnes, a state senator and a member of the Education Committee from predominantly suburban Morris County, led the charge. MacInnes spoke frequently against the proposal, writing in an op-ed piece that "the administration's proposal would shatter the very school districts that should be emulated for their high academic standards and commendable student achievement" (MacInnes 1996). His primary concerns were that the standards promulgated by the state department of education did not reflect the true cost of delivering a top-flight education and that the voter approval necessary for any "excess spending" would necessarily drive down spending in the suburbs, as voters recoiled from the property tax increases necessary to maintain those programs. These two objections emerge directly from the geopolitics of education in New Jersey. The fragmented governance and tax structure in New Jersey meant that a large number of low-enrollment districts with high tax bases could present a formidable resistance to Whitman's plan. Their political influence stemmed from one of the necessary corollaries of the new proposal: in high-spending districts, local voters would have to increase local taxes to maintain current educational offerings. The state plan to fund only the core curriculum meant that affluent districts faced either program cuts or local property tax hikes. The Garden State Coalition, dominated by educational interests and parents who supported high spending levels, sought to diminish the likelihood of either. Along with MacInnes's steady drumbeat of opposition, this pressure influenced many suburban GOP legislators, especially those fearful of igniting local property tax revolt if the bill passed (Burton 1996, McGrath 1996).

In the end, the affluent districts secured a number of compromises that advanced their interests, while the central city districts won few concessions from the Republican-dominated state legislature. The Republicans added $51 million to Whitman's original proposal to fund relief and exemption packages to districts that posed especially thorny political obstacles to the CEIFA. Among the changes were additional funds for property tax relief in middle-class districts and more money for districts with a high percentage of senior citizens. But most important, Republicans substantially changed Whitman's original plan of submitting to voters the costs of exceeding the core curriculum. Instead, voters were given the opportunity to vote up or down the *entire* district budget, blurring the distinctions between local add-ons and the constitutionally required core curriculum. In addition, if residents voted down the budget and the town council imposed any cuts in accordance with voters' wishes, the school board could appeal to the state education commissioner to reinstate those funds, despite voter and municipal denials. In the original plan, no appeal was allowed. In sum, the changes to the bill largely left intact the existing scheme of voter approval with an appeal to the commissioner and thereby met the Garden State Coalition's objective of preserving high spending within affluent districts. Affluent districts also achieved guarantees of "stabilization funds" to ensure that there would be no sudden decreases in state aid and a process by which they could increase their permissible rate of growth in spending (McLaughlin 1996b, Senate Budget and Appropriations Committee 1996).

At the bill's signing, Whitman waxed on about the merits of the legislation: It would ensure that "every child . . . will receive a superior education" but that "nothing in this plan will cause property taxes to rise." And, of course, the kids: "For the first time, we are putting children first" (New Jersey State Law Library 1996). Meanwhile commentators complained that the bill would do little to change the existing distribution of educational opportunities, and lawyers at the Education Law Center hurried to refile their claim that the newly enacted legislation did not meet the *Abbott II* mandate. In other words, little appeared to have changed. Legislators legislated, the governor crowed about the new plan, and lawyers relitigated. But the CEIFA did mark a turning point in the struggle for educational opportunity in New Jersey because it allowed the New Jersey Supreme Court to turns its focus away from structural change in school financing and toward oversight and implementation issues in the new structure. While the court may have done so out of fatigue or political shifts within the court, this reorientation marked a meaningful change in judicial politics of educational financing in New Jersey. The jurisprudential logic of that change was traced out in chapter 5, but here I just want to conclude this case study with some comments on the changing nature of the judicial task in the wake of the CEIFA.

The Judicial Turn to Administrative Oversight

In January 1997 the Education Law Center returned to the state supreme court, contending that the CEIFA failed to provide substantial parity between the special needs districts and suburban districts. In May 1997 the court struck down the CEIFA, declaring that while the core curriculum is an "essential component of a thorough and efficient education," the act is nonetheless "incapable of assuring [educational] opportunity for children in the special needs districts for any time in the foreseeable future."[48] The state failed, according to the court, to show any meaningful connection between the funding levels in the special needs districts and their capacity to help students master the core curriculum and its skills. Establishing the components of a thorough and efficient education was only one half of the constitutional equation, the court stated. The other half consisted in providing enough resources to enable students to learn those skills and subjects. In short, the court rejected the state's price tag for the core curriculum, *especially* given the enormous educational needs of the children in the special needs districts. In those districts, the court contended, more resources would be needed to master the core curriculum. The court also found that the state had not adequately responded to the issues of school facilities and it ordered additional compliance.

It is important to note that the court *did* accept the basic structure of the CEIFA, particularly its effort to move away from a funding-based notion of parity and toward a standards-based notion. It simply rejected the state's estimate of the funding required to achieve those standards within the special needs districts. And, in the absence of any other pricing information for education in the special needs districts, the court reasserted its claim that the affluent suburbs provide a proper benchmark for the cost of a thorough and efficient education in the twenty-eight special needs districts. The court then ordered equivalent spending between the two groups of districts by the 1997–98 school year, only four months away.[49] More important, however, the court ordered judicial, rather than legislative, relief for the continuing constitutional violations. To determine what form this relief should take, the court remanded the matter back to superior court and ordered the Department of Education to develop a detailed plan to further address the special educational needs of children in central-city schools, along with a cost estimate and an implementation plan for effecting the necessary changes in the school districts. It ordered the superior court to rule by 31 December 1997 on the sufficiency of the state's plan to achieve long-term parity. In undertaking judicial relief, *Abbott IV* placed the state judiciary in the position of managing an educational reform agenda in a few troubled districts, outside the influence of legislative and executive politics that had marked both the QEA and CEIFA reform projects. By taking on the role of administrative oversight, the New Jersey Supreme Court ensured that the subsequent *Abbott V* ruling would have a profoundly different tone and quality.

During the course of the lower court hearings, it quickly became apparent that the two sides in this dispute had profoundly different perceptions of the changes needed in the special needs districts.[50] In November, Education Commissioner Leo Klagholz testified that a phased-in program of "whole school reform" for elementary schools would meet the court's mandate of providing additional educational opportunity without costing any additional money.[51] This program, dubbed "Success for All" requires administrators, staff, and teachers to undertake intensive reading instruction and tutoring to prevent any student from falling behind in reading skills.[52] At the junior high and high school level, the state, in essence, would provide more remedial instruction.

In contrast, lawyers for the Education Law Center (ELC) argued that these districts needed all-day preschools for three- and four-year-olds, class sizes of fifteen or fewer in kindergarten through third grade, a lengthened school day and school year, social workers and health clinics at school, along with extensive summer and after-school programs and tutoring. According to ELC Executive Director David Sciarra, the goal would be "schools that serve not just students but their families and their communities" (Glovin 1997, Goodnough 1997b, 1998). The state quickly calculated that these programs would cost over $800 million a year (*New York Times* 1997).

Aided by school financing expert Allan Odden, who served as a special master, Judge Michael Patrick King pursued a middle course, ruling that the state would need to spend an additional $312 million (on top of the $247 million released in September 1997) in the special needs districts to ensure substantial parity with affluent districts. Among the programs he said the state needed to implement were whole school reform with Success for All as the instructional foundation, full-day kindergarten for five-year-olds, full-day prekindergarten for three- and four-year-olds, summer school, school-based health and social services, added security measures, and a program of fiscal and academic accountability for school districts.[53] He also ordered further review of facilities improvement and construction.[54]

Upon appeal, the New Jersey Supreme Court indicated, somewhat prematurely, that this would be its last ruling in the *Abbott* litigation. Wrote the court: "[T]his decision should be the last major judicial involvement in the long and tortuous history of the State's extraordinary effort to bring a thorough and efficient education to the children in its poorest school districts."[55] Although its prediction of final closure was wrong, the court did lay the foundation for terminating the litigation. In *Abbott V*, the court substantially adopted the Department of Education's proposals for reforming the special needs district. Approved by the court were the whole school reform proposal, including "Success for All," along with a full-day kindergarten program. The court reduced the full-day prekindergarten program to a half-day requirement and adopted the Department of Education's argument that on-site social and medical services were not necessary, but that each middle and high school should hire a "community services coordinator" to refer students to existing agencies for assistance. In addition, the court directed the education commissioner to authorize a variety of supplemental programs (school-to-work, college transition, alternative schools, security measures, technology reforms, accountability mechanisms, etc.) in special needs schools, if individual schools could demonstrate a need for such programs. The court also adopted the commission's plans for facilities improvement and construction. In short, the court stripped away several expensive programs recommended by the special master and Judge King and largely sided with the Department of Education that such programs would be adopted after schools demonstrated a need for them and specifically requested additional funding from the Department of Education. More important, the court specifically declined jurisdiction over future conflicts in the administration of these reforms. Instead, aggrieved parents, schools, or districts would appeal within the Department of Education to the commissioner and then, under the Administrative Procedure Act, transfer the action to an administrative law judge. The conflict could then be appealed in the state courts. Although in the spring of 2000 the New Jersey Supreme Court handed down two additional *Abbott* decisions, *Abbott V* indicated that the state would soon be free from state supreme court oversight of its school finance system.[56]

With a collective judicial sigh, the New Jersey Supreme Court signaled that its campaign to restructure the financing of public education in the Garden State was nearly at an end. The progression from the lofty rhetoric of *Abbott II* to the detailed policy prescriptions of *Abbott V* highlights the inability of the court to do more than pump more money through the existing institutional framework of educational governance. The twenty-eight Abbott districts (and the nearly 265,000 students in those districts) saw substantial increases in funding during the life of this litigation. They gained new programs, new resources, new buildings, and possibly new hopes for a broader educational vision. What they did not see was a transformation in how those services and programs are paid for within the state. Reliance on the property tax for educational funding in New Jersey has increased over the life of the *Abbott* litigation. The inability of the court to achieve this transformation stems from both the targeted nature of the court's rulings and the geopolitics of education that entrenches the interests of key districts, school administrators, and educational interest groups within the educational policy-making process. These structural dimensions of the regimes of inequality have been attacked through two other lawsuits winding their way through the New Jersey judicial system. This time, taxpayers in middle-class and rural districts have claimed, separately, that the CEIFA discriminates against them by imposing unequal tax burdens and insufficient state resources, respectively.[57] The political logic of the policy response to the *Abbott* could be severely challenged if the New Jersey judiciary seriously entertains these claims. Given the experience of the past twenty-five years, it appears unlikely the courts in New Jersey will have the energy and desire to undertake yet another effort at systemic reform. But stranger things have happened in a New Jersey courtroom.

Conclusion

When we think of how constitutions order a regime — allocating power, assigning responsibilities, creating mechanisms for change — we typically think of a group of founders, dignified folks, typically men, engaged in the craft of statesmanship. James Madison is perhaps the patron saint of this form of constitutional ordering. His vision and theory of governance shaped the U.S. Constitution far more than any other. Yet other forms of constitutional regime ordering exist in the United States, outside the purview of the founders of 1789 and outside the scope of the U.S. Constitution. State constitutions and the forms of political organization that emerge under them are important dimensions of constitutional governance in the United States. And at the state level, perhaps no other political issue is as important or central as public education. The judicial effort by state courts to reshape the fundamental assumptions of the regime of public education has placed enormous strain on legislators, citizens, policy-makers, and interest groups. In many places, not just in New Jersey, state supreme courts have sought to change the rules by which educational resources are distributed and controlled. That effort — while it has increased the flow of money through the educational system and has in general made that flow more equitable — has not changed the fundamental assumptions of the regime of public education : the primacy of local control of local resources. The interlocking ties of property wealth, home rule, and governmental fragmentation are simple, but robust, organizational rules that courts have not been able to alter, let alone erase. As judges have sought to make property wealth irrelevant to a child's education, they have confronted an educational regime that is well entrenched in American life. That regime enables a relatively narrow band of actors to preserve both their influence in public education and the advantages they accrue under its existing design.

The judicial inability to restructure the constitutional regime of public education in the United States does not mean, however, that the judiciary has not effected meaningful changes. It does mean, however, that judges do not meet the "founders test" of constitutional design. But that may be an unfair test. These courts *have* placed before citizens and their representatives a normative injunction that educational opportunities be made more equitable and that greater educational resources be provided for the worst off in our society. This mandate pursues constitutional ordering in more ways than the redesign of the existing regime of public education. The next chapter reviews how the judicial efforts at constitutional ordering within public education have been successful and how they might be made more successful. Of course, *Brown v. Board of Education* hovers over the entire project of the constitutional ordering of public education, and, as a result, the next chapter begins with an exploration of the connections between race and class inequality in educational opportunity.

8

CONCLUSION:

CONSTITUTING EDUCATION IN AMERICA

I N HIS BOOK *Savage Inequalities,* Jonathan Kozol relates a conversation
he had with an East St. Louis high school student named Samantha
about her school choices: "'If you don't live up there in the hills,' she
said, 'or further back, you can't attend their schools. That, at least, is what
they told my mother.'

"'Is that a matter of race?' I ask. 'Or money?'

"'Well,' she says . . . 'the two things, race and money, go so close together—what's the difference?'" (Kozol 1991, 31).

Up to this point, this book has focused on the differences between these
two forms of inequality. That is, I have taken lessons from the convulsive
judicial struggle to desegregate America's schools and applied them to a less
visible, but similarly divisive effort by courts to provide more educational
resources to America's poor children. In doing so, I have kept the two problems—race and class—analytically distinct. Of course, as Samantha re-
minds us, the two go so close together. From the perspectives of courts and
legal actors, the two *are* different: different legal theories apply, different
constitutional texts are available for interpretation, different remedies are
available, different actors may be ultimately responsible for the disparities.
So far, this book has sought to highlight those differences. Yet race and class
disadvantages, combined, produce a common core of inequality that blurs
those legal and theoretical differences. From a political and educational
perspective, the two go so close together. Perceptions of inequality are filtered through racial and class lenses, and disparities of wealth and racial
isolation both produce inadequate educational outcomes. When the two
forms of inequality are combined, the effects are doubly devastating.

In this concluding chapter, I want to put the two forms of educational
inequality in the United States back together and reexamine their common-
alities. The first part of this reexamination explores how race and class tensions reinforce one another in the remedial phase of school finance litigation. What starts out as an argument about money becomes in some
places an argument about race and the relative worth of the reform beneficiaries. The second part of the chapter briefly discusses an emergent legal approach to combined racial and economic inequalities, and summarizes the
strengths and weaknesses of court efforts to restructure public school financ-

ing. The third part of this chapter outlines two policy proposals to address both racial and economic inequality in public education. The proposals, aimed at creating "magnet neighborhoods" to redress both the racial and economic isolation of schoolchildren, acknowledge the lessons of the school desegregation struggles and the judicial campaign for greater resources in education. Only by learning from these two nearly intractable problems can we begin to unravel the binding ties of racial and economic inequality in education. The chapter ends with some thoughts on how educations and constitutions knit communities together and how we might remove the thread of inequality without unraveling the dense fabric of schools, communities, and our diverse constitutional commitments.

Racial Perception in School Finance Cases

Although school finance cases revolve around the resources available to school districts, there is often a racial dimension to the political conflict over school financing. Beneath the dry discussion of formulas, local add-ons, and student weights, there runs a bitter current of racial animosity over the distribution of educational resources. These comments pop up in legislative debates, letters to the editor, and community hearings. Sometimes frank and sometimes guarded, they reveal two things. First, some opponents of greater equality in education see poverty through a racial lens and view governmental efforts to redress that poverty as an unworthy goal. Second, many beneficiaries of school finance reform efforts see opponents of these measures — whatever their motivation — as racially antagonistic. In either case, the racial segregation of communities and the geopolitics of education can transform political battles over educational resources into explicitly racial contests.

In 1992, after the Texas Supreme Court struck down yet another legislative reform, Texas State Representative John Culberson (R-Houston) introduced an amendment to the Texas Constitution that would have prevented the courts from reviewing any school funding plan adopted by the legislature. His bill would have also prohibited the redistribution of tax revenues from property-rich districts to property-poor districts. "Enough is enough," said Culberson. "It is time to get school finance out of the courthouse and back in the hands of parents and taxpayers." Culberson's proposal immediately drew fire from a number of legislators, some of whom called the proposal racist. Representative Gregory Luna (D-San Antonio) said the proposal would push "civil rights back 20 years." State Senator Carl Parker (D-Port Arthur), chair of the Senate Education Committee, claimed that the proposal was "racially motivated" (Stutz and Hoppe 1992). Culberson denied the racial motivation, but his proposal nonetheless soon died. It is important to note that critics of Culberson's proposal did not decry its effects on poor children, but on students of color, particularly Hispanic and African American. Despite the financial origins of the legislative stalemate that prompted Culberson's proposed amendment, the cleavage was not cast in terms of rich versus poor, but of white versus black and Hispanic. A racial thread winds around the core of class conflict over the distribution of educational money — in Texas and elsewhere.

In Connecticut, during the final debates to push through a school financing bill in response to the state supreme court's *Horton* decision, State Senator Richard Bozzuto (R-32d, Waterbury) spoke in opposition to the equalization plan. His language invoked a vivid series of racial code words:

> The majority party in this Circle today is about to commit a travesty on every taxpaying citizen in the State of Connecticut. . . . Today, you are legislating a tax that is going to cost every citizen in this state more money and you're funneling it into a cesspool, a political cesspool that spends and spends because they know they're not responsible. (Connecticut General Assembly 1979, 1785–88)

Bozzuto equated school finance reform with theft — theft from upstanding folks, folks from the suburbs. He blasted his fellow lawmakers, insisting that

> [Y]ou put your hands in their [the taxpayers'] pocket and stole their money. That's the simplicity of it. You, indeed, have stolen money from hardworking citizens in East Hartford and Manchester, in Watertown and Waterbury and from all over this State because you were prevailed upon by outstanding lobbyists in Hartford. (Ibid., 1788).

The themes of Bozzuto's objections were clear: Residents of the small towns and suburbs were "honest" and "hardworking"; they were "citizens." Most important, they were "taxpayers." Unlike the residents of Hartford, they contributed to the fiscal and moral well-being of the state. The cities were "wasteful" and "inefficient"; residents of cities got off "scot-free" from obligations that fell to the other, more responsible residents of the state. The politics of cities was dominated by "lobbyists" and political chicanery. The cities were morally suspect.

These comments made a deep and lasting impression on Bozzuto's fellow lawmakers. State Senator (and future vice-presidential candidate) Joe Lieberman, representing New Haven, called Bozzuto's comments "one of the worst, most wrong-headed, most partisan and irresponsible speeches I have ever heard in this Chamber and I think more of him than to believe that he means what he says" (Ibid., 1797). In an interview over thirteen years after the enactment of the 1979 reforms, Representative Dorothy Goodwin still vividly recalled the remarks Bozzuto made on the senate floor: "Bozzuto got up and said . . . 'Why should we send all that money to the cesspools of the cities?' Now that's a pretty racist remark, and it's really hardly disguised" (Goodwin 1992).

Whites are not the only ones to see a racial divide on this issue. A summer 1996 public hearing in Newark, New Jersey, saw a large crowd condemn Governor Whitman's proposed Comprehensive Educational Improvement and Financing Act (CEIFA). Many of those testifying argued that the reduction of funding to Newark and other central cities under the Whitman proposal was a racist attack on minority children. James Harris, representing the New Jersey State Conferences of the NAACP, claimed that the proposed legislation "is a bad bill because it is racially divisive." He added "You know that when there is a discussion of urban anything (*sic*) in this State, people see black and Latino faces. So when the bill talks about downsizing or taking away from the rural districts and giving to the urbans, it is pitting white folks against black folks and Latino folks, and that is unnecessary." Targeting his comments at the state lawmakers in attendance, Harris continued:

> Are you saying in this bill that African-Americans and urban children are of less value than children in suburban, wealthy districts? Are you saying that the children in Newark and other urban cities do not deserve the same type of facilities, the same types of opportunity, the same type of safety? If that is what the public policy is saying, then the NAACP is prepared to fight you to death — to death. (New Jersey Legislature 1996, 36–37)

Others saw the *Abbott* litigation as part of a long trajectory in the campaign for racial justice, an arc that stretched from Jim Crow and *Plessy v. Ferguson*, through *Brown v. Board of Education* and the end of separate but equal, the *Robinson* litigation, and finally to the *Abbott* case. After invoking a legacy of slavery and *Brown v. Board of Education*, Lawrence Hamm, state chair of the New Jersey Million Man March coalition said:

> [I]t wasn't enough simply to say that it was wrong to have separate and unequal schools, we needed the resources to, in fact, make that happen. That is why the *Abbott v. Burke* decision is as significant, even more significant, than *Brown* . . . Because it would give us the resources that we need to correct an unequal and unjust situation.
>
> So we took a small step forward with *Abbott*, [a decision] that said 'We have, in New Jersey still, after slavery, after the Civil Rights Movement, after the Black Power Movement — we still have an apartheid school system in this State, and under the Constitution of this State, the State government is legally bound to correct that situation.' It took a small step forward to do so, but now [this proposal] has taken ten steps back. They want to go back to the situation that existed prior to that (New Jersey Legislature 1996, 14).

A few minutes later, Andaiye Foluke took the floor on behalf of the Pro-Child Coalition, an education advocacy group in Newark. Her comments also invoked themes of oppression and racial conflict.:

> We had our day in court, and the courts ruled on our behalf. . . . [T]here is . . . a great fund of enthusiasm for education in our communities. It is the fruits of a heritage of struggle. It is the legacy, sometimes written in blood, of the many thousands gone. We are personally offended by the S-40 and the A-20 bills, which are racist, discriminatory, and perpetuate the vicious cycles within our communities. Like our sister, Rosa Parks . . . we say 'No more. Enough is enough.' If you say cut back, we will say fight back." (Ibid., 18).

For many within predominantly African American and Latino communities, the connections between the legal movements of school desegregation and school finance reform are not simply academic or theoretical. *Brown* and *Abbott* are more than different legal tactics by which lawyers seek educational reform; they are touchstones of constitutional promises. They represent links in a chain of struggle for civil rights, and as such, any attack or attempt to reverse these decisions is seen as an attack on the civil rights movement itself. The invocations of Rosa Parks, lynching, Jim Crow, and other symbols of racial oppression are not merely racial grandstanding. They reveal the close and deeply felt connections between race and class disparities in American education and how the provision of resources to poor schools is, in many ways, the culmination of a much longer struggle for educational opportunity.

The flip side of this perspective, of course, is Bozzuto's. His white suspicion of school finance reform as merely public assistance for unworthy minorities invoked many of the arguments used against welfare and affirmative action. And Bozzuto's attitudes are not confined simply to the Northeast. University of Houston Professor Kent Tedin found them in Texas as well. In a study that highlighted connections between attitudes toward school finance equalization and symbolic racism, Tedin found in two Houston school districts that racial prejudice was as good a predictor of white attitudes toward school finance reform as economic self-interest (Tedin 1994). Tedin surveyed 1,032 whites in two school districts near Houston about their support for the proposed school finance equalization plan, as well as other issues designed to measure racial prejudice. He concluded that white views about minorities had a substantial effect on attitudes toward school finance equalization — independent of whether respondents thought their own district would win or lose money in the reform process. Tedin also found that respondents viewed the beneficiaries of school finance equalization in racial terms: Eighty-two percent of his survey respondents (all whites) thought predominantly Hispanic districts would gain a lot or a little from a 1991 equalization plan.[1] Eighty-three percent though predominantly black districts would gain a lot or a little. Meanwhile, only 9 percent thought white districts would gain a lot or a little, whereas 73 percent thought white districts would lose a lot or a little (Tedin 1994, 23, note 20).

Just as a class dimension existed in the racial conflict over school desegregation, these episodes and attitudes highlight the racial dimensions of redistributing educational resources. There is no denying that segregated housing markets, combined with economic disparities among communities, will produce a racial divide in the geopolitics of education. That divide is the by-product of a struggle over educational resources in a context of segregated communities. Over the past few years, however, a few school finance activists have pursued a litigation strategy that directly targets the combined racial and economic divide among school districts. The most prominent of these cases, the *Sheff v. O'Neill* case from Connecticut, argues that one form of inequality cannot be isolated from the other.[2] In many ways, cases like *Sheff* combine the political fireworks of school desegregation with the geopolitics of school finance reform.[3]

Sheff v. O'Neill emerged against the background of two primary facts about Hartford, Connecticut's schools. First, the school finance litigation effort of the 1970s and 1980s had ensured that Hartford schools had resources comparable and in some cases exceeding those of the surrounding suburbs.[4] Yet by all indicators, the money had not placed Hartford's schools on a par with its neighbors'. Instead, test scores were lower, dropout rates were much higher, and college attendance rates paled in comparison. As a result, educational activists and parents in Hartford began to think beyond educational spending and to pay greater attention to the contexts of public schooling in Hartford and the surrounding areas. And here a second fact became most central: the Hartford school system is an island of poor Hispanic and African American students within a ring of largely white suburbs.

Typically, this kind of de facto segregation would have been attacked in federal court with an equal protection argument that aimed at forcing the state into compliance with *Brown*. Instead, the plaintiffs in *Sheff* claimed that as a matter of state constitutional law, Connecticut was not meeting its obligation to provide all students with equal educational opportunities, a right won in the 1977 school finance case of *Horton v. Meskill*. The problem for the plaintiffs was that the schools that were the worst off academically were relatively well funded: the Hartford school district was spending *more* per pupil than its neighboring suburban districts. The conventional school finance suit that sought more funding on adequacy grounds or more equal funding on equality or education clause grounds would not work for Hartford. Indeed, Hartford's funding was comparatively high because *Horton* ultimately produced greater revenue for Hartford.[5] The inequality of Hartford's schools lay beyond the financing issue.

By a variety of measures, the Hartford school system provided an obviously inferior education to its neighboring suburbs. Its graduation rates were lower, its dropout rates were higher, its achievement scores were lower, and its subsequent educational attainment of students was lower. The *Sheff* plaintiffs contended that these inequalities stemmed from the organization of school districts along municipal lines, a governing arrangement dating back to 1909 that reinforced the racial and economic segregation of students between Hartford and the surrounding suburbs. That is, by allowing residential segregation to entrench the Hartford school district's racial and economic segregation, the state of Connecticut had not lived up to its affirmative duty to provide Hartford students with an equal educational opportunity, even if it did fund that district relatively well.

The plaintiffs lost at the trial level, but in July 1996 the Connecticut Supreme Court, in a closely divided 4-3 vote, reversed that decision and found that the racial segregation in Hartford's schools violated the state constitution. It ordered the legislature to "fashion the remedy that will most appropriately respond to the constitutional violations."[6] The court specifically took the issue of economic isolation off the judicial and legislative agenda, however, forcing the state to focus most closely on the racial disparities in Connecticut's schools. It fused the plaintiffs' claims for an equal educational opportunity with the state constitution's ban on segregation to remove the question of class disparities in school district populations. In doing so, the court may have been on more solid jurisprudential ground, but it recast the policy problem as *strictly* a racial issue, one in which local control and the racial composition of school districts were directly being assaulted. The plaintiffs' legal theory had been more subtle, drawing attention to multiple forms of educational disadvantage; the Connecticut Supreme Court's opinion transformed that subtlety into a stark conflict between black and white, a social and political conflict much more difficult to address in the context of severe residential segregation. The political fallout was both predictable and disheartening.

At the time of the lower court ruling, Connecticut Governor John Rowland literally popped champagne bottles at a press conference to celebrate the state's victory. His opposition to the supreme court decision was, not surprisingly, abundantly clear. He did, however, appoint a twenty-two-member panel chaired by the state education commissioner to develop proposals for the legislature to consider. When those proposals arrived, they largely failed to address the difficult question of racial segregation. Instead, the commission proposed early childhood education, school readiness programs, and a statewide program of school choice. Despite their relatively limited ambition, the state legislature enacted only a few of the commission's proposals. Not surprisingly, the substantive effects on the racial and economic composition of the Hartford schools (and other central-city, predominantly minority schools) were negligible. The centerpiece of the Connecticut legislature's reform package, an expanded interdistrict school choice program, included funds for only one thousand schoolchildren spread throughout Hartford, New Haven, and Bridgeport. (Ironically the new choice program replaced an existing program that offered suburban choice to five hundred Hartford students alone.) The resulting, "expanded" program could affect, at most, 1 percent of Hartford's students. The plaintiffs returned to court in 1998 to force greater reforms, but the district court judge ruled that it was too early in the five-year reform plan for the court to compel any new measures and that the state had responded in good faith. The attorneys for the *Sheff* plaintiffs opted not to appeal that decision, possibly because new appointees by Republican governor John Rowland to the Connecticut Supreme Court had dimmed the chances of a favorable review. The plaintiffs and their attorneys vowed to continue their legislative efforts to force greater changes in the racial and economic segregation of Connecticut's schoolchildren. "We're in this for the long haul," said plaintiffs' attorney Philip D. Tegler (Gural 1999).

Can Courts Achieve Greater Educational Opportunity?

Given this relatively discouraging outcome for a case that proposed such novel and intriguing legal arguments, what conclusions can we draw about the effectiveness of judicial interventions to achieve greater equality in educational opportunity? Clearly, *Sheff v. O'Neill* has yet to produce dramatic changes in the racial and class composition of the Hartford schools, but that case presents only one window on the judicial campaign for greater educational opportunity. We need to take a broader view of the entire project of judicial efforts to ensure educational opportunity before we arrive at any definitive conclusions about judicial efficacy. Chapter 2 of this book showed rather convincingly that when state supreme courts strike down financing systems, more funds flow to public education, and those funds are generally distributed more equitably than they were prior to the court decision. Of course, not all courts have enjoyed dramatic success, but when we review the trajectory of the school financing cases, we see that courts, in general, have significant influence over the policy outcomes of these cases. Moreover, we see that courts can heighten their influence by remaining aware of some central lessons.

A key lesson of the foregoing chapters is that judges need to stay focused on their agenda-setting powers, rather than micromanaging particular outcomes. Legislatures are quite willing to avoid this difficult issue and courts are often the only institutional force that can keep the issue at the forefront of the policy agenda. Through the use of declaratory relief—especially when used in conjunction with the threat of injunctive relief — courts can focus the attention of a legislature unwilling to attend to the unpleasant task of altering the distribution of educational resources. This is especially important when the advocates of reform — the poor, minority groups, and others lacking power — have few other political venues in which to seek redress. In this sense, the agenda-setting power of courts acts as a representational proxy for those whose interests are systematically excluded by the geopolitics of education. This lesson reinforces the findings of other scholars, such as William Gormley, who see agenda-setting as perhaps the most fruitful use of judicial power.[7]

Two techniques often help courts enhance their agenda-setting powers. First, courts should make clear the ultimate aim of reform, giving the legislature a meaningful target. While noble pronouncements of the goals and ideals of an educational system comport well with the expected function of courts as the constitutional conscience of a polity, a decision that is too vague or lacks specific reform objectives is virtually meaningless to a legislature. These objectives can be expressed in high language, but they must simultaneously be politically realistic and give legislators a concrete formulation of the problem. By remaining focused on goals and outcomes, without dictating means, judges simultaneously respect the policy-making authority of legislators and executives and increase the likelihood that the legislature will take the decision seriously. Second, judges should make extensive use of meaningful, yet respectful deadlines. By giving sufficient time to pull together a legislative coalition, but not too much time to allow other issues to divert attention, courts can ensure that reforms are kept on track. In establishing those deadlines, courts should keep the electoral calendar firmly in mind. Often, the most significant advances in school finance reforms take place when legislators are not yet worrying about the next election. Threats of injunctive relief and retaining jurisdiction over a lawsuit make these deadlines much more credible. Together, a clear task and a clear timetable, backed by ominous threats of extensive judicial intervention, can quickly focus a legislator's attention.

These techniques of maintaining the agenda-setting powers of a court must be complemented, however, by a clear awareness that courts should focus on the first principles of institutional design. That is, judges must remember at all times that their decisions will act as policy blueprints and they should be prepared to sketch out a vision of what a constitutional program of educational financing would look like. While producing that sketch, they should also expect that their words will be parroted back at them, as legislators and policy-makers seek to bend judicial language to the difficult political realities of increasing funding to one set of districts while holding others constant, or worse, decreasing state aid. This notion of a "policy blueprint" reinforces the clear objective requirement stated above, while recognizing that court decisions strongly influence the institutional design of school financing systems. Thus, courts not only must be prepared to state what the reforms should accomplish, but must provide a quick overview of the mechanisms and institutions that would attain those objectives. Clearly, legislatures and executives could reject that blueprint, but more likely than not they will adopt those design elements in an effort to meet constitutional muster and then try to reconcile that institutional framework with the political pressures of educational geopolitics.

The foregoing chapters also illustrate that unanticipated consequences are inevitable in structural reforms as complex as these. What, for example, was one of the consequences of New Jersey's efforts to pump more money into inner-city schools? The reliance on local property taxes for educational revenues increased across the state. Moreover, this increasing reliance on local property tax fueled such ire in middle-income districts that they filed their own lawsuit against the state, saying that the existing system imposes unequal burdens on taxpayers across the state.[8] The point here is that as courts seek reforms, they cannot assume that all remaining elements of the system will stay constant. These revenue and spending decisions are interrelated, and changes in one area will result in unanticipated changes in other areas. Because of this, court reforms should promote school financing changes that do not require court supervision or maintenance in order to be effective. These changes need to be self-executing and rely on forces other than judicial oversight to keep them in place. Ideally, judges might harness market mechanisms to achieve judicial objectives.[9]

Perhaps the strongest lesson is, finally, that popular support for financing reforms significantly decreases when the reforms diminish local control. This finding places courts in a difficult situation because a property tax regime based on local control is, in effect, what generates inadequate and/or unequal resources. Courts have addressed the issue of local control, but generally those arguments have been advanced by the state as reasons not to intervene in school financing issues. Courts that do intervene typically dismiss issues of local control, claiming that it is either illusory because property-poor districts have control over nothing without sufficient resources or that its importance does not trump the constitutional mandate of providing greater educational opportunity. There are at least two reasons why courts that do strike down existing school finance regimes need to take local control into account. First, the public opinion data surveyed in chapter 6 shows that local-control concerns transcend questions of class and geography. That is, residents living in poor districts want local control just as much as residents in affluent districts. Of course, they also want additional resources, but they want to have influence over the administration over those funds. Second, the issues surrounding local control constitute perhaps the largest obstacle to legislative compliance. Where funds come from and who controls the use of those funds are central policy issues that need to be resolved in any reform effort. Judicial deference on this issue means that courts will be less likely to induce significant changes. A court that wants to change the distribution of resources simply cannot dismiss the local control question.

Often, a state legislator who is confronted with an unconstitutional financing system will design a system in which the state asserts greater control over the provision and administration of education. School financing changes generally result in greater state involvement. This again runs counter to the expressed desires of constituents, as evidenced by the polls. Courts and legislatures need to balance increased state responsibility against citizen and parental desires for maintaining local control.

Finally, courts need to pay greater attention to the multiple causes of inadequate or unequal educational opportunity. Resources matter tremendously, but so do the learning environments of communities. Schools exist within broader social contexts than financing alone can address. Healthy and vital communities are prerequisites for healthy and vital schools. This is not to say that the education clauses of state constitutions empower judges to embark on large-scale social reform simply to ensure that adequate learning takes place within classrooms. It does suggest, however, that state and local policies that influence the broader community may merit judicial attention, even if they are not directly related to educational policies. In particular, the ruling in the *Sheff* decision points toward the connection between racial isolation and poor learning environments. Educational research illustrates that compounded forms of inequality (racial, economic, social) pose tremendous obstacles to student achievement and learning. To focus exclusively on the provision of educational funds in those districts facing a myriad of ills often does not meet the state's obligation to provide an adequate or equal educational opportunity. While money alone provides important opportunities to students, it cannot generate the community attention, political power, and educational capital that ensure successful schools. In this sense, a key difference between affluent and poor districts is not simply that affluent ones have money. They also have fewer of the conflicts and ills that place obstacles in the paths of parents and students seeking quality education. In many poor districts where parents and children are concerned with economic and physical survival, the luxuries of time, attention, and parental oversight are quite dear indeed. If courts seek to improve the educational opportunities in these districts, more money is necessary but not sufficient to achieve that judicial ambition. Attention must be paid to the broader community context in which schools are situated.

Creating "Magnet Neighborhoods"

To foster stronger schools in areas that suffer from racial and economic isolation, we need to foster stronger neighborhoods. The reform ideas proposed here are designed to advance equal educational opportunity by focusing on the community dimensions of public education. At base, these reforms share a common goal: to reduce the racial and economic homogeneity of classrooms in an effort to promote better learning and increased life opportunities, while simultaneously acknowledging the real concerns that parents have for local control of education. Integrating schools on racial and class lines increases the chances that children from all backgrounds will broaden their educational horizons, that parents will focus on educational achievement, and that schools will respond to community needs and demands. The aspiration, then, is to focus on proposals that can help magnetize entire neighborhoods, making them more attractive to parents with school-age children. The use of inducements, rather than sanctions, also helps us to respect local control, an important dimension of parental views toward public education.

Combining these forces is not simple; economic and racial integration do not easily reconcile with local control. Racial and economic exclusivity, it seems, is a by-product, if not a primary aim, of local control policies. In order to weaken that nexus, these reforms provide incentives for either school districts or individuals to actively mingle students of different racial and class backgrounds. The reforms aim to maximize the impact of court-ordered funding changes by linking the infusion of new money to peer exchanges in classrooms and to parental expectations outside classrooms.

Every educational experience is a blend of two inputs: the resources a child brings to the classroom and the resources a community devotes to that classroom. The court decisions that are the primary focus of this book have meaningfully increased the latter, but to achieve greater educational opportunity, we need to enrich those financial classroom inputs with the more intangible resources that children bring to school and that they share with their peers — through their classroom discussions, their collaborations, their homework assignments, their social networks, and their future plans and dreams. The following proposals seek to bolster peer and parental effects in classrooms. Certainly not panaceas and certainly not applicable or desirable in all settings, these reforms can nonetheless, I argue, help us to constitute a more equal education for children most at-risk.

Proposal One: Create a Public School Attendance Property Tax Credit in School Attendance Zones That Are Predominantly Minority and/or Poor

One reform to address the race and class dimensions of educational inequality in the post-*Brown* era is a public education property tax credit for parents of children enrolled in schools where the percentage of minority children and children in poverty exceeds the metropolitan area average. This property tax credit would, in effect, create a property-tax free zone for parents in areas that on average have higher concentrations of poor and minority children.

The goal of the policy is twofold. First, the proposal could provide incentives for greater economic and racial mixing in our housing markets, helping to "magnetize" particular neighborhoods. To the extent that parents and those expecting to be parents make housing decisions on the basis of marginal costs, this promise of a long-term tax credit (as long as twelve years per child) could significantly change the nature of housing markets in economically distressed and racially isolated areas. By fostering class and racial diversity, these neighborhoods could reverse declining property values, racial segregation, and limited economic development. To the extent that whites and more affluent residents are drawn to these areas, the social, business, and educational networks of the existing residents would increase and, hopefully, provide greater educational opportunities in the long run. Moreover, the new parents may be better situated to demand better schools from teachers, administrators, and school-board members. Middle- and upper-middle-class efforts to improve the local public school may well have greater effect than similar efforts by poor parents. While that disparity may not be fair, it could improve the educational opportunities for all students.[10] Similarly, children from higher socioeconomic backgrounds can raise the expectations in schools for teachers, administrators, parents, and students alike. In this sense, the proposal is aimed at increasing the educational capital as well as the political and economic capital in these communities. Research has shown that integrated educational environments hold out the promise of long-term transformations of the life opportunities for these students. While they are not panaceas for the educational fortunes of poor and minority children (Schofield 1989), they are clearly better than segregated environments.[11]

Critics may object that minority students do not need to sit next to white students to obtain an excellent education, and that urging an influx of white middle-class kids is an insult to these communities and to their children. Why not simply boost the resources, energies, and facilities that we devote to our racially isolated schools? Why rely on an indirect, perhaps even Rube Goldbergesque, contraption to achieve greater educational opportunity? The objection is an important one that I have long grappled with. My response emerges from the simple recognition that what takes place inside schools is significantly shaped by what takes place outside schools, and if this nation's poor, minority children are to have a fighting chance in American society, we need to pay greater heed to the collective institutional inequalities of our neighborhood schools. *Neighborhood* schools are precisely that; they reflect the strengths and weaknesses of our social and economic ties. If local control and localist sentiment in public education are more or less fixed public sentiments, then we need to pay attention to the localities that build and support our schools. More equal educational opportunity, in this context, is the product of integrated housing markets and diminished class disparities in school districts. Without these changes, excellence in poor, predominantly minority public schools will be rare, and white America's collective insistence on de facto racial and economic segregation will contribute to those continued failings. The question, then, is which is a worse insult? To insist that minority academic achievement emerge in settings where the odds are stacked against it, or to contend that minority and white academic accomplishment are best achieved jointly and collaboratively?

A second goal of this reform will be the immediate redress it offers the residents and students who are suffering from racial and economic isolation.[12] Many children and parents have endured years of legal and political struggle to achieve school finance reform or school desegregation. An immediate residential property tax credit, even if it does nothing to change the composition of the neighborhood, at least provides some measure of remedy for those who suffer the worst abuses of a segregated and class-based educational system.

A central virtue of the proposal is that it does not coerce parents to live in any particular neighborhood or send their children to any particular school. New white residents who move to an integrated neighborhood to benefit from this tax credit do so by choice, induced both by the reduction in property taxes and, hopefully, the opportunity to live in an integrated neighborhood.[13] In effect, the proposal rewards individuals who pursue the kind of racial and economic equality we claim our nation espouses, rather than forcing integrated schools and neighborhoods on whites who do not want them. It may offend our constitutional sensibilities to recognize that many Americans do not want integrated schools and communities, but the hard lessons of white flight suggest that whites do not often meet the challenge of our constitutional commitments. Rather than accept those lessons as given, this proposal seeks to induce, rather than coerce, white middle-class participation in the education of poorer minority children. The current housing and schooling decisions in the United States clearly indicate that many whites do prefer segregation, but this proposal may affect those preferences.

The effects of this proposal on the housing and schooling decisions of black and other minority parents is less clear. It could generate some perverse incentives, drawing middle-class minority parents out of integrated schools and into predominantly minority schools in order to gain the tax advantage. This draw may be stronger if these parents are unsatisfied with their children's integrated schools, but that concern is dampened somewhat by the significantly higher value that blacks and other minorities place on the value of integrated neighborhoods and schools (Massey and Denton 1993). Given Black parents' preference for integrated schools, the chances that they would forgo an integrated education for their children simply to take advantage of the property tax credit are most likely small.[14] The larger question is whether white parents would forgo a *segregated* education for their children to take advantage of the property tax credit. That, in a nut-shell, is the great difficulty of this proposal. This question forces us to at least acknowledge that many whites value segregation and to raise the troub-ling specter that no tax credit is sufficient to overcome that value.[15]

For the black parents already living in these neighborhoods, there could be at least two counterproductive reactions. First, because the tax credit would give them a financial incentive to stay in the neighborhood, the proposal might further anchor minorities and the poor in underperforming public schools. Moreover, if the tax credit is not sufficient to draw whites to these neighborhoods, the policy could produce the worst of all possible outcomes: continued or entrenched minority attendance in these schools and no white or middle-class in-migration. Second, substantial white in-migration could produce resistance among the existing residents as that mi-gration would, eventually, reduce their tax credit. However, the likelihood of these two possible outcomes is, at best, small. In many parts of the coun-try, especially the large cities of the Northeast and Midwest, African Ameri-cans *could not be more anchored* to segregated communities. Segregation, in many instances, simply cannot get much worse. Outside central cities, seg-regation is less acute, but still profound. Black suburbanization, particularly, is relatively modest (Farley and Frey 1994) and is typically clustered in older suburbs adjacent to central cities (Massey and Denton 1993). In short, Afri-can Americans are already severely confined by segregation. It is doubtful this proposal would intensify that segregation.

A number of institutional safeguards must be in place, however, if this proposal is not to harm existing residents and their communities. First, pol-icy-makers must not reduce educational spending in affected districts in order to pay for the public school attendance property tax credit. Courts and legislatures will need to continue to provide additional material resources to these low-wealth and racially isolated districts to ensure that parental and peer effects can take root in a rich and ample educational environment. Second, there must be safeguards against rapid transformation and/or gen-trification of existing urban areas if this public school attendance tax credit attracts large numbers of in-migrants. Typically, when urban areas are "eco-nomically developed" through tourism, business development, or gentrifica-tion, the existing poor and minority residents are priced out of the housing market and shunted back into other areas of extreme poverty and segrega-tion. Those most vulnerable are renters, who see rising rents as property values increase. Homeowners, in contrast, are better situated to benefit from this transformation. This proposal would work best in areas where rates of home ownership are relatively high, but policy-makers could easily include renters in the program by requiring landlords to document that the tax credit has been passed on to renters. In order to minimize hardships on existing residents, this public school attendance tax credit may need to be phased in over a few years, rewarding first, longtime residents and then extending the program to newcomers as they stay longer in the local public school.[16]

Policy-makers would also have to address the geographic reach of the property tax credit. In many cases, a tax credit for attendance in an entire school district that is predominantly minority or poor would not be appropriate because school districts often exhibit marked racial and class extremes, particularly in large metropolitan districts. If a tax credit were available to parents in an entire district, especially one with substantial disparities among schools, there would be no incentive for middle-class parents of white children to move to the schools suffering from racial and class isolation. Thus, it is important that the tax credit be focused on the most narrowly drawn unit possible, preferably the school attendance zone.

Proposal Two: Explicitly Link Magnet and Charter Schools with Magnet Neighborhoods

Perhaps the most widely touted education reform of the 1990s was school choice. Choice, along with its policy cousins, the charter movement and publicly paid vouchers for private education, has captured the fancy of policy-makers and parents alike. Of course, for particular segments of the population school choice has always existed; parents with sizable incomes could always opt for private education, and others, typically less affluent, but still comfortable, could choose the best public schools for their children simply by moving to that attendance zone. Taking into account new choice programs, charter schools, private schools, and the residential options of some families, Jeffrey Henig and Stephen Sugarman have estimated that nearly 60 percent of all parents choose their children's schools (Henig and Sugarman 1999, 29). Extending this range of choice to those lower on the socioeconomic ladder has some superficial appeal.

But school choice in all its forms is not without cost. Because students learn a good deal from their peers, and schools benefit from the consistent attention of parents, the use of the exit option by talented students and involved parents will necessarily diminish the education of those left behind. And when we acknowledge that those with broader educational horizons and aspirations typically come from families with higher incomes, it becomes increasingly clear that school choice will exacerbate not only the educational inequalities of the existing public school system, but also compound the growing economic isolation of many students. Because education is a social enterprise, the use of school choice, in whatever form, affects not

simply the student and parents exercising that choice, but those who actively decide to stay or passively stay in their neighborhoods schools because
of inertia or lack of interest. The irony of school choice is that the aggregate
effects of individual decisions to seek a better education could produce a
worse educational system, as larger and larger chunks of student populations
are left behind. Should we then simply deny parents and students the opportunity to make these choices? That, clearly, is not a desirable outcome,
either educationally or politically. For the foreseeable future, education reformers must acknowledge and accept the reality of school choice.

What we can do, however, is to structure the educational and social contexts of those decisions so that economic and racial inequalities are not
exacerbated by the legitimate quest for a better education. One way of doing
this is to explicitly link the creation of magnet and charter schools with the
program of magnet neighborhoods detailed above. By introducing into the
array of choices currently available to parents, innovative and well-funded
educational programs that combine either strong educational themes or racial and economic diversity (or both) *with* a reduced or eliminated property
tax burden, judges and policy-makers could provide a major boost to some
marginal communities. Moreover, if students who lived within the magnet
or charter neighborhood automatically qualified for attendance in these dy-
namic programs, while those living outside the neighborhoods were on wait-
ing lists, the financial incentive offered by the residential property tax credit
could be coupled with the educational incentive of a strong academic program. It is also important that students be able to choose these magnet and
charter schools in magnetized neighborhoods across existing school-district
lines. In places like Newark, New Jersey, or Hartford, Connecticut, school-
district lines reinforce racial and class disparities, and by not allowing cross-
district attendance, the pool of potential students would be relatively homogeneous. In places where jurisdictional boundaries map out class and racial
boundaries as well, this kind of cross-district attendance is essential to promoting more equitable educational contexts.[17]

Magnet schools have a long history of promoting academic innovation
and achieving a significant measure of racial integration. Charter schools,
too, hold some measure of promise for promoting greater educational innovation in school systems that are not meeting the needs of their students. Of
course, neither charters nor magnets can help build the surrounding neighborhoods the way that strong neighborhood schools can. But with the bonds
of geography increasingly weakened in school systems that are promoting
choice, and the bonds of geography trapping some students where choice
does not exist, we should not overly romanticize the local schoolhouse. Local control is a good thing to the extent that it improves educational performance and builds strong communities; to the extent that it isolates, ex-
cludes, and homogenizes our schools, rendering them grossly unequal,

localism is a problem. The difficulty, of course, is that the virtues of local control produce its vices. This proposal aims to minimize the harms of localism and enhance its virtues by structuring the choice option to possibly help reinforce communities ties. By creating incentives for parents to move into the neighborhoods where innovative school programs exist, this reform can possibly further "magnetize" neighborhoods and allow for a meaningful alternative in public education.

In sum, the combination of a property-tax abatement for racially and economically isolated districts and innovative and challenging magnet and charter schools might, in the long-run, achieve a more significant transformation in troubled urban school districts than the kind of limited remedies pursued in *Sheff v. O'Neill*, which to date have done little to alter the demographics of the schools in Hartford, Connecticut. Imagine a network of twenty top-flight new elementary schools, sprinkled around Hartford, open to all, with free transportation to all, but with enrollment preference given to those who live in the neighborhood and in which local residents who enroll their children at the magnet or charter schools will pay no property taxes. This kind of educational reform could be either wholly locally run or run by the state, depending on the characteristics of the local district. It may not address the needs of all children in a district like Hartford, but it would clearly improve the education of more students than the reforms enacted in the wake of *Sheff*. Magnetized neighborhoods and magnet schools could have a combined effect of bringing in new residents, new money, and new educational goals, while aiding longtime residents who have been profoundly harmed by mediocre or failing schools in racially and economically isolated neighborhoods. The key elements of this program would appeal to a public that endorses the notion of equal schooling, but is deeply troubled by judicial usurpation of local control and has a strong desire for school choice. And it might, just might, open the door to a significant institutional change in a system of public education that has not yet delivered on its constitutional promises of educational opportunity.

Conclusion

Programs of property tax credits and magnet schools, by themselves, will not, of course, generate a groundswell of support for educational equality. It is never popular to provide more resources to communities dying, not thriving, with the American dream. Those communities, and in particular their schools, lay bare the myth that everyone has a chance to succeed in American society. Without greater resources, schools in these communities cannot provide even a semblance of equal opportunity. With greater resources, they are subjected to greater oversight by the state. A public school property tax credit and a vigorous magnet program in racially and economically isolated communities might, and I stress the uncertainty here, create conditions in communities that improve the prospects for educational opportunity. The causal link is perhaps tenuous, but the idea is a structural response to a structural problem in our educational system. Previous and continuing judicial efforts have successfully procured more resources, and those efforts should be continued, even expanded. But simultaneously, these decisions have not paid sufficient attention to the contexts of education and the health of the communities upon which schools depend.

Public education is not dead. There is tremendous support for the notion of publicly funded community schools. The current trend toward choice and charter schools does not mean the abandonment of public education; it simply means that the public is groping toward a way to cut the connection between geography and schooling. That is why there is significant support for educational alternatives in central cities, where geography offers little to enhance the viability of education. In areas where geography and class coalesce to provide excellent educations, there is diminished support for these measures. Greenwich, Connecticut, Montgomery County, Maryland, and Plano, Texas, all very much enjoy their well-funded public schools, and residents there support the *notion* of public school. The problem is simply that their support rests on the existing framework of local control, extreme disparities in property wealth, and fragmented jurisdictional boundaries, the very mechanisms that systematically generate unequal chances for children. Thus, the citizen support that exists for public education backs the very local control mechanism that generates huge disparities for children. Efforts to unravel those connections produce a vociferous yelping from privileged parties who fear the demise of local control, but also endorse, at least implicitly, the idea of equal educational opportunity, Therein lies the contradiction of educational opportunity in America today.

What does our constitutional life have to do with these arrangements? In short, until state supreme courts began striking down school finance systems, our constitutional commitments — interpretative, normative, and institutional — reinforced those contradictions. The judicial effort to make geography irrelevant to the educational fortunes of children tried to remove one leg of that constitutional triad by articulating a judicial constitutional vision of educational opportunity that was consonant with previous constitutional interpretations of equal education. That broader interpretative view necessarily borrowed extensively from *Brown v. Board of Education*, but it also extensively clashed with our localist vision of education as expressed in our attitudes toward local control of schools and in our institutions that entrench local control. The interpretative frameworks these courts advanced were not startling theoretical innovations; they are, rather, a straightforward judicial expression of the sentiments found in the Declaration of Independence: "We hold these truths to be self-evident: that all men are created equal." The implicit radicalism of that sentiment cannot be easily suppressed, however. The political fallout from these decisions partly reveals that equality is not tremendously valued in American life, at least not in the early twenty-first century.

The U.S. Supreme Court's directive in *Brown* that educational opportunity, where the state undertakes it, must be provided "on equal terms," has not been fully implemented. Whether it ever will be depends on the creation of a new constitutional vision for education in American life, a vision in which the ties of geography no longer bind students to a dismal future, but in which community control, a treasured American sentiment, is allowed to flourish. Reconciling these tensions and constituting that kind of education in the United States means further development of jurisprudential approaches to the problem of educational opportunity, but it also requires the construction of a normative commitment and an institutional plan to realize the aspirations of *Brown* and its progeny. Constituting education in the United States has never been easy; great school wars ravaged New York in the Nineteenth century, rural districts resisted the creation of the common school, Northern and Southern school districts alike bitterly fought desegregation. And in our time, ideological and religious conflicts have led some parents to leave the public arena and to homeschool their children. Yet if publicly funded education is to be a public institution, it must draw on some common ideals. Some contend there is no longer sufficient public will to pursue a common aspiration of educational opportunity for all children, but I think that is an overly pessimistic view. Constituting public education will require a collective assessment of what is important in our educational systems and the design of imaginative institutions that can overcome political and normative resistance to change. Perhaps even our understanding of "equal terms" must change. But the need to educate our children and to live collective and public lives will not disappear; these two insistent social requirements mean that the task of constituting education will remain with us for some time.

APPENDIX A
EQUITY AND ADEQUACY ANALYSIS FOR CHAPTER 2

TO ANALYZE TRENDS in school financing equity and adequacy, I obtained school financing data for each school district in each state. These data generally came from the state departments of education, although Connecticut data was obtained from the Connecticut Public Expenditure Council, a well-regarded fiscal watchdog group, and the Illinois data came from the National Center for Educational Statistics, a division of the U.S. Department of Education. Also, because the New Jersey decision was restricted to only particular socioeconomic classes of school districts, I have applied my analysis only to those districts that are the focus of the court's ruling: the 30 so-called special needs districts (largely inner-city districts) and the roughly 110 affluent districts that fall into the New Jersey Department of Education's "I" and "J" categories of district wealth (the two most affluent categories). New Jersey presents particular methodological difficulties because many of the I & J districts are non-K12 districts. These districts cannot be fairly compared with K12 districts because of different revenue needs for elementary and secondary education. As a result, I constructed hypothetical K12 I & J districts by pooling the revenues of the I & J K6 and K8 districts that fed into I & J 9–12 regional high schools. The resulting hypothetical districts are thus directly comparable to the K12 special needs districts. See Berne and Stiefel 1984 for a discussion of this methodology.

Once I had obtained the data, I then calculated the per pupil combined state and local revenues. Because state supreme courts have sought to alter the distribution of resources provided by state and local sources, I omitted federal revenues from these district-level per pupil calculations. This gives a more accurate assessment of the educational resources actually controlled by a state legislature as it grapples with the court decision. In two states, I had to rely on expenditure data rather than revenue figures. In the case of Texas, I was forced to use total operating expenditure minus federal revenue because of significant data errors in the reporting of local revenues. In North Carolina, only state and local expenditure data were readily available in electronic form from the North Carolina Department of Education. I then weighted each district for the number of students within that district in order to obtain a per pupil rather than a per district analysis. After adjusting the figure for inflation, I calculated the median and range of expenditures for each state over a period of years, as well as the Gini coefficient. The Gini coefficient was calculated using the formula found in Equation Eight in Pyatt et al. 1980, 456.

APPENDIX B
PUBLIC OPINION ANALYSES IN CHAPTER 6

THE POLLS USED in this chapter were gathered from a variety of sources, including the University of Connecticut, Roper Center; the Center for Public Interest Polling, Eagleton Institute of Politics, Rutgers University; the Survey Research Center, University of Kentucky; Social Science Research Center, University of Tennessee. With the exception of the Connecticut polls, all original data and survey questions are available free of charge over the World Wide Web from the University of North Carolina's Institute for Research in Social Science Data Archive (http://www.irss.unc.edu/data—archive/). The Connecticut poll data is available from the Roper Center at the University of Connecticut.

PUBLIC OPINION DATA

The data sets listed here were used at some point in the analyses in this chapter. In all regression analyses, "don't know" responses were treated as missing. In the data analysis, the data from each state's polls were pooled and analyzed together.

> Connecticut: Connecticut Poll 1, 15–21 March 1979, sample size 500; Connecticut Poll 7, 11–18 June 1980, sample size 500.
> New Jersey: Eagleton Poll 79, 2–10 July 1990, sample size 800; Eagleton Poll 94, 10–15 September 1993, sample size 801; Eagleton Poll 106, 22–29 February 1996, sample size 804.
> Kentucky: Kentucky Spring Poll Survey 1992, 20–May 12 April 1992, sample size 664; Kentucky Fall Poll Survey, 1993, 18 November–22 December 1993, sample size 655; Kentucky Spring Poll Survey, Part I, 1994, 12 May–2 June 1994, sample size 629; Kentucky Fall Poll Survey, 1994, November 1994, sample size 649.
> Tennessee: Tennessee Survey, Winter 1990, 1–7 December 1990, sample size 799; Tennessee Survey Fall 1991, 20–25 October 1991, sample size 802; Tennessee Survey, Spring 1992, 22 February–2 March 1992, sample size 802.

THE DEPENDENT VARIABLES: QUESTIONS CONCERNING SCHOOL FINANCE

Connecticut Poll 1

Some people feel that the same amount ought to be spent for the public schools throughout Connecticut. Others think that the citizens of each town should be able to decide how much they want to spend on education.

Which do you think is more important, (1) to fund schools equally, or (2) to let towns decide how much to spend on their schools?

Connecticut Poll 7

Some people say that the state should see to it that rich communities and poor communities have the same amount of money per student to spend on their schools. In general do you favor this or oppose it?

Eagleton Poll 79

In June the New Jersey Supreme Court decided in the *Abbott vs. Burke* case that the state's present system of financing public education is unconstitutional because of the wide differences in funding between the rich and the poor school districts. The court decision also said that a new system of financing public education was needed to give students in poorer school districts an opportunity for an education that was equal to that of students in richer school districts. In general, do you agree or disagree with the decision made by the court? Do you agree/disagree mildly or strongly? (Asked only of those who indicated they had heard of the *Abbott v. Burke* case.)

Eagleton Poll 94 and 106

In general, do you agree or disagree that spending for education must be equal in all of New Jersey's school districts? Do you agree/disagree mildly or strongly?

Kentucky Poll 027

KERA has two basic goals: to provide equal educational opportunities for each child, and to expect each child in Kentucky to perform at a high level. If only one of these goals had to be chosen, which one would you consider more important?

Kentucky Poll 027, 032, 033, and 035

Next I'd like to ask some questions about school reform. Would you say you strongly approve, somewhat approve, somewhat disapprove, or strongly disapprove of the Kentucky Educational Reform Act, also known as KERA, which was designed to change the educational system in the state?

Tennessee Poll 002

Some have suggested changing the ways schools are paid for by having the state of Tennessee see that all students receive the same level of funding, regardless of whether they live in a rich or poor school county, while others would like to leave the funding of schools as it is now, to be determined by the citizens in each county. How do you feel? (Leave as is / Have same level in all schools / Unsure / DK)

Tennessee Poll 006 and 007

Have you heard or read anything about the court decision that requires that all students receive the same level of funding regardless of whether they live in a rich or poor school district? (No /Yes)

Do you agree or disagree with the court decision to equalize school funding? (Disagree /Agree) (Asked only of those who said yes to the prior question.)

THE MODEL

Both the logistic and OLS analyses draw on roughly comparable demographic measures to build a basic explanatory model that relies on the usual demographic data plus party affiliation and self-reported ideology. The Connecticut Polls did not record community type or parental status of respondents, and the Tennessee polls did not report parental status, but these were included in the other polls. Coding for all variables is available from the respective data sources; space considerations prevent their presentation here. In general, I avoided collapsing variables in order to preserve information.

In addition, I used questions from each poll that touched on local control concerns to test for their salience to attitudes toward equal funding or education reform more generally. These poll-specific questions varied, but they were all used to determine the extent to which local control concerns mattered to respondents. In Connecticut the Local Control Phrasing variable is the Poll Date control variable. The nature of these local control variables is detailed in chapter 6.

Despite these few state-by-state differences, in all four states the structure of attitudes toward funding schools equally are modeled similarly, with the attitudes posited as a function of self-interest demographic variables, symbolic demographic variables, perceived self-interest variables, plus perceived effect of reforms on local control. Stated more formally: Opposition to funding school equally = α + $\beta 1$(Age) + $\beta 2$(Community Type) + $\beta 3$(Education Level) + $\beta 4$(Ideology) + $\beta 5$(Income) + $\beta 6$(Parents of school age children) + $\beta 7$(Party Affiliation) + $\beta 8$(Race) + $\beta 9$(Poll Date Control) + $\beta 10$(Local Control) + ϵ. In this equation, self-interest demographic variables include age, community type, income, and parental status while symbolic demographic variables include party affiliation, ideology, and race.

TEXAS ELECTION RETURN DATA

The analysis of the results of Proposition 1 in Texas is substantially different from the analysis of public opinion in Connecticut, New Jersey, Kentucky, and Tennessee. In analyzing these election returns, I obtained demographic data on each of Texas's 150 House of Representative districts from the Texas

Legislative Council, which is responsible for providing the state legislature with demographic information for legislative reapportionment. These demographic data, in turn, were based on United States Census Bureau data gathered in the 1990 census. I also obtained the election returns for each of the precincts in Texas from the 1 May 1993 constitutional amendment referendum and the 1 June 1993 U.S. Senate run-off election between Kay Bailey Hutchison and Robert Kreuger from the Texas Legislative Council, and those returns were aggregated into 150 district totals. Ideally, we would want to regress the election returns from each precinct in Texas against the demographic data for that precinct. This fine-grained analysis would come closer to an individual level survey, and would provide several thousand more data points. Unfortunately, demographic data are not available from the Texas Legislative Council at the precinct level. As a result, the election returns were aggregated to state representative districts.

Using the percentage of no votes cast against Proposition 1 as the dependent variable, I performed an OLS regression analysis using the following model: % Votes No in District $= \alpha + \beta 1$(District Per Capita Income) $+ \beta 2$(Party of District Representative) $+ \beta 3$(% of Non-Hispanic Blacks in District) $+ \beta 4$(% of Hispanics in District) $+ \beta 5$(% of Housing in District that is Owner-Occupied) $+ \beta 6$(% of Urban Residents in District) $+ \epsilon$. In a second model, I substituted $\beta 2$(% of Vote for Hutchison) in the above equation for reasons described in the chapter. The results are found in table 6.7.

APPENDIX C
SIGNIFICANT STATE SUPREME COURT RULINGS
ON SCHOOL FINANCE

BELOW ARE THE significant state supreme court rulings that have either struck down the existing school finance system or upheld it. Many cases have had several state supreme court rulings; the citations listed below are to either the initial or the most important ruling affecting school financing within a state.

STATE SUPREME COURTS RULING IN FAVOR OF GREATER EQUITY AND/OR ADEQUACY, IN ALPHABETICAL ORDER OF STATE

Alabama: *Ex Parte James,* 713 So. 2d 869 (1997)

Arizona: *Roosevelt Elem. Sch. Dist. No. 66 v. Bishop* 179 Ariz. 233, 877 P.2d 806 (1994)

Arkansas: *Dupree v. Alma School District No. 30* 29 Ark. 340, 651 S.W.2d 90 (1983)

California: *Serrano v. Priest* 5 Cal.3d 584, 487 P.2d 1241 (1971) (*Serrano I*); *Serrano v. Priest* 18 Cal.3d 728, 557 P.2d 929 (1976) (*Serrano II*) (*Serrano I* was based on federal grounds held to be invalid under *Rodriguez. Serrano II* is based on state constitutional provisions.)

Connecticut: *Horton v. Meskill* 172 Conn 615, 376 A.2d 359 (1977) (*Horton I*)

Idaho: *Idaho Schools for Equal Educ. Opportunity v. Idaho State Bd. of Educ.* 128 Idaho 276, 912P.2d 644 (1996)

Kentucky: *Rose v. Council for Better Education* 790 S.W. 2d 186 (1989)

Massachusetts: *McDuffy v. Secretary of the Executive Office of Education* 415 Mass. 545, 615 N.E.2d 516 (1993)

Montana: *State ex rel. Woodahl v. Straub* 161 Mont. 141, 520 P.2d 776 (1974); *Helena Elementary School Dist. No. One v. State* 769 P.2d 684 (1989) (*State ex. rel Woodahl* found that a modest equalization scheme was constitutional; *Helena* found the existing scheme unconstitutional)

New Hampshire: *Claremont School District v. Governor* 138 N.H. 183, 635 A.2d 1375 (1993)

New Jersey: *Robinson v. Cahill* 62 N.J. 473, 303 A.2d 273 (1973) (*Robinson I*); *Abbott v. Burke* 119 N.J. 287, 575 A.2d 359 (1990) (*Abbott II*)

North Carolina: *Leandro v. State,* 346 N.C. 336, 488 S.E.2d 249 (1997)

Ohio: *DeRolph v. State,* 78 Ohio St. 3d 193, 677 N.E.2d 733 (1997)

Tennessee: *Tennessee Small School Systems v. McWherter* 851 S.W.2d 139 (1993)

Texas: *Edgewood Independent School Dist. v. Kirby* 33 Tex. Sup. J. 12, 777
   S.W.2d 391 (1989) (*Edgewood I*)
Vermont: *Brigham v. State*, 692 A.2d 384 (1997)
Washington: *Seattle School Dist. No. 1 v. State of Washington* 90 Wash. 2d 476,
   585 P.2d 71 (1978)
West Virginia: *Pauley v. Kelly* 162 W.Va. 672, 255 S.E.2d 859 (1979)
Wyoming: *Washakie County School Dist. No. One v. Herschler* 606 P.2d 310
   (1980); *Campbell v. State* 907 P.2d 1238 (1995)

STATE SUPREME COURTS RULING AGAINST GREATER EQUITY AND/OR ADEQUACY, IN ALPHABETICAL ORDER OF STATE

Alaska: *Matanuska-Susitna Borough School District v. Alaska* 931 P.2d 391
   (1997)
Arizona: *Shofstall v. Hollins* 110 Ariz. 88, 515 P.2d 590 (1973)
Colorado: *Lujan v. Colorado State Bd. of Educ..* 649 P.2d 1005 (1982)
Florida: *Coalition for Adequacy and Fairness in School Funding v. Chiles*, 6909
   So. 2d 400 (1996)
Georgia: *McDaniel v. Thomas* 248 Ga. 632, 285 S.E.2d 156 (1982)
Idaho: *Thompson v. Engelking* 96 Idaho 793, 537 P.2d 635 (1975)
Illinois: *Blase v. State* 55 Ill.2d 94, 302 N.E.2d 46 (1973); *Committee for Educ.
   Rights v. Edgar*, 174 Ill. 2d. 1, 672 N.E. 2d 1178 (1996)
Maine: *School Administrative Dist. No. 1 v. Commissioner, Dept. of Education*
   659 A.2d 854 (1995)
Maryland: Hornbeck v. Somerset County Bd. of Educ.. 295 Md. 597, 458 A.2d
   758 (1983)
Michigan: *Milliken v. Green* 390 Mich. 389; 212 N.W.2d 711 (1973)
Minnesota: *Skeen v. State*, 505 N.W. 2d 299 (1993)
New York: *Bd. of Educ.., Levittown Union Free School Dist. v. Nyquist* 57
   N.Y.2d 127, 439 N.E.2d 359 (1982)
North Carolina: *Britt v. North Carolina State Bd. of Educ.* 86 NC App 282, 357
   S.E.2d 432 *aff'd mem* 320 N.C. 790, 361 S.E.2d 71 (1987)
North Dakota: *Bismarck Pub. Sch. Dist. #1 v. State* 511 N.W. 2d 247 (1994)
Ohio: *Board of Education v. Walter* 58 Ohio St.2d 368, 390 N.E.2d 813
   (1979)
Oklahoma: *Fair School Finance Council of Oklahoma, Inc. v. State* 746 P.2d
   1135 (1987)
Oregon: *Olsen v. State ex rel Johnson* 276 Ore. 9, 554 P.2d 139 (1976); *Coalition for Equitable Sch. Funding v. State of Oregon*, 311 Ore. 300, 811 P.2d
   116 (1991)
Pennsylvania: *Danson v. Casey* 484 Pa. 415, 399 A.2d 360 (1979)
Rhode Island: *City of Pawtucket v. Sundlun* 662 A.2d 40 (1995)

South Carolina: *Richland County v. Campbell* 294 S.C. 346, 364 S.E.2d 470 (1988)

Virginia: *Scott v. Commonwealth* 247 Va. 379; 443 S.E.2d 138 (1994)

Washington: *Northshore School Dist. No. 417 v. Kinnear*, 84 Wash. 2d 685, 530 P.2d 178 (1974)

Wisconsin: *Buse v. Smith* 74 Wis.2d 550, 247 N.W. 2d 141 (1976); *Kukor v. Grover* 148 Wisc.2d 469, 436 N.W.2d 568 (1989)

NOTES

INTRODUCTION

1. For an overview of various efforts to use courts and legal strategies to achieve educational reforms, see Flicker 1990.

2. 411 U.S. 1 (1973)

3. *Rose v. Council for Better Education*, 790 S.W.2d 186 (1989).

4. *Rose*, 190. In a 1997 decision, the Vermont Supreme Court also explicitly invoked *Brown* as judicial inspiration for the expansion of educational opportunity. See *Brigham v. State*, 166 Vt. 246, 692 A.2d 384 (1997).

CHAPTER 1
COURTS AND EDUCATIONAL OPPORTUNITY

1. *Milliken v. Bradley*, 418 U.S. 717 (1974).

2. In the late 1970s a parallel effort emerged to use desegregation suits in federal courts to obtain additional resources for school districts that had been harmed by racial segregation. This strategy emerged in response to the Supreme Court's refusal in *Milliken v. Bradley* to allow the district court to include suburban districts in the desegregation order. On remand, the plaintiffs in *Milliken* sought additional money from the state of Michigan to remedy the state-imposed segregation. This approach was upheld by the U.S. Supreme Court in a second *Milliken* decision, *Milliken v. Bradley*, 433 U.S. 267 (1977) (*Milliken II*). As a result, successful desegregation lawsuits could also generate additional revenues as part of a desegregation remedy. Unfortunately, *Milliken II* remedies have not successfully targeted the central resource inequities in public education, nor substantially improved resources for predominantly minority districts. According to one scholar, "*Milliken II*–type programs have not evolved as systemic changes to the unequal opportunity structure *Brown* sought to eradicate, but as transitory extras of questionable utility" (Eaton et al. 1996, 146). Not until the state supreme court decisions on school finance is there any systematic legal attention paid to resource inequities in public education.

3. *Edwards v. California*, 314 U.S. 160 (1941).

4. *Griffin v. Illinois*, 351 U.S. 12 (1956).

5. *Gideon v. Wainwright*, 372 U.S. 335 (1963).

6. *Serrano v. Priest*, 96 Cal. Rptr. 601, 487 P.2d 1241 (1971).

7. *Rodriguez v. San Antonio Independent School District* 337 F. Supp. 280 (1971). The U.S. Supreme Court's ruling can be found at *San Antonio Independent School District v. Rodriguez* 411 U.S. 1 (1973). All subsequent citations to *Rodriguez* refer to the U.S. Supreme Court ruling.

8. *Swann v. Charlotte-Mecklenburg Board of Education*, 402 U.S. 1 (1971).

9. *Roe v. Wade*, 410 U.S. 113 (1973).

10. *Dandridge v. Williams*, 397 U.S. 471 (1970).

11. *Brown v. Board of Education*, 347 U.S. 483 (1954).

12. *Rodriguez*, 30, 35.

13. Ibid., 23.

14. The Court here relied on a study done in Connecticut on the correlation between the property wealth of a district and the cash poverty of the families within that district (Churgin et al. 1972). That article states that the poor (in Connecticut at least) often live in urban centers that produce property-rich districts. The article, however, does not support the Court's larger claim that such evidence means that urban districts are adequately funded.

15. *Rodriguez*, 23.

16. Justice Potter Stewart's concurrence called the scheme "chaotic and unjust" (*Rodriguez*, 59). He nonetheless deemed it constitutional.

17. *Rodriguez*, 58.

18. Ibid., 58–59.

19. See, in particular, Tractenberg 1974.

20. Since the 1875 case of *Murdock v. City of Memphis*, 87 U.S. (20 Wall.) 590 (1875), the Supreme Court traditionally has declined to review state court decisions that are based on an "adequate and independent state ground." For a discussion of the relationship between state supreme courts and the U.S. Supreme Court, see Pollock 1985.

21. *Robinson v. Cahill*, 62 N.J. 473 (1973).

22. New Jersey Constitution, art. 8, sec. 4, para. 1. It reads as follows: "The legislature shall provide for the maintenance and support of a thorough and efficient system of free public schools for the instruction of all the children in the State between the ages of five and eighteen years." For further discussion, see Williams 1990.

23. For an overview of these developments, see Pollock 1983 and Brennan 1986.

24. Brennan's 1977 *Harvard Law Review* article (Brennan 1977) was dubbed the "Magna Carta" of state constitutionalism by New Jersey Supreme Court Justice Stewart G. Pollock in a 1983 article (Pollock 1983).

25. For an exhaustive listing of articles relating to the new judicial federalism, see Pifler 1996, notes 1–17.

26. One exception to this statement may be the right to die. For an examination of the development of state-level judicial policy-making in this area, see Glick 1991, 1992.

27. Montana Constitution, art. 10, sec. 1, para. 1.

28. Alabama Constitution, art. 14, sec. 256, amend. 111.

29. For a comprehensive review of state equality provisions, see Williams 1985.

30. The first *Serrano* decision combined federal constitutional arguments and state claims. After *Rodriguez* declared the federal claims inapplicable, the California Supreme Court restated the holding of *Serrano* expressly and exclusively in terms of state constitutional provisions, particularly state equality guarantees. To date, California is the only state to declare its financing scheme unconstitutional on equality grounds alone. All others have either combined equality provisions with educational provisions or based their decisions entirely on educational clauses.

31. See, in particular, the New Jersey Supreme Court's rationale in *Robinson v. Cahill*. There, the court argued that a judicial search for fundamental rights "was not helpful" and that disparate expenditures among various political subunits are, in essence, a political fact of life. If the strictures of the state equality provisions declared those disparities unconstitutional, then New Jersey's "political structure [would] be fundamentally changed." *Robinson I*, 282–83.

32. *McDaniel v. Thomas*, 248 Ga. 632 (1981) is a good example of the application of federal equal protection jurisprudence to state equality provisions within the context of school finance. For an overview of "lockstep" interpretation of state constitutional provisions, see Maltz 1988. For a contrasting analysis of the independence of state equality provisions, see Williams 1992.

33. The recent Vermont decision, *Brigham v. State*, bucks this trend in a decisive manner, arguing strongly that the Vermont school finance system violates students' rights to equal educational opportunities. *Brigham v. State*, 166 Vt. 246 (1997).

34. See, for example, Oklahoma Constitution, art. 13, sec. 1.

35. Washington Constitution, art. 9, sec. 1.

36. States with "thorough and efficient" language include Maryland, New Jersey, Ohio, Pennsylvania, and West Virginia. For a comprehensive comparison of state educational clauses, see Hubsch 1992 and Thro 1989.

37. This language is found in the Indiana, Minnesota, North Carolina, Oregon, South Dakota, and Washington constitutions. See Hubsch 1992 for an overview of the provisions.

38. Other states in this middle range borrow similar language, relying on such terms as "general, uniform and thorough" (Idaho), "uniform and general" (Oregon), an "efficient" and "high quality" system (Illinois), "suitable provision" for an "efficient" system (Texas), "thorough and uniform" (Colorado), "adequate" (Georgia), "uniform (Florida, Utah), "complete and uniform" (Wyoming), "sufficient" (New Mexico), "high quality" (Virginia), "general and efficient" (Delaware). Although these terms exhibit significant range ("high quality" is probably more demanding than "sufficient"), they nonetheless fall between the mere creation of a schooling system and the creation of a fundamental right. Hubsch 1992 at 1343–48 excerpts the education-clause language from all fifty states. See also Grubb 1974 and Thro 1989 for discussions of variations among state educational clauses.

39. *Brigham v. State*, 166 Vt. 246 (1997), 249, 268.

40. *Roosevelt Elementary School District Number 66 v. Bishop*, 877 P.2d 806 (Ariz. 1994); Arizona Constitution, art. 11, sec. 1; *Roosevelt v. Bishop*, 814 (emphasis added).

41. Rose v. Council for Better Education, 790 S.W.2d 186 (1989).

42. Ibid., 211. Emphasis in original.

43. Indeed, in the Kentucky Supreme Court's nine-point definition of an "efficient" school system, point 5 reads: "Common schools shall provide equal educational opportunities to all Kentucky children, regardless of place of residence or economic circumstances." *Rose*, 212.

44. Judges have not paid careful attention to this important project of defining what equality actually means in the context of school finance reform. Notions of vertical equity, horizontal equity, per pupil equality, and taxpayer equality all need to be carefully specified if legislators are to have a clear vision of their task.

CHAPTER 2
THE JUDICIAL IMPACT ON SCHOOL FINANCE REFORM

1. See Rosenberg 1991, 9–36 for his enumeration of the constraints operating on courts as they seek social and political change and the conditions under which they can achieve success.

2. See Feeley 1992, McCann 1992, Sanders 1995 for criticisms of Rosenberg's argument. Also, others have argued that different, indirect, mechanisms may have been at work: see Klarman 1994.

3. Political philosophers made much hay over this distinction in the late 1970s and 1980s — primarily because of the influence of John Rawls. His *Theory of Justice* concluded that rational actors in an "original position," in which they did not know their interests or future lives, would choose for themselves principles of distribution that maximized equality. An important question remained unanswered in Rawls's theory, however: equality of what? If we simply equalize resources, we have failed to take into account individual capacities to utilize those resources. The welfarist conception of equality is dubbed "welfarist" not because it consists of an extra allotment to a needy person (here, the political rhetoric of "welfare reform" risks conflation with terms in political theory). Instead, a welfarist conception is dubbed "welfarist" because it is centrally concerned with an individual's capacity to utilize his or her allotment; it is concerned, that is, with the welfare and well-being that the allotment produces for that individual. An intuitive example of this is the felt need to provide additional resources to disabled or handicapped children to ensure that they derive the same welfare (the same amount of learning) from their education as able-bodied children. Amartya Sen, Ronald Dworkin, and G. A. Cohen have contributed a great deal to this debate. See Cohen 1989, Dworkin 1981, Dworkin 1981, Sen 1980 for illustrative examples.

4. This distinction might be generalized as the difference between "lot-regarding equality" and "person-regarding equality." That is, are we seeking to provide students the same educational inputs (identical curricula) or are we seeking to provide students the same level of intellectual challenge (equal opportunities to learn). In the first instance, we can provide identical allotments; in the second instance, we have to adjust those allotments to take into account different intellectual capacities of students. This is similar to Amartya Sen's distinction between equality of resources and equality of welfare.

5. This is done by calculating the mean enrollment of school districts within a state and then dividing each district's enrollment by the mean. The resulting figure then becomes the weight for the equity analysis. In effect, I am calculating a pupil-level equity rather than a district-level equity. See Berne and Stiefel 1984 for illustrations of the difference between the two.

6. In general, I use revenue figures because they are more directly comparable. I also, however, analyze expenditure data in appendix A to illustrate the similar equity trends among both revenue and expenditure levels in each state.

7. For an overview of the debate, see Card and Krueger 1998.

8. Richard Murnane offers a good illustration of this point: "Consider student writing as an example. It seems logical that students must write frequently and have their writing corrected in order to learn to write well. Consequently, improving writing may require hiring graders, or even reducing the size of English classes, both of which cost money. Thus, more money may be a necessary condition for improving student writing. It is not, however, a sufficient condition; increasing per-pupil expenditures may result in smaller class sizes, but not in an increase in the amount of writing that students do" (Murnane 1991, 462). Murnane's point is that the efficiency of the level of expenditure depends, in turn, on *how* the money is spent. As a result, not all increases yield results, but cuts can certainly do significant harm.

9. See Berne and Stiefel 1984 for an explication of horizontal equity — and the welfarist conception of "vertical equity." Vertical equity is the term used in school finance circles to describe the condition attained when students with special needs (in particular, handicapped students) are able to learn at the same rate and level as students without special needs. In short, vertical equity means that one cannot provide the same resources to a handicapped child and a nonhandicapped child and claim to be treating them equally. They have different needs; therefore they require different levels of resources to derive equal educational attainment. Berne and Stiefel stress that vertical equity requires an explicit normative assertion about the level to which special needs students must be raised. That is, there can be no internal metric by which to judge equity among students who are not equal in needs. This presents a real problem for judges as they strive to create equitable standards among different populations of students — especially as the educational establishment shifts its definition of what constitutes a learning disability. See chapter 6 for a more detailed explication of judicial difficulties with vertical equity and special needs students.

10. Ensuring that students with special needs receive the same level of educational welfare as students without special needs is the aim of vertical equity. See Berne and Stiefel 1984.

11. This assumes that moving from an equality of resources to an equality of welfare is not a zero-sum movement. That is, I assume that the politics of school finance will ensure that the additional resources provided to ensure the welfarist equality will not come directly from the allotment distributed to non–special needs students.

12. It is most useful to think of the Gini coefficient in graphic terms. Say we rank each child within a state according to the expenditures spent on that child, and we plot that expenditure level on a horizontal axis. On a vertical axis, we tally the percentage of total expenditures "consumed" by each child at each expenditure level. The resulting line is known as a Lorenz curve. The Gini coefficient is simply the area between the Lorenz curve and a 45-degree line drawn through the origin of the two axes. As with the coefficient of variation, as the Gini coefficient nears zero, the distribution of funds approaches perfect equality.

13. Indeed, both these measures are particularly good at examining equity changes over time, because they are relatively immune to inflation. Nonetheless, I have adjusted all the figures used in this book for inflation, using the CPI-U index.

14. *DeRolph v. State*, 78 Ohio St. 3d 193, (1997) at 205.

15. Ohio Constitution, sec. 2, art 6.

16. *Coalition for Adequacy and Fairness in School Funding v. Chiles* 680 So. 2d 400, (1996) at 406.

17. Many judges refuse to take on this task, seeing it as more a legislative function than a judicial one. Others, who defend the task of discerning adequacy, claim that constitutional language of such social importance must be amenable to judicial interpretation — otherwise, there is no justification for its placement within a state constitution. This debate hinges, in essence, on theories of constitutionalism and the nature of the judicial role within constitutional interpretation. See chapter 5 for a full discussion.

18. Indeed, courts can compel legislatures to specify more carefully what constitutes an adequate, or efficient, or thorough educational system. New Jersey pursued this tack in its first round of school finance decisions. See, in particular, *Robinson v.*

Cahill where the court ruled "[T]he State must define in some discernible way the educational obligation and must compel the local school districts to raise the money necessary to provide that opportunity. The State has never spelled out the content of the constitutionally mandated educational opportunity. Nor has the State required the school districts to raise moneys needed to achieve that unstated standard." *Robinson v. Cahill*, 62 N.J. 473 (1973) (*Robinson I*), 519.

19. I will return to this issue in chapter 5 when I address the problems of judicial interpretation in school finance cases.

20. This assumes, of course, that more resources indicate greater adequacy.

21. However, California may be in this situation. After the *Serrano* decision and Proposition 13, California has, in the estimation of some analysts, produced a funding system that is relatively equal, but woefully underfunded. Indeed, California's national expenditure ranking has slipped from sixteenth in 1970 to thirty-seventh in 1997. (Digest of Educational Statistics, 1999, table 171). Simultaneously, however, the system has become increasingly equal, garnering most of its revenue from state, rather than local sources.

22. This is because, as I mentioned above, the range compares the spending levels of only two districts — the most well-off and the least well-off. If, over time, these two data points remain the same, the range will remain the same — even if all other districts have achieved full equality. Thus, the range does not capture changes in the relative position of districts between the two extremes. See Berne and Stiefel 1984 for further comment on the relative strengths and weaknesses of various equity measures.

23. In each state, I sought data, whenever possible, for two years prior to the state supreme court decision to the most recent data available. (Fiscal years are used, meaning that the 1989–90 academic year, for example, is listed in the tables as 1990.) This selection of data years produced a spread of at least five years (Tennessee) and as many as ten years (Connecticut). In the case of Connecticut, I began the data analysis with the year of the decision (1977) and carried it forward for ten years.

24. Or expenditure figures in the case of Texas.

25. This finding endorses the conclusions drawn by Michael Heise in his study of Connecticut and Wyoming (Heise 1995a) and (Heise 1995b). Heise's more recent work, however, suggests that court decisions relying on equity alone cannot be identified as independent causes of increased real educational spending in states where plaintiffs have won. See Heise 1998.

26. It is important to remember that not all school districts in New Jersey were included within the scope of the Court's ruling. See Appendix A for details. Although most districts in the state saw their financing changed in the wake of the Quality Education Act only the special needs and I & J districts were, technically, subject to the Court's ruling.

27. Expenditures in the case of North Carolina.

28. The average annual median percentage increase for the five states where the state supreme court ordered reform was 14.2 percent, while in the three states where the courts did not order reform it was 12.3 percent.

29. Relying on state-level, rather than district-level data, Heise contends that equity suits in Connecticut, Wyoming, and Arkansas cannot be identified as an independent cause of either greater centralization of educational revenues or increased aggregated spending in those states. Writes Heise, the observed increases in real

spending "cannot be properly attributed to the independent influence of successful equity school finance court decisions in any of these states. Because none of the coefficients achieves statistical significance, random chance endures as a viable explanation for the relation between the court decisions and educational spending levels" (Heise 1998 at 627).

CHAPTER 3
RACE, CLASS, AND THE LIMITS OF JUSTICE

1. *Milliken v. Bradley*, 418 U.S. 717 (1974), 741–42, citations omitted.

2. There is an extensive literature on white opposition to busing and whether it stems from symbolic racism or a more direct threat to whites. For two contrasting views of this controversy, see Bobo 1983 and Sears et al. 1979. For a more recent account that extensively reviews the literature and provides a synthesis of these theories of white opposition to racial policies, see Bobo and Kluegel 1993.

3. David Armor and Christine Rossell have put forward another theory about white flight, one that dismisses the role of racism and the role of local control and jurisdictional fragmentation that *Milliken* protected. Their argument contends that white flight is not a product of racism, per se, but a reaction to the heavy-handed techniques that federal judges have used to effect desegregation, particularly mandatory busing (Armor 1995, Rossell 1990, Rossell and Armor 1996). They contend that court-ordered busing has made segregation worse because it left whites with no option but to flee. While their account may account for the early stages of white flight, it cannot explain why white flight persists even as court-ordered busing has ground to a halt in many areas. Moreover, white flight took place in many cities that did not experience court-ordered busing.

4. Wendy Parker, however, contends that while many of the court orders on school desegregation are languishing, few school districts wish to end court-ordered desegregation. In her study of all federal desegregation lawsuits against some 189 school districts in the six states comprising the Fifth and Eleventh Circuit Courts of Appeal, Parker found that "few school districts have sought unitary status" (Parker 2000, 1189).

5. See Massey and Denton 1993 for a powerful assessment of the role of housing segregation in American public and political life.

6. The relationship between jurisdictional boundaries and racial and economic segregation are thoroughly covered in Danielson 1976, Harr 1996, Hill 1974, Kirp et al. 1995, Massey and Denton 1993, McKenzie 1994, Weiher 1991.

7. See *Board of Education of Oklahoma City Public Schools v. Dowell* 498 U.S. 237 (1991) and *Freeman v. Pitts*, 503 U.S. 467 (1992).

8. As we will see in chapter 5, New Jersey is a singular exception to this practice of establishing statewide reforms.

9. On the other hand, if the result of school financing reforms is to produce *lowered* levels of educational spending throughout the state, then it appears that parents will turn to private schools. This appears to be the case in California, where the combination of *Serrano v. Priest* and Proposition 13 has produced relatively equal, but substantially lower levels of spending on public education (Downs and Schoeman 1998). Based on the rising median levels of school spending reported in chapter 2, it is clear that California's response is not the typical one.

10. *Claremont School District v. Governor*, 138 N.H. 183 (1993), (*Claremont I*) 192–93.

11. Quoted in Alexander 1992, 1.

12. In Texas, where school financing disputes dragged on for many years, state voters have been surprisingly kind to state supreme court justices despite the justices' rather bungled efforts at judicial policy-making (see chapter 5). Matthew Bosworth reports from his interviews with Texas lawmakers that Texas Supreme Court elections "are determined by the conflict between business defendants and plaintiff lawyers on civil law issues. School finance was only a minor player" (Bosworth 1997, 161).

13. So far, only one lawsuit has merged the racial and class dimensions of educational opportunity. The politics of that suit, *Sheff v. O'Neill* from Hartford, Connecticut, appears to have blended both the public hostility of a school desegregation suit with the legislative consternation of a school finance suit. For an overview of the legal and political issues in the case, see chapter 8.

CHAPTER 4
HOW DOES A CONSTITUTION MEAN?

1. This emergent literature is growing and politically diverse. For important works in the field, see Levinson 1988, Griffin 1996, Moore 1996, Levin 1999, Whittington 1999, Tushnet 1999.

2. For a fuller account of the constitutional complexity of the American state constitutions, see Reed 1999.

3. *Pierce v. Society of Sisters*, 268 U.S. 510 (1925), 534–35.

4. *Brown v. Board of Education of Topeka*, 347 U.S. 483 (1954) (*Brown I*), 493.

5. Alan Tarr's *Understanding State Constitutions* (Tarr 1998) provides the best and most comprehensive overview of the forms and dimensions of state constitutions.

6. A 1977 article by Brennan (Brennan 1977) has been dubbed the "Magna Carta" of the new judicial federalism (Pollock 1983).

7. *Brown v. Board of Education of Topeka*, 347 U.S. 483 (1954) (*Brown I*), 494.

8. Martin Luther King Jr., "Give Us the Ballot" speech at the Prayer Pilgrimage for Freedom, 17 May 1957, Washington, D.C. [from website: http://www.stanford.edu/group/King

9. Southern Manifesto, 102 *Congressional Record* 4515–16 (1956).

10. That implicit injunction was made explicit in later decisions, most notably *Green v. County School Board of New Kent County*, 391 U.S. 430 (1968) where the court wrote that *Brown II* compelled school boards operating segregated schools "with the affirmative duty to take whatever steps might be necessary to convert to a unitary system in which racial discrimination would be eliminated root and branch" (*Green*, 437–38).

11. In a constitutional sense, we see the close connection between public education and a regime of racial inequality when we see that the Supreme Court's per curiam decisions banning all forms of Jim Crow segregation within public facilities followed quickly on the heels of *Brown*. The attack on segregated public education formed the implicit foundation for a judicial assault on all forms of "separate but equal" treatment. The educational context proved sufficiently expansive to cover virtually all other public facilities.

12. Indeed, none other than Thurgood Marshall himself stated shortly after *Brown I* that the national elimination of segregated public education might take "up to five years" (quoted in Rosenberg 1991, 43).

13. See, for example, the Supreme Court rulings in *Board of Education of Oklahoma City Public Schools v. Dowell*, 498 U.S. 237 (1991), and *Freeman v. Pitts*, 503 U.S. 467 (1992).

CHAPTER 5
A BOUNDED AMBITION

1. Declaratory relief, in contrast to injunctive relief, simply declares that a plaintiff enjoys a particular right; under declaratory relief a court typically leaves the realization of that right up to the legislative or executive branches. Injunctive relief either requires another actor to uphold those rights or to cease violating those rights. Declaratory relief simply asserts that such a right exists. For an overview of the forms and nature of declaratory relief see Borchard 2000.

2. Specifically, the court wrote that "an efficient system of education must have as its goal to provide each and every child with at least the seven following capacities: (i) sufficient oral and written communication skills to enable students to function in a complex and rapidly changing civilization; (ii) sufficient knowledge of economic, social, and political systems to enable the student to make informed choices; (iii) sufficient understanding of governmental processes to enable the student to understand the issues that affect his or her community, state, and nation; (iv) sufficient self-knowledge and knowledge of his or her mental and physical wellness; (v) sufficient grounding in the arts to enable each student to appreciate his or her cultural and historical heritage; (vi) sufficient training or preparation for advanced training in either academic or vocational fields so as to enable each child to choose and pursue life work intelligently; and (vii) sufficient levels of academic or vocational skills to enable public school students to compete favorably with their counterparts in surrounding states, in academics or in the job market" *Rose v. Council for Better Education*, 212.

3. The influence of a state supreme court as an explicit policy-maker can extend substantially beyond the borders of a single state. For example, the Massachusetts Supreme Court adopted wholesale the Kentucky Supreme Court's seven-point definition of an efficient system of education, writing, "As has been done by the courts of some of our sister States, we shall articulate broad guidelines and assume that the Commonwealth will fulfil its duty to remedy the constitutional violations that we have identified. The guidelines set forth by the Supreme Court of Kentucky fairly reflect our view of the matter and are consistent with the judicial pronouncements found in other decisions" *McDuffy v. Secretary of the Executive Office of Education*, 415 Mass. 545 (1993), 618.

4. *Rose v. Council for Better Education*, 212.

5. The cases are, in chronological order: *Edgewood Independent School District et al. v. Kirby*, 777 S.W.2d 391 (1989) (*Edgewood I*); *Edgewood Independent School District et al. v. Kirby*, 804 S.W.2d 491 (1991) (*Edgewood II*); *Edgewood Independent School District et al. v. Kirby*, 1991 Tex. LEXIS 21 (1991) (*Edgewood IIA*) (Opinion on Motion for Reconsideration); *Carrollton-Farmers Branch Independent School Dis-*

trict et al. v. Edgewood Independent School District et al., 826 S.W.2d 489 (1992) (*Edgewood III*); *Edgewood Independent School District et al. v. Meno*, 893 S.W.2d 450 (1995) (*Edgewood IV*).

6. (Lutz 1994, table A-1, 367). Lutz's research shows that the average U.S. state constitution runs over 19,000 words and has been amended an average of 117 times, as of 1991. In contrast, the U.S. Constitution has been amended only 26 times and runs a skimpy 4,300 words.

7. *Edgewood Independent School District v. Kirby*, 777 S.W.2d 391 (1989) (*Edgewood I*), 392, 393, 397. Emphasis added.

8. Ibid., 496.

9. Ibid., 497.

10. The court quoted with disapproval District Court Judge McCown's rejection of tax base consolidation. McCown had ruled that tax base consolidation ran afoul of constitutional provisions related to taxation and that it violated the court's sixty-year-old ruling of *Love v. Dallas*, 40 S.W.2d 20, 120 351 (1931).

11. *Edgewood II* 497.

12. *Edgewood Independent School District et al. v. Kirby*, 1991 Tex. LEXIS 21 34 Tex. Sup. J. 368 (1991) (*Edgewood IIA*), 1991 Tex. LEXIS 13.

13. *Edgewood IIA*, 3–4. The plaintiff-intervenors in their brief for the motion on reconsideration argued that all taxes raised at the local level are, in effect, taxes levied by the state. The court here quoted from the plaintiff-intervenors' language.

14. Ibid., 5.

15. In particular, the timing of *Edgewood IIA* was highly suspect. The decision came down on Monday evening, 25 February 1991, the very day the House Education Committee had voted in favor of a Robin Hood proposal, SB351. The morning after *Edgewood IIA* was announced, Representative Ernestine Glossbrenner (D-Alice) asked Texas Education Agency lawyers at a hastily called meeting of the House Education committee what the latest decision meant. Responded TEA General Counsel Kevin O'Hanlon: "That the Supreme Court reads the newspapers" (Elliott 1991b). One state senator dismissed the court's majority ruling as "political posturing" (Elliott 1991b).

16. In the wake of *Edgewood IIA*, it was unclear whether *any* form of "revenue capture" was permissible. The court had taken statewide recapture off the table in *Edgewood IIA*, but *Edgewood II* still suggested that a countywide redistribution of tax revenues might be constitutionally acceptable. Not until *Edgewood III* rejected SB351 and its system of 188 county-based taxation districts did the court make it clear that *any* recapture plan that was forced upon local districts was unconstitutional because it was, in effect, a statewide property tax. The current system, adopted in the wake of the rejection of Proposition 1 in May 1993, allows for local districts to choose among five methods to reduce their per pupil property tax base to a state-mandated level. The Texas Supreme Court approved that plan in *Edgewood IV*.

17. The details of this entire convoluted series of decisions can be found in Reed 1995, 267–300. For a similar account, see also Bosworth 1997 118–50.

18. New Hampshire Constitution, part 2, art. 74.

19. *Opinion of the Justices (School Financing)*, 142 N.H. 892; 712 A.2d 1080 (1998).

20. One journalist told me that the legislative session that ensued in the wake of the Court's advisory opinion was "as ugly a legislative session as anyone can remember" (Jimenez 1999).

21. Of course, the New Hampshire picture is further complicated by the impeachment and subsequent trial of Chief Justice David Brock in 2000. Some contend that the legislature was less concerned with the ethics of the New Hampshire High Court and more determined to seek political revenge for the school financing decisions. Clearly, however, there were some serious ethical breaches on the New Hampshire Supreme Court and many legislators who supported school finance reform were also deeply concerned about those ethical lapses.

22. *Abbott v. Burke*, 136 N.J. 444 (1994) (*Abbott III*).

23. *Thompson v. Engelking*, 96 Idaho 793 (1975), 798–99.

24. *Brigham v. State*, 166 Vt. 246 (1997), 249.

25. *Pauley v. Kelly*, 162 W.Va. 672 (1979), 749.

26. *Roosevelt Elementary School District No. 66 v. Bishop*, 179 Ariz. 233 (1994), 250. Emphasis added.

27. Of course, this is not to say that Arizona's constitutional provisions concerning education are the same as West Virginia's or hold the same force. Different texts can have different commitments, but it is this differing understanding of the fundamental nature of the educational provisions within state constitutions that shapes this conflict within states. Indeed, Feldman's concurrence was largely an argument that education is a fundamental right under Arizona's constitution and that disparities in facilities expenditures should be viewed under Arizona's equal protection provisions, not the education clauses.

28. *Horton v. Meskill*, 172 Conn. 615 (1977) (*Horton I*), 658, Justice Loiselle dissenting.

29. *Claremont School District v. Governor*, 142 N.H. 462 (1997) (*Claremont II*), 476.

30. For details of these amendments and their political settings, see Reed 1995, 131–40, especially table 3.3.

31. As Horton reopened his lawsuit, the City of Hartford immediately moved to intervene, as did a number of suburban districts throughout the state. In earlier stages of the lawsuit, Horton had secured "an unwritten agreement" with the town counsels in Hartford and elsewhere that if Hartford stayed out of the lawsuit, "the suburban towns and the rich towns down in Fairfield County" would stay out. Hartford's motion blew apart that implicit agreement and created, in Horton's opinion, "a three ring circus" (Horton 1992a). The basic problem stemmed from conflicting rulings on the motions to intervene. One judge approved some of the motions, while another denied others. The losing towns appealed those denials all the way to the state supreme court, which resolved the conflicting approvals in a largely procedural decision, *Horton v. Meskill*, 187 Conn. 187, 445 A.2d 579 (1982) (*Horton II*).

32. *Horton v. Meskill* (memorandum of decision), Docket No. 185283, 24 April 1984, reprinted in *Connecticut Law Tribune* 10(19) (7 May 1984), 6–20, 8.

33. In *Horton I*, the Connecticut Supreme Court wrote: "in Connecticut the right to education is so basic and fundamental that any infringement of that right must be strictly scrutinized." *Horton v. Meskill*, 172 Conn. 615, 376 A.2d 359 (1977) (*Horton I*), 646.

34. Ibid., 8.

35. *Horton v. Meskill*, 195 Conn. 24 (1985) (*Horton III*), 35–36, 38, 47.

36. Ibid., 47, quoting *CEUI v. CSEA*, 183 Conn. 235, 248–49 (1981).

37. Wes Horton claims he could have prevailed under the revised standard, but he chose not to pursue the matter in the lower courts. The legislature, still under the threat of a re-activated litigation, decided to devote more money to the equalization effort after *Horton III*.

38. Since *Horton III*, other events have overtaken litigation on school finance reform in Connecticut. In 1986 the state fully funded the GTB formula for the first time and created an additional program to equalize teachers' salaries throughout the state. The reason for the newfound beneficence was, most likely, a booming state economy. As Wesley Horton put it, the state was "awash in money." (Horton 1992a) In 1988 the state scrapped the GTB formula and constructed a new foundation-type plan, dubbed Educational Cost Sharing (Public Act 88–358). In addition, a new lawsuit (endorsed by Wesley Horton) has churned the waters of public education in Connecticut since 1996. The *Sheff v. O'Neill* case focused on both regional racial segregation and broader inequalities in educational opportunity within the state, especially between central cities and their suburban neighbors. I discuss the *Sheff* litigation more fully in chapter 8.

39. New Jersey Constitution, art. 8, sec. 4, para. 1. The passage reads as follows: "The legislature shall provide for the maintenance and support of a thorough and efficient system of free public schools for the instruction of all the children in the State between the ages of five and eighteen years" (Williams 1990, 120).

40. *Robinson v. Cahill*, 62 N.J. 473 (1973) (*Robinson I*), 513.

41. *Robinson I*, 515.

42. *Abbott II*, 306–307.

43. Ibid., 313, 374, 343.

44. Ibid., 385.

45. This, in many respects, is a central conclusion of the New Jersey case study explored in chapter 7.

46. *Abbott v. Burke*, 149 N.J. 145 (1997) (*Abbott IV*), 189.

47. *Abbott v. Burke* 153 N.J. 480 (1998) (*Abbott V*), 528.

48. Ibid., 490.

49. *Abbott v. Burke*, 163 N.J. 95 (2000) (*Abbott VI*) and *Abbott v. Burke*, 164 N.J. 84 (2000) *Abbott VII*.

50. The literature on the new judicial federalism is vast, but for a sampling see the following: Howard 1976, Brennan 1977, Scheiber 1980, Sturm 1982, Pollock 1983, Abrahamson 1985, Brennan 1986, Hall 1991, Tarr 1994, Kincaid 1995. For the most comprehensive study to date on state constitutions in general, see Tarr 1998.

51. This view is so pervasive, it is almost hard to find a theorist who explicitly makes the case rather than assumes it. Perhaps the closest example is Rostow 1962, published at the height of the Warren era. Recent counterarguments, however, abound. See, generally, Griffin 1996, Whittington 1999, Tushnet 1999.

52. Gardner 1992 makes a number of these claims, and more.

53. Lutz 1996, 32–34, table 2.1.

54. An amendment rate is defined as the number of amendments adopted per year of a constitution's existence. For the U.S. Constitution, it is 0.13 for the years 1776–1979, while for states the amendment rate is 1.23. See, generally, Lutz 1996, 34, 40, table 2.7.

55. Of course, the constitutional history of a few states runs longer than even U.S. constitutional history. Massachusetts provides perhaps the best example of relying on originalist sentiments to construe the meaning of a state education clause. In *Duffy v. Secretary of the Executive Office of Education*, Chief Justice Liacos relied on a rich documentary history of education in Massachusetts dating back to the 1600s to determine the duty the state constitution imposed on the state legislature, even consulting the written statements by towns upon ratification of the 1780 Massachusetts Constitution. Such a well-developed constitutional record, however, is anomalous in state constitutional history. See *Duffy v. Secretary of the Executive Office of Education* 415 Mass. 545 (1993), 578–99.

56. For an overview of this "popular constitutionalism" in Hawaii and elsewhere, see Reed 1999.

57. *Brigham v. State*, 166 Vt. 246 (1997), 256.

58. *Claremont School District v. Governor*, 142 N.H. 462 (1997) (*Claremont II*), 477–78, 479.

59. In Vermont, the state supreme court construed the education clause of the Vermont Constitution in light of the common benefits clause to reach a fundamental rights analysis within an equal protection framework. In New Hampshire, in contrast, the state supreme court relied on the encouragement of a literature clause (adapted from the Massachusetts Constitution in 1784) to find that the state had a constitutional duty to provide an adequate education to its citizens. *Claremont School District v. Governor*, 138 N.H. 183 (1993) (*Claremont I*). Justice Horton's quote came from his dissent in the *Claremont* decision.

60. For further treatment of this point, see Reed 1999.

CHAPTER 6
THE PUBLIC'S OPINION

1. Because some of the analyses are rather technical, Appendix A contains the full model specifications for each regression, as well as the polling questions themselves and information on data sources and sample sizes.

2. A search of the Social Science Index on the subject classification "Public Schools, Finance — Public Opinion" yields only two articles: Tedin 1994, and Teske et al. 1993.

3. Cataldo and Holm, 1983.

4. This point is driven home by the periodic reports of state departments of education that, on occasion, make substantial errors in their calculations of state aid to local school districts. The complex formulas that make up school funding mechanisms are numbing in their detail and a slight alteration can change the distribution of funds dramatically. For an example of a $10.7 million screwup in Connecticut, see *Hartford Courant* 1981.

5. See, for example, Green and Gerken 1989, for an account of the connection between self-interest and cigarette taxes. In one important area of educational policy,

however, self-interest has not been shown to dominate public opinion: school busing for desegregation. While the academic controversy over this issue has raged for over two decades now, it has become increasingly clear that exposure to busing plans has little to do with one's attitudes toward busing in general. See Bobo 1983, Sears et al. 1979, Bobo and Kluegel 1993. A significant body of research indicates that white nonparents and white parents of school-age children exhibit similar levels of opposition to desegregation busing plans within their community. Although the logic of self-interest would suggest that the costs of a busing plan (extra travel time, educational disruption, possible conflicts within schools, weaker school-community ties, less parental involvement, etc.) would induce greater opposition among white parents than among white nonparents, it appears that opposition is consistent across the board. Instead, either symbolic racism or old-fashioned prejudice or simple political conservativism largely explain white opposition — among both parents and non-parents alike. Rather than defeat the self-interest argument about political attitudes, this body of work may, instead, illustrate the depths of racial animosity within American political and educational life.

6. Texas is omitted here because among the polls to which I have access no question directly broached the question of support for funding schools equally. See appendix B for data sources of Texas election results on school finance reform quetions.

7. In some instances, the phrasing of the question on equality forces respondents to choose between two options. In these situations, because the responses are dichotomous, we need to use a logistic regression to analyze respondents' answers. A standard multiple regression equation enables us to calculate the size of the average effect of each independent variable on the dependent variable, in this case attitudes toward equality. But when there are only two possible outcomes, the choices are too constrained for a multiple regression to produce reliable estimates of the average effect. As a result, we need to use logistic regression, a technique that better handles dichotomous dependent variables. A logistic regression can help us calculate the degree to which a particular characteristic (say, a conservative ideology) is likely to reduce (or increase) the probability that a respondent will support one answer over another, holding all other factors constant.

8. In the earliest poll, conducted in July 1990 at the height of the tax revolt against Florio, the question was lengthier and phrased slightly differently: "In June, the New Jersey Supreme Court decided in the *Abbott vs. Burke* case that the state's present system of financing public education is unconstitutional because of the wide differences in funding between the rich and the poor school districts. The court decision also said that a new system of financing public education was needed to give students in poorer school districts an opportunity for an education that was equal to that of students in richer school districts. In general, do you agree or disagree with the decision made by the court? Do you (agree/disagree) strongly or mildly?" This question was asked only of respondents who indicated that they had heard of the *Abbott v. Burke* case.

The similarities in these phrasings of school funding questions enables us to pool these responses, as long as we control for the different time frames of each poll. The resulting merged data set has over 2,100 respondents.

9. Responses to the question range from strongly agree, mildly agree, mildly disagree, to strongly disagree. In all cases, "don't know" responses were treated as missing data.

10. The fact that race is salient in the pooled analysis, however, suggests that nonwhites outside the central cities are just as supportive as nonwhites within the central cities, despite the fact that they will bear a greater burden of the costs of the equalization plan. In this sense, it appears that race trumps geographically defined financial self-interest. This finding suggests that just because a nonwhite respondent lives in the suburbs does not mean that he or she exclusively identifies with the material self-interest of that suburb. Although the size of the relationship between race and support for *Abbott II* is not large, the fact that it is significant (and twice the size of the relationship between central city residence and funding schools equally) shows a durability to this racial cleavage beyond jurisdictional boundaries.

11. Connecticut Poll 7, 11–18 June 1990, Institute of Social Inquiry, University of Connecticut. Pooling these responses with those on funding schools equally from the first poll is legitimate, as long as one assumes that the questions tap into the same underlying issue, or, in more technical terms, the issue dimensions are equivalent. I am making that assumption here. For my purposes, these questions are sufficiently alike and sufficiently explore attitudes toward equality that we can pool them without too much concern. Moreover, the differences in the phrasing allow us to test the extent to which removing the cost of local control contributes to greater support for equality. Additionally, the greater number of responses increases the statistical strength of the claims.

12. On one level this finding is counterintuitive. Most Kentuckians agreed that schools needed reforming and the KERA provided funds to for those reforms. One would think that parents would support this. On the other hand, parents typically do not like to see educational experiments being conducted on their children. Perhaps parents in Kentucky, on average, saw the KERA as more of an experiment than a needed reform.

13. The first question asked the following: "KERA has two basic goals: to provide equal educational opportunities for each child, and to expect each child in Kentucky to perform at a high level. Do you think it is possible to try to achieve both of these goals at the same time?" To this question 65.40 percent responded yes, 22.40 percent responded no, and 12.2 percent indicated they did not know.

14. The topic of school funding was covered in two questions, exact phrasings of which are as follows: Question 19: "Have you heard or read anything about the court decision which requires that all students receive the same level of funding regardless of whether they live in a rich or a poor school district?" Question 20: "Do you agree or disagree with the court decision to equalize school funding?" Identical phrasings were used in both the fall 1991 poll and the spring 1992 poll.

15. Community type, it will be recalled, ranged (in the Tennessee surveys) from central city to rural (both farm and nonfarm).

16. As noted in chapter 5, the string of decisions by the Texas Supreme Court on school finance is staggering. For the complete list, see footnote 5 in chapter 5. For present purposes, the relevant case is *Carrollton-Farmers Branch Independent School District et al. v. Edgewood Independent School District et al.*, 826 S.W.2d 489 (1992) (*Edgewood III*).

17. The poll surveyed 790 individuals and had a margin of error of plus or minus four points (Rugeley 1993).

18. The Mason-Dixon poll surveyed 819 likely voters and had a margin of error of plus or minus 3.5 points (Associated Press 1993).

19. Professor Kent Tedin of the University of Houston has conducted surveys of Houston-area residents to determine their support for school finance equalization. Some of this work is directly relevant to my own, and I discuss it in chapter 8.

20. For a detailed discussion of how this data was prepared, see appendix B.

21. Of course, other factors than party strength — such as candidate-specific factors, the economy, etc. — may play a significant role in the level of support that Hutchison received. In this respect, this measure may overstate Republican support in traditionally Democratic Texas.

22. Ideally, we would include among our independent variables the effect of Proposition 1 on each district's school budget. Unfortunately, at the time of Proposition 1, such information did not exist. Proposition 1 was only a constitutional amendment that would have allowed funds to be transferred; it did not actually set up the mechanisms or means of the transfer. As a result, there could be no reliable or accurate predictions of who would be harmed and who would be aided by the amendment, or to what degree. Instead, the electorate could only guess whether their school districts would be better off with consolidated education districts, or worse off. Here I have used per capita income and home ownership rates to estimate that calculation.

23. It should also be noted that the R^2 value for the multiple regressions equations is rather low, typically in the 0.125 to 0.15 range, with the exception of Texas. (The logistic regressions do not report an R^2). This low value suggests that overall these models may not be the best predictors of variation in attitudes toward school finance reforms. However, I am less interested in building the "best" predictive model, than I am in testing the relevance of some theoretically interesting cleavages in American life to the issue of school spending. That is, we have some sense that race and class might have some influence on attitudes toward school finance reform. To leave those variables out, in order to produce a higher R^2, does not allow us to test whether race or class, in themselves, are relevant to divisions over funding greater educational opportunity. I am more interested in the salience of particular variables than I am in building the best predictive model.

CHAPTER 7
REGIMES OF INEQUALITY

1. *Abbott v. Burke*, 119 N.J. 287 (1990), 375.

2. *Opinion of the Justices (School Financing)* 142 N.H. 892 (1998), 902.

3. Arizona probably represents the clearest example of a court decision seeking increased spending in property poor districts, but not seeking to control expenditures at the top end. As Justice Frederick Martone wrote for a majority of the Arizona Supreme Court in 1994, "There is nothing unconstitutional about relying on a property tax. There is nothing unconstitutional about creating school districts. But if together they produce a public school system that cannot be said to be general and uniform throughout the state, then the laws chosen by the legislature to implement its constitutional obligation . . . fail in their purpose." The Arizona Supreme Court limited its decision to the financing system for capital expenditures and expressly

ruled that local districts are within their constitutional rights to spend beyond the minimal level required by the state constitution. *Roosevelt Elementary School Dist. No. 66 v. Bishop*, 179 Ariz. 233 (1994), at 242.

4. In 1958 Congress enacted the National Defense Education Act (NDEA), which directed money to local school districts for science and math education. The Civil Rights Act of 1964 provided funds for school districts that were undergoing desegregation (and threatened to withhold funds from those that did not desegregate). Most important, the Elementary and Secondary Education Act of 1965 provided federal funds to state and local authorities to provide educational programs to low-income children. Between the 1957–58 and 1967–68 school years, the federal share of total public educational expenditures in elementary and secondary schools jumped from 4.0 percent to 8.8 percent. It peaked at 9.8 percent in the last years of the Carter administration, then dropped sharply to a little above 6 percent during the Reagan and Bush administrations. Currently, it hovers around 7 percent (National Center for Education Statistics 1998, table 157).

5. Between 1972–73 and 1987–88, the national average of educational revenue coming from state sources jumped from just under 40 percent to almost 50 percent. Correspondingly, the local share declined from nearly 52 percent to a shade over 44 percent (National Center for Education Statistics 1998, table 157).

6. United States. National Commission on Excellence in Education 1983.

7. Parker 2000. Parker's analysis includes all public opinions reported in Westlaw from the two circuits between 1983 and 1999 (eighty-nine school districts) and all docket sheets from three federal district courts in Alabama, Georgia, and Mississippi between 1963 and 1999 (one hundred school districts). Because the docket sheets uncovered far more school districts under court order than the published opinions, the actual number of school districts operating under court order in the Fifth and Eleventh Circuits is undoubtedly much higher than 189.

8. For an overview of the effects of teacher contracts on educational policy-making, see Goldschmidt and Stuart 1986.

9. Over the past ten years, a few states, independent of state court pressures, have deviated from this principle. For example, in 1992 Kansas enacted legislation that established a statewide property tax and placed a cap on local tax revenues. The new program also allowed the state to recapture tax revenues raised in a district that exceeded that cap. Those funds are then distributed to other districts. This scheme was upheld by the Kansas Supreme Court in 1994 *Unified School District No. 229 v. Kansas*, 256 Kan 232, 885 P.2d. 1170 (1994). For further details on incursions on local control in other states, see Fulton 1997.

10. See, for example, the 1999 legislation passed by the House amending the Elementary and Secondary Education Act, the Academic Achievement for All Act (H.R. 2300), known informally as "Straight As."

11. See, for example, Polinard et al. 1990, Abrams 1993, and Spring 1988. A useful review of approaches can be found in Stewart 1991. From the perspective of competitive pluralism, the politics of education is typically seen as a struggle among groups. Scholars in this tradition typically emphasize how groups in public education advance and protect their interests through compromise, bargaining, and negotiation. In this sense, education policy is simply the product of clashes between organized interests in education. Within this framework, the relative political

strength of each group determines the course of educational policy. Essential to this framework is the capacity of groups to readily mobilize to advance their interests. This assumes, in turn, that unorganized individuals holding latent interests can accurately perceive those interests and then overcome the collective action problems that inhibit their coalescence into an effective group.

12. Some representative works from this perspective are Chubb and Moe 1990, Schneider et al. 1997, 2000, Witte 2000. The unifying theme of this approach is the application of economic principles to politics. Within the framework of public education, the rational choice model typically focuses on the capacity of individual-level actors in the educational system to exercise influence over the policy process, either singly or in aggregate. There are two main variants of this line of analysis. The first focuses on the effects that incentive structures in institutions have on the behavior of individual actors. The second explores the impact that consumers of education — parents and students, especially — can have on public education. This second variant is the most common. Its central claim is that individuals can effect (or retard) policy changes by either withdrawing or threatening to withdraw from a public school. This withdrawal can take one of two forms: either leaving public schools in toto and enrolling in private schools or relocating to another school district. This model has become increasingly popular just as (or perhaps because) market-based proposals for educational reform have hit political agendas. The underlying logic of rational choice models as applied to education holds that individuals can inspire and induce changes in either the quality of education or its organization if they are given the capacity to exit a public school system. In short, that potential to leave — multiplied by the preferences of thousands of dissatisfied and ill-served parents and students — will alter the behavior of leadership within schools and school districts to respond to declining enrollments.

13. This theory, known as the Tiebout Model, was first put forward in the 1950s and then refined in the early 1960s. See Tiebout 1956 and Ostrom et al. 1961. Since then, it has sparked a considerable debate among economists and a few political scientists. For recent contributions to the debate, see Lowery and Lyons 1989, Percy and Hawkins 1992, Percy et al. 1995.

14. At times, these implicitly racial arguments intersect with existing theories of what makes for a quality education to produce a robust and disturbing theory of how to distribute money for public education. To quickly summarize the argument: A substantial body of research shows that household characteristics (educational levels of parents, family income, parents' attention to homework, etc.) contribute substantively to the educational performance of the child. In communities that are poor, where parents are working two or more jobs, where parents may not have finished high school, more money may not be able to help children overcome these significant obstacles to academic achievement. In those situations, some residents of other communities suggest that the courts are forcing the legislatures to "waste" money in these schools. As we will see, even some state legislators make this argument during debates over school finance reform.

15. *Robinson v. Cahill*, 62 N.J. 473 (1973) (*Robinson I*); *Robinson v. Cahill*, 63 N.J. 196 (1973) (*Robinson II*); *Robinson v. Cahill*, 67 N.J. 35 (1975) (*Robinson III*); *Robinson v. Cahill*, 69 N.J. 133 (1975) (*Robinson IV*); *Robinson v. Cahill*, 69 N.J. 449 (1976) (*Robinson V*); *Robinson v. Cahill*, 70 N.J. 155 (1976) (*Robinson VI*);

Robinson v. Cahill, 70 N.J. 465 (1976) (*Robinson VII*); *Abbott v. Burke*, 100 N.J. 269 (1985) (*Abbott I*); *Abbott v. Burke*, 119 N.J. 287 (1990) (*Abbott II*); *Abbott v. Burke*, 136 N.J. 444 (1994) (*Abbott III*); *Abbott v. Burke*, 149 N.J. 145 (1997) (*Abbott IV*); *Abbott v. Burke*, 153 N.J. 480 (1998) (*Abbott V*); *Abbott v. Burke*, 163 N.J. 95 (2000) (*Abbott VI*); *Abbott v. Burke*, 164 N.J. 84 (2000) (*Abbott VII*).

16. For a comprehensive account of the New Jersey struggle, see Paris 1998. A useful older account of the *Robinson v. Cahill* conflict is found in Lehne 1978, while Firestone et al. 1997 provides an illuminating assessment of the financial impact of Jim Florio's Quality Education Act (QEA) on school districts in New Jersey. For an overview of public reaction to *Abbott II* and the QEA, see Reed 1994.

17. *Abbott II* came down on 5 June 1990. The legislature passed the QEA on 21 June 1990. At passage, it was scheduled to take effect in fall 1991, for the 1991–92 school year. Between January and March 1991, however, the legislature substantially amended the QEA. The original QEA never took effect, as QEA II was implemented in its place in Fall 1991. The list in the text detailing QEA's provisions is adapted from both the New Jersey Legislature 1990 and from secondary sources, primarily Goertz 1992 and Firestone et al. 1993 and from *New York Times* articles on the QEA from March 1990 through October 1990. See also Salmore and Salmore 1993b, 273–78, for additional details.

18. Foundation aid is the general equalization fund and is largely unrestricted, unlike categorical state funds, which must be spent on particular programs.

19. A distinctive form of communication apparently helped mobilize public opinion in the course of this tax revolt: talk radio. A crowd of six thousand people rallied at the state capital against the new taxes only nine and a half days after John Budzash, a thirty-nine-year-old postal worker from Howell Township, suggested on the air that something should be done to demonstrate New Jerseyans' ire over new taxes. WKXW-FM 101.5 deejay John Kobylt encouraged Budzash to give his telephone number over the air and organize like-minded citizens. The rally grew out of this effort, aided by publicity from WKXW-FM 101.5, which is owned by the *Asbury Park Press*. See DePalma 1990 for additional details.

20. The NJEA PAC ranked first among non-candidate-controlled PACs in 1985, 1987, and 1991, contributing $268,000 to New Jersey elections in 1991 (Salmore and Salmore 1993b, 100); (Salmore and Salmore 1993a, 247). Candidate-controlled PACs ranked higher in 1991, an election year for the state legislature.

21. NJEA President Betty Kraemer had stated at a press conference announcing the endorsement: "Jim Florio is the crystal-clear choice of educators. . . . NJEA is ready to go all out for the man who has shown he is ready to lead our state into the 1990s" (Shearman 1989).

22. Presumably, it hurt him even more in the 1993 gubernatorial race against Christine Whitman when the NJEA decided to endorse neither candidate (Van Tassel 1993).

23. Hanley 1990d. In *Abbott II*, the New Jersey Supreme Court identified twenty-eight special needs districts as the target for financing reforms. In the course of determining a remedy, the New Jersey legislature added two more, Plainfield City and Neptune Township. Thus, while there are twenty-eight "*Abbott* districts," thirty districts are included in the remedies. In *Abbott VI*, the New Jersey Supreme Court authorized the legislature to drop any district from the special needs list, if its finan-

cial and socioeconomic condition improved. Currently, the legislature is considering whether to drop Hoboken from the special needs list.

24. The eight are Irvington, Milville, Passaic, Union City, Phillipsburg, Garfield, West New York, and Vineland. Irvington, according to press reports, would have to raise $6.1 million in local revenues in order to qualify for a $5.3 million increase in foundation aid (Hanley 1990d).

25. For an overview of the New Jersey tax revolt of 1990–91, see Kehler 1992.

26. There is some evidence that these districts are developing a third option: private funding of public schools. A letter in January 1994 by William S. Palmer, superintendent of the Essex Fells School District (which runs one K-8 school), to the residents of the town stated that

> Essex Fells School must generate resources that extend *beyond the limitations* of the Board of Education school budget. Therefore, the Board of Education is now exploring various avenues of *alternate funding*. . . . For example, the P.T.A. will be asked to lend its fund-raising expertise to help the school begin an endowment fund. . . .
>
> One avenue of alternate funding that has been quite successful in many New Jersey school districts is an education foundation. An education foundation exists as a non-profit, non-political entity independent of the Board of Education. Its mission involves the development of supportive community and private sector relationships with a school or school system. . . .
>
> Perhaps an education foundation, which provides *private support* for public education is an idea whose time has come for the Essex Fells School. (Palmer 1994, emphasis in original)

For additional information about education foundations, see Celis 1991.

27. Hanley 1990c. A study of five of the thirty special needs districts conducted during the 1991–92 academic year found an average of 67 percent of students eligible for at-risk aid (Natriello and Collins 1993, 27).

28. *Abbott II* 383, 385.

29. Indeed, the NJEA abandoned support for Democratic legislators in the mid-term 1991 legislative elections, endorsing a record forty-six Republican candidates and only three Democrats. As Betty Kraemer, president of the NJEA, stated: "Democrats turned their backs on educators, our schools and our students when they slashed $360 million from the original Quality Education Act" (King 1991a).

30. Governor Florio conceded as much in early November 1990 when he allowed the Department of Education to engage in planning discussions with school districts (Hanley 1990d); (Hanley 1990e). It became a certainty in January when the Democratic leadership in the General Assembly broke with Florio and introduced its own plan to overhaul the QEA (Hanley 1991).

31. Total Maximum School Aid is basically the money the state spends on elementary and secondary education. For the years discussed here, it does not include some debt service aid, but those small sums are immaterial to the analysis here.

32. Foundation aid is the general equalization fund and is largely unrestricted, unlike categorical state funds, which must be spent on particular programs.

33. King 1991b. One analysis of the voters' reaction to QEA I and II indicates the QEA II did little to alter the electorate's mood. See Bogart and VanDoren 1993. Using household-level income and property tax data, Bogart and VanDoren modeled

the 1991 state senate election to determine whether voters punished New Jersey state legislators for voting against their constituents' economic interests. By regressing the percentage vote obtained by a candidate in the election against whether the legislator voted in favor of the QEA, the candidate's party and incumbent status and whether the candidate was unopposed, as well as the effect of the QEA on household income, Bogart and VanDoren conclude that a legislator's support for the QEA II revisions accounted for little of the variation in the percentage of the vote won by the candidate. Indeed, "The legislators' attempt to curry favor with their constituents through revisions to the QEA that diluted its redistributive character was discounted by voters whose reactions toward incumbents were governed mainly by the senators' behavior toward the original QEA in June 1990" (Bogart and VanDoren 1993, 371). Instead of being appeased by the QEA II, it appears that voters were deeply angry at Democrats and simply voted them out of office.

34. It is conceivable that Democrats could have lost by a *greater* margin in the fall 1991 elections without the QEA revisions, although it seems like it would have been a difficult feat to pull off.

35. Florio's top education advisor, Tom Corcoran, told Paris in an interview that "we failed to really think about the internal organization of the NJEA. . . . Suburban teachers control it" (Paris 1998, 333).

36. Reilly 1992. See also Hendrie 1992 and Paris 1998, 375–76.

37. Of course, there was still some money freed up by the annual 25 percent reduction in "transition aid" to affluent districts, but that money paled in comparison to the new funds promised in the original QEA and the pot of money spent on state contributions to teachers' pensions.

38. In January 1993 Republican legislators and Florio created a bipartisan School Funding Review Commission to take the issue off the fall electoral agenda. That commission, chaired by former state legislator Al Burstein, was supposed to consider alternatives to the QEA and report back by 15 November 1993, two weeks after elections for governor and the state legislature. Internal divisions prevented the group from giving any plan its stamp of approval by that date and forced several delays. It approved its report on 13 April 1994 by a narrow 8-6 margin. Meanwhile, shortly after her election, Governor-elect Whitman appointed former New Jersey Commission of Education Saul Cooperman as chair of an education funding task force to develop a legislative proposal. Cooperman's task force issued its recommendations on April 7, 1994. Whitman, however, was cool to Cooperman's central recommendation that local districts pick up teacher pension and Social Security costs, an element of the original QEA that put Florio in hot water with the New Jersey Education Association.

39. *Abbott v. Burke*, 136 N.J. 444 (*Abbott III*) (1994).

40. The State Department of Education assumed control of the Jersey City school district in 1989 and the Paterson school district in 1991. In July 1995 the state took over the Newark School District. See Reilly 1995c, Stewart 1995. For a general discussion of state takeovers of public schools, see Berman 1995.

It should be noted that many of these accusations of "waste" had a racial dimension, as Paris 1998 amply shows. The racial tensions that undergird New Jersey educational politics are often intense. The criticisms of excessive waste in New Jersey's central-city districts were, in many instances unfounded, as Firestone et al. 1997 show. Their analysis of the spending that took place with the infusion of QEA money reveals that much of it went for needed and essential programs.

41. Braun 1995. See also Reilly 1995a. In January 1995 the Whitman administration also adopted a policy that fined local school districts if their administrative overhead exceeded the median noninstructional expenditure by more than 30 percent. This fell particularly hard on a few small, affluent districts that provided extensive services. See Reilly 1995b.

42. New Jersey has consistently ranked among the highest per pupil expenditure in the fifty states. (Digest of Education Statistics, 1999. table 171).

43. There were three reports that came out of Klagholz's office with virtually the same title. The first arrived in February 1995 and contained only the barest details. The second was released on 22 November 1995 and was a much longer, more substantive description of the components of the core curriculum. The third report finally put a price tag on the core curriculum, but it was not released until May 1996, four months before the state supreme court deadline. The first is most readily available in a series of excerpts published in the Newark *Star-Ledger*. See Klagholz, 1995a, 1995b, and 1995c.

44. Klagholz 1995a

45. Klagholz 1995c

46. The court eventually denied the motion in September 1996 and at the same time extended the state's deadline to 31 December 1996. While considering the ELC's motion, the court was undoubtedly unsettled by the sudden retirement of Chief Justice Robert Wilentz in mid-June due to illness. He died in late July of cancer. Wilentz had been the chief architect of the *Abbott II* decision and his departure from the court may explain the supreme court's shift in tone beginning in September 1996.

47. New Jersey State Supreme Court justices have a mandatory retirement age of seventy.

48. *Abbott v. Burke*, 149 N.J. 145 (1997) (*Abbott IV*), 152.

49. Shortly after the *Abbott IV* decision, state officials estimated that it would cost $247 million in new funding to comply with the decision (Pristin 1997). After receiving spending plans from the districts, the state department of education rather quickly released those funds, drawing them from unanticipated tax revenues. The court battle continued over how those, and possibly additional funds, should be spent.

50. As Judge King wrote in his eventual opinion,"The State's vision is likely driven by a certain measure of political pragmatism; the plaintiff's vision is likely driven by optimistic, well-meaning idealism." *Abbott v. Burke*, 153 N.J. 480 (1998), 604.

51. Goodnough 1997. See also Judge Michael Patrick King's Superior Court decision dated 22 January 1998. Although unpublished, it was printed as appendix I in *Abbott v. Burke*, 153 N.J. 480 (1998), 529–635. The discussion of the state's funding requirements for "Success for All" can be found at 565–68.

52. "Success for All" is a respected language arts and communications skills reform program developed in the late 1980s by Robert Slavin at Johns Hopkins' Center for Research on the Education of Students Placed at Risk. The program is now a joint operation of Johns Hopkins and Howard University. Its aim is to harness the

existing resources within a school to develop the reading and language skills of a child who might otherwise fall behind. In doing so, it significantly changes the administration and instruction in elementary schools, often to dramatic effects. It has significantly improved reading scores in Camden, New Jersey, where it was adopted in the early 1990s. As of 1996, over four hundred schools nationwide had adopted the program. Pilot programs have been adopted in Miami, Albuquerque, and Memphis. A complementary program, "Roots and Wings," uses similar techniques for math instruction, science, and social studies. See Center for Research on the Education of Students Placed at Risk 1996.

53. *Abbott v. Burke*, 153 N.J. 480 (1998) (*Abbott V*), 607–13.

54. The issue of school facilities is complex, because facilities needs are driven by a number of factors: simple age and neglected maintenance; growing enrollments in a number of special needs districts; new space needs for new full-day prekindergarten and kindergarten offerings; and new space needs to achieve core curriculum standards, particularly in the sciences where laboratory space is needed. Judge King indicated that the DOE's fall 1997 survey of existing facilities needs, while fair and accurate, was not extensive enough to encompass all these concerns. As a result, he ordered a school-by-school evaluation of needs and costs.

55. *Abbott v. Burke*, 153 N.J. 480 (1998) (*Abbott V*), 490.

56. *Abbott VI* clarified the early education requirements imposed by *Abbott V* and directed the Department of Education to meet those requirements. *Abbott v. Burke*, 163 N.J. 95 (2000) (*Abbott VI*). *Abbott VII* determined that the state was fully responsible for the construction costs of new school facilities in special needs districts. *Abbott v. Burke* 164 N.J. 84 (2000) (*Abbott VII*).

57. In *Stubaus v. Whitman*, twenty-five middle-class districts filed suit in 1998 claiming that the CEIFA created wide disparities in property tax rates and forced too great a reliance on the property tax to fund public education. A superior court dismissed the suit in February 2000. As of August 2000, it is unclear whether the plaintiffs will appeal. In *Keaveney v. New Jersey Department of Education*, twenty poor rural districts filed suit against the state claiming that the state's aid package did not enable them to meet the newly imposed curricular standards and that they should receive additional *Abbott* aid because their poverty rates, test scores, and graduation rates are similar to the twenty-eight special needs districts. That case has been split and the Group I plaintiffs' case is pending before the state Office of Administrative Law, while the Group II plaintiffs' claims are still under review by the state education commissioner.

CHAPTER 8
CONCLUSION

1. The 1993 constitutional referendum would have essentially preserved the 1991 plan that formed the basis of Tedin's inquiries.

2. *Sheff v. O'Neill* 238 Conn 1 (1996). Minnesota saw a similar set of claims proposed in two cases, *NAACP et al. v. State of Minnesota et al.* (Fourth Judicial District Court, File No. MC 95-14800, Judge Gary Larson) and *Xiong et al. v. State of Minnesota et al.* (Fourth Judicial District Court, File No. MC 98-002816, Judge Gary Larson). The cases never proceeded to trial, but were instead settled by the

state and the NAACP. The Minneapolis chapter of the NAACP saw intense internal divisions over the cases, and there was substantial disagreement between the lawyers for the case, the lead plaintiffs, and the leadership of the NAACP. For details of the conflict, see Hawkins 2000. (Available on line at http://citypages.com/databank/21/1015/article8664.asp, visited 24 July 2000.) The settlement included the creation of a limited Open Enrollment program for some five hundred students from eight Minneapolis schools, allowing them to attend suburban schools.

3. For an overview of the *Sheff* decision and its significance to the school finance cases, see Ryan 1999. Kathryn McDermott (1999) also has a rich and vivid account of the politics of the reaction to the *Sheff* lawsuit. Many of her arguments echo those made in chapter 7.

4. Of course, in the 1970s and 1980s, Hartford was never at the bottom end of the resource distribution in Connecticut schools. Ironically, the most severe poverty, in terms of property wealth, was in the Naugatuck Valley, populated by declining industrial towns like Ansonia and Derby. Eastern Connecticut was also quite property poor, contending with significant rural poverty.

5. Astute readers will recall that Connecticut's inequality did not change as dramatically as other states in the wake of its school financing decision (see chapter 2 for details). But, interestingly, Hartford's funding did grow substantially. Part of the reason that Connecticut's overall measures of inequality did not drop so dramatically in the wake of *Horton* is that there were and are other property-poor areas in the state (notably the rural areas of eastern Connecticut and the decaying industrial towns of the Naugatuck Valley) that did not benefit as much from the legislative response to the *Horton* decision. Thus, while overall inequality did not improve as much as in other states, the relative inequality between the four large central cities in Connecticut (Hartford, New Haven, Bridgeport, and Norwich) and their surrounding suburbs *did* improve.

6. *Sheff v. O'Neill*, 238 Conn. 1 (1996), 3.

7. Gormley argues that judicial coercion of bureaucratic organizations can be misplaced or even counterproductive if courts misapprehend the causes of bureaucratic delay. According to Gormley, the issue context and bureaucratic characteristics matter significantly, and the failure of courts to appreciate those features can actually thwart compliance, or produce worse policy outcomes. Within the language of Gormley's analysis, I see school finance issues as a policy issue of low complexity and high conflict (that is, it is easy administratively to equalize expenditures, but politically very difficult) and the bureaucratic characteristics required are generally high skill, low support. In this policy issue, it is more relevant to consider the legislature as the institution the courts seek to coerce, rather than the state educational bureaucracy. In short, the legislature has the skills to accomplish the task, but not the political desire. According to Gormley, in such situations judicial coercion is justifiable, but should be used as a last resort. See Gormley 1989, 22–23.

8. That case, *Stubaus v. Whitman*, was dismissed by the superior court in February 2000.

9. Gerald Rosenberg came to a similar conclusion in his book *The Hollow Hope* (Rosenberg 1991).

10. This assumes, of course, that affluent and nonaffluent students (or white and minority students) are not resegregated in neighborhood schools through tracking programs or other sorting mechanisms. Research on magnet schools shows that inter-

nal segregation can be quite severe and that the benefits of integrated schools diminish substantially when children are ostensibly re-sorted on achievement lines, but in reality are sorted on class and racial lines (Schofield 1989, 75–97).

11. See, for example, the following: Bankston and Caldas 1996; Braddock and Dawkins 1981; Dawkins and Braddock 1994; Entwisle and Alexander 1992, 1994; Trent 1997; Wells 1996; Wells and Crain 1994, 1997.

12. While there is a long debate in the black community about both the need for integration with whites and the trade-offs that accompany integration, most commentators have agreed that racial isolation, in conjunction with poverty, has profound consequences on the health of the community. See, in particular, Massey and Denton 1993. In addition, this proposal is not simply targeted at black-white segregation, but at any racial or ethnic group that experiences extreme isolation compounded by economic hardship.

13. Policy-makers who wish to target the most racially isolated neighborhoods could adjust the tax credit according to the degree of racial and class isolation in the school attendance zone, with, for example, parents receiving only 20 percent of the tax credit when their children are enrolled in schools that are only 20 percent more segregated than the median school.

14. In order to avoid long-term unanticipated or harmful consequences, the property tax credit should be enacted with a sunset provision so that it will end after five years unless policy-makers feel it merits renewal. Similarly, if the program enjoys success and produces more integrated neighborhoods and schools, the program should be phased out. Of course, the politics of tax credits typically creates constituencies that lobby or mobilize for their continuation. Because of this, it may be difficult to eliminate the tax credit if the program enjoys any measure of success.

15. An alternative proposal that would cost significantly less, but cause perhaps greater controversy, would be to limit the percentage of poor children in any one school. Once a school's percentage of children in poverty reached greater than, say, 40 percent, students in that school would be chosen by lottery to be bused to the nearest neighborhood school where poverty rates were below that level. In some cities, of course, the rates of poverty are so high that it would be impossible to reduce the percentage significantly below the existing levels. In that situation, cross-district busing would have to occur to significantly reduce the poverty levels of some schools. This proposal is probably best suited to small and medium-size school districts in which student poverty is not the norm and is located in pockets around the city. A few districts have experimented with socioeconomic busing, to great controversy and some meaningful effect, the most notable being La Crosse, Wisconsin. In many cities, busing by socioeconomic class would be the virtual equivalent of busing by race. I have yet to see an academic study of the La Crosse busing program, but there are journalistic accounts. See Walters 1993. Other districts that implemented or proposed busing by class include Wake County, North Carolina, and Coweta County, Georgia.

16. One alternative to the public school attendance property tax credit is a complete property tax abatement in school attendance zones suffering from racial and economic isolation. While such an abatement might achieve an even greater neighborhood transformation it might also result in development that does not immediately translate into increased demands for better educational services. Home buyers without children, the elderly, and gay residents all might seek out the advantages of a

property-tax-free home, but not mobilize on behalf of better schools, simply because it is not in their immediate interest to do so. Even without that political mobilization, however, the community could conceivably benefit from greater racial and economic integration, which could indirectly lead to better neighborhood schools.

17. Some may contend that this policy proposal is simply a rerun of the remedies imposed by Federal District Judge Russell G. Clark in the Kansas City school desegregation case of *Missouri v. Jenkins*. In that case, Judge Clark ordered a $1.15 billion desegregation plan that overhauled facilities and educational programs in an effort to draw white suburban students to Kansas City central-city magnet schools. The program has had mixed results, not producing any meaningful racial desegregation and somewhat boosting test scores of students, especially elementary students (Morantz 1996). While the experience of Kansas City is certainly sobering, I would urge two cautions. First, the Kansas City program did not focus on any of the residential aspects of segregation, and, as a result, it neglected community influences on educational performance. In fact, as a result of Clark's desegregation order, property taxes in the Kansas City, Missouri, school district nearly doubled (Ibid., 251), making white relocation to the city even less likely. The combination of a property-tax-free residence *and* dramatically improved magnet school offerings might induce the changes Clark sought. Second, the plan was in effect for only a few years before the U.S. Supreme Court ruled in 1995 that Clark had overstepped his judicial authority by ordering increases in teachers' salaries (*Missouri v. Jenkins*, 515 U.S. 70 (1995) (*Jenkins II*)). The fallout of that decision has been a negotiated end to the increased spending program due to its high cost. As a result, the infusion of resources was only temporary and not sustained. It is little wonder then that results were, at best, mixed.

BIBLIOGRAPHY

"State Constitutional Law: Selected Secondary and Source Materials." *National Law Journal*, 29 September 1986, S-15.

Abrahamson, Shirley S. "Criminal Law and State Constitutions: The Emergence of State Constitutional Law." *Texas Law Review* 63, 6, 7 (1985): 1141–93.

Abrams, Douglas M. *Conflict, Competition, or Cooperation: Dilemmas of State Education Policymaking*. Albany: State University of New York Press, 1993.

Armor, David J. *Forced Justice: School Desegregation and the Law*. New York: Oxford University Press, 1995.

Associated Press. "Backers of School Proposal Face a Tough Sale, Poll Finds." *Dallas Morning News*, 11 April 1993, 26A.

Associated Press. "Sticking Points Remain in School Funding Talks." *The Record* (Bergen, NJ), 3 October 1996, A5.

Baldassare, Mark. *Trouble in Paradise: The Suburban Transformation in America*. New York: Columbia University Press, 1986.

Bankston, Carl L., III, and Stephen J. Caldas. "Majority African-American Schools and Social Injustice: The Influence of De Facto Segregation on Academic Achievement." *Social Forces* 75, 2 (1996): 535–55.

———. "The American School Dilemma: Race and Scholastic Performance." *Sociological Quarterly* 38, 3 (1997): 423–29.

Berman, David R. "Takeovers of Local Governments: An Overview and Evaluation of State Policies." *Publius* 25, 3 (1995): 55–70.

Berne, Robert, and Leanna Stiefel. *The Measurement of Equity in School Finance*. Baltimore, Md.: The Johns Hopkins University Press, 1984.

Bird, Kathleen. "Abbott Lawyer Set to Challenge QEA Overhaul; Says Plan to Use Funds for Tax Relief Violates Court's Mandate." *New Jersey Law Journal*, 28 March 1991, 3.

Bobo, Lawrence. "Whites' Opposition to Busing: Symbolic Racism or Realistic Group Conflict?" *Journal of Personality and Social Psychology* 45, 6 (1983): 1196–210.

Bobo, Lawrence, and James R. Kluegel. "Opposition to Race-Targeting: Self-Interest, Stratification Ideology or Racial Attitudes?" *American Sociological Review* 58, August (1993): 443–64.

Bogart, William T., David F. Bradford, and Michael G. Williams. "Incidence Effects of a State Fiscal Policy Shift: The Florio Initiatives in New Jersey." *National Tax Journal* 45, 4 (1992): 371–87.

Bogart, William T., and Peter M. VanDoren. "Do Legislators Vote Their Constituents' Wallets? (And How Would We Know If They Did?)" *Southern Economic Journal* 60, 2 (1993): 357–75.

Borchard, Edwin Montefiore. *Declaratory Judgments*. 2d ed, reprint of 1941 ed. Buffalo, N.Y.: William S. Hein, 2000.

Bosworth, Matthew H. "Do Courts Matter? Public School Finance Reform in Texas, Kentucky and North Dakota." Ph.d. diss., University of Wisconsin, 1997.

Braddock, Jomills Henry, II, and Marvin P. Dawkins. "Predicting Black Academic Achievement in Higher Education." *Journal of Negro Education* 50, 3 (1981): 319–27.

Braden, George D., ed. *The Constitution of the State of Texas: An Annotated and Comparative Analysis.* Vol. 1. Austin, Tex.: Texas Advisory Commission on Intergovernmental Relations, 1977.

Braun, Robert J. "Klagholz Wants Funding Tied to School Necessities." *Star-Ledger,* 16 January 1995.

Brennan, William J., Jr. "State Constitutions and the Protection of Individual Rights." *Harvard Law Review* 90, 3 (1977): 489–504.

———. "The Bill of Rights and the States: The Revival of State Constitutions As Guardians of Individual Rights." *New York University Law Review* 61, 4 (1986): 535–53.

Burton, Cynthia. "Whitman Approves School Aid Overhaul." *Star-Ledger,* 21 December 1996, 11.

Caldas, Stephen J., and Carl Bankston, III. "The Inequality of Separation: Racial Composition of Schools and Academic Achievement." *Education Administration Quarterly* 34, 4 (1998): 533–57.

Card, David, and Alan B. Krueger. "School Resources and Student Outcomes." *Annals of the American Academy of Political and Social Science* 559 (1998): 39–53.

Cataldo, Everett F, and John D. Holm. "Voting on School Finances: A Test of Competing Theories." *Western Political Quarterly* 36, 4 (1983): 619–31.

Celis, William, III. "Schools Go Outside Districts for Money." *New York Times,* 16 October 1991, B9.

Center for Research on the Education of Students Placed at Risk. "CRESPAR Research and Development Report." Baltimore, Md.: Johns Hopkins University and Howard University, 1996.

Chiles, Nick. "Scorn for Education Funding Plan Prompts Call for Legislative Action." *Star-Ledger,* 13 December 1995.

———. "Whitman Plan Lowers Funds for Top Schools." *Star-Ledger,* 19 May 1996, 1.

Chubb, John E., and Terry M. Moe. *Politics, Markets, and America's Schools.* Washington, D.C.: Brookings Institution, 1990.

Churgin, Michael J., Peter H. Ehrenberg, and Peter T. Grossi, Jr. "Note: A Statistical Analysis of the School Finance Decisions: On Winning Battles and Losing Wars." *Yale Law Journal* 81, 7 (1972): 1303–391.

Clotfelter, Charles T. "Are Whites Still 'Fleeing'? Racial Patterns and Enrollment Shifts in Urban Public Schools, 1987–1996." Cambridge, Mass.: National Bureau of Economic Research, 1999a.

Clotfelter, Charles T. "Public School Segregation in Metropolitan Areas." *Land Economics* 75, 4 (1999b): 487–504.

Cohen, G. A. "Equality of What? On Welfare, Goods and Capabilities." All Souls College, Oxford, unpublished manuscript, 1989.

Coleman, James Samuel. United States. Office of Education, and National Center for Education Statistics. *Equality of Educational Opportunity.* Washington: U.S. Department of Health, Education, and Welfare Office of Education; for sale by the Superintendent of Documents U.S. Government Printing Office, 1966.

Connecticut General Assembly. *House of Representatives Proceedings*: 24 H.R. Proc., 1979.

Connecticut General Assembly. *Senate Proceedings*: 22 S. Proc., 1979.

Cook, Thomas, David Armor, Robert Crain, Norman Miller, Walter Stephan, Herbert Walberg, and Paul Wortman, eds. *School Desegregation and Black Achievement*. Washington, D.C.: National Institute of Education, 1984.

Crain, Robert L. "School Integration and Occupational Achievement of Negroes." *American Journal of Sociology* 75, 4, part 2 (1970): 593–606.

Crain, Robert L., and Rita E. Mahard. "The Effect of Research Metholodogy on Desegregation-Achievement Studies: A Meta-Analysis." *American Journal of Sociology* 88, 5 (1983): 839–54.

Danielson, Michael N. *The Politics of Exclusion*. New York: Columbia University Press, 1976.

Dawkins, Marvin P., and Jomills Henry Braddock, II. "The Continuing Significance of Desegregation: School Racial Composition and African-American Inclusion in American Society." *Journal of Negro Education* 63, 3 (1994): 394–405.

DePalma, Anthony. "Anti-Tax Protesters Demand Florio's Recall, for Starters." *New York Times*, 2 July 1990, B4.

Digest of Education Statistics. U.S. Department of Education, National Center for Education Statistics, Washington, D.C.: GPO, 1999.

Donahue, Terry. "House Rejects School Finance Bill." *United Press International*, 27 March 1991.

Downs, T.A., and D. Schoeman. "School Finance Reform and Private School Enrollment: Evidence from California." *Journal of Urban Economics* 43, 3 (1998): 418–43.

Dworkin, Ronald. "What Is Equality? Part 1: Equality of Welfare." *Philosophy and Public Affairs* 10, 3 (1981): 185–246.

―――. "What Is Equality? Part 2: Equality of Resources." *Philosophy and Public Affairs* 10, 4 (1981): 283–345.

Eaton, Susan E., Joseph Feldman, and Edward Kirby. "Still Separate, Still Unequal." In *Dismantling Desegregation*, edited by Gary Orfield, Susan E. Eaton, and Harvard Project on School Desegregation. New York: The New Press, 1996.

Elliott, Janet. "Edgewood II Offers Same Vote, New Activist Advice." *Texas Lawyer*, 28 January 1991a, 8.

Elliott, Janet. "Edgewood III Foes Blame Ruling on Public Pressure." *Texas Lawyer*, 4 March 1991b, 15.

Enrich, P. "Leaving Equality Behind: New Directions in School Finance Reform." *Vanderbilt Law Review* 48, (1995): 101–194.

Entwisle, Doris R., and Karl L. Alexander. "Summer Setback: Race, Poverty, School Composition, and Mathematics Achievement in the First Two Years of School." *American Sociological Review* 57, 1 (1992): 72–84.

―――. "Winter Setback: The Racial Composition of Schools and Learning to Read." *American Sociological Review* 59, 3 (1994): 446–60.

Farley, Reynolds, Howard Schuman, Suzanne Bianci, Diane Colasanto, and Shirley Hatchett. "Chocolate City, Vanilla Suburbs: Will the Trend toward Racially Separate Communities Continue?" *Social Science Research* 7 (1978): 319–44.

Farley, Reynolds, and William H. Frey. "Changes in the Segregation of Whites from

Blacks during the 1980s: Small steps toward a More Integrated Society." *American Sociological Review* 59, 1 (1994): 23–45.

Feeley, Malcom M. "Hollow Hopes, Flypaper and Metaphors." *Law and Social Inquiry* 17, 4 (1992): 745–60.

Feiffer, Jules. "Op-Art." *New York Times*, 8 September 1999, A23.

Firestone, William A., Susan H. Fuhrman, and Michael W. Kirst. "State Educational Reform since 1983: Appraisal and the Future." *Educational Policy* 5, 3 (1991): 233–50.

Firestone, William A., Margaret E. Goertz, Brianna Nagle, and Marcy F. Smelkinson. "Where Did the $800 Million Go? The First Year of New Jersey's Quality Education Act." Center for Educational Policy Analysis, 1993.

Firestone, William A., Margaret E. Goertz, and Gary Natriello. *From Cashbox to Classroom: The Struggle for Fiscal Reform and Educational Change in New Jersey*. New York: Teachers College Press, 1997.

Flicker, Barbara, ed. *Justice and School Systems: The Role of Courts in Education Litigation*. Philadelphia: Temple University Press, 1990.

Frug, Gerald E. *City Making: Building Communities without Building Walls*. Princeton, N.J.: Princeton University Press, 1999.

Fulton, Mary F. *State School Finance System Changes* (April) [World Wide Web]. Education Commission of the States, 1997 [visited 15 August 2000].

Gardner, James A. "The Failed Discourse of State Constitutionalism." *Michigan Law Review* 90, 4 (1992): 761–837.

Glick, Henry R. "Policy Making and State Supreme Courts." In *The American Courts: A Critical Assessment*, edited by John B. Gates and Charles A. Johnson, 87–118. Washington, D.C.: CQ Press, 1991.

———. *The Right to Die: Policy Innovation and Its Consequences*. New York: Columbia University Press, 1992.

Glovin, David. "Klagholz: No Intent to Cut Aid; Defends School Funding Proposal." *The Record*, 8 December 1995, A5.

———. "Poor Districts Propose Schools That Serve Family, Community." *The Record*, 2 December 1997, A2.

Goertz, Margaret E. "The Development and Implementation of the Quality Education Act of 1990." Center for Educational Policy Analysis, 1992.

Goldschmidt, Steven M., and Leland E. Stuart. "The Extent and Impact of Educational Policy Bargaining." *Industrial and Labor Relations Review* 39, 3 (1986): 350–60.

Goodnough, Abby. "Schools Chief in New Jersey Is Pressed on Education Plan." *New York Times*, 20 November 1997a, B4.

———. "Urban Schools Do Not Need More Money, State Argues." *New York Times*, 22 December 1997b, B5.

———. "Judge Weighing New Jersey's Spending on Urban Schools Offers Few Clues on Ruling." *New York Times*, 4 January 1998, 21.

Goodwin, Dorothy. Interview with author, 28 September 1992, Storrs, Conn.

Gormley, William T., Jr. *Taming the Bureaucracy*. Princeton, N.J.: Princeton University Press, 1989.

Green, Donald Philip, and Ann Elizabeth Gerken. "Self-Interest and Public Opinion toward Smoking Restrictions and Cigarette Taxes." *Public Opinion Quarterly* 53, Spring (1989): 1–16.

Griffin, Stephen M. *American Constitutionalism: From Theory to Politics*. Princeton, N.J.: Princeton University Press, 1996.

Grubb, Erica Black. "Breaking the Language Barrier: The Right to Bilingual Education." *Harvard Civil Rights–Civil Liberties Law Review* 9, 1 (1974): 52–94.

Gural, Natasha. "Lawyers, Plaintiffs in Landmark Case Will Not Appeal." *Associated Press*, 23 March 1999.

Hall, Kermit L. "Mostly Anchor and Little Sail: The Evolution of American State Constitutions." In *Toward a Usable Past: Liberty under State Constitutions*, edited by Paul Finkelman and Stephen E. Gottleib, 388–417. Athens: University of Georgia Press, 1991.

Halpern, Stephen C. *On the Limits of the Law*. Baltimore: Johns Hopkins University Press, 1995.

Hanley, Robert. "Florio's School Aid Dream Is Town's Nightmare." *New York Times*, 12 July 1990a, B2.

———. "Foes of Florio's School Plan Are Hopeful about Changes." *New York Times*, 10 November 1990e, A26.

———. "New Jersey Shifts Plan for 'At Risk' Students." *New York Times*, 6 October 1990c, A27.

———. "New Jersey's Wealthy School Districts Gird for Battle on State Aid." *New York Times*, 1 September 1990b, A23.

———. "Plan to Revise Aid to Schools Deepens New Jersey Tumult." *New York Times*, 12 January 1991, A28.

———. "School Officials Vent Anger on New Jersey Financing Law." *New York Times*, 1 November 1990d, B1.

Hansen, Chris. "Are the Courts Giving Up? Current Issues in School Desegregation." *Emory Law Journal* 42, Summer (1993): 863–75.

Harr, Charles M. *Suburbs under Siege: Race, Space and Audacious Judges*. Princeton, N.J.: Princeton University Press, 1996.

Hartford Courant. "School Aid Error, Tax Shortfall Complicate State's Fiscal Outlook." *Hartford Courant*, 20 February 1981, A1.

Hawkins, Beth. "Magic Bus." *City Pages*, 17 May 2000.

Hawkins, Brett W., and Stephen L. Percy. "On Anti-Suburban Orthodoxy." *Social Science Quarterly* 72, 3 (1991): 478–90.

Heise, Michael. "The Effect of Constitutional Litigation on Education Finance: More Preliminary Analyses and Modeling." *Journal of Education Finance* 21, 2 (1995a): 195–216.

———. "State Constitutional Litigation, Educational Finance and Legal Impact: An Empirical Analysis." *University of Cincinnati Law Review* 63, 4 (1995b): 1735–65.

———. "Equal Educational Opportunity, Hollow Victories, and the Demise of School Finance Equity Theory: An Empirical Perspective and Alternative Explanation." *Georgia Law Review* 32, 2 (1998): 543–631.

Hendrie, Caroline. "Teachers, Activist Agree on Pensions." *The Record*, 17 July 1992, A3.

Henig, Jeffrey R., and Stephen D. Sugarman. "The Nature and Extent of School Choice." In *School Choice and Social Controversy*, edited by Stephen D. Sugarman and Frank R. Kemerer, 13–35. Washington, D.C.: Brookings Institution, 1999.

Hill, Richard Child. "Separate and Unequal: Governmental Inequality in the Metropolis." *American Political Science Review* 68, 4 (1974): 1557–68.

Hobby, William P., and Mark G. Yudof. "Texas Got Itself into This School-Finance Mess, How's It Going to Get Out?" *Houston Chronicle*, 15 December 1991, Outlook sec., 5.

Horton, Wesley W. Interview with author, 17 August 1992a, West Hartford, Conn.

Horton, Wesley W. "Memoirs of a Connecticut School Finance Lawyer." *Connecticut Law Review* 24, 3 (1992b): 703–19.

Howard, A. E. Dick. "State Courts and Constitutional Rights in the Day of the Burger Court." *Virginia Law Review* 62, 5 (1976): 873–944.

Hubsch, Allen W. "The Emerging Right to Education under State Constitutional Law." *Temple Law Review* 65, 4 (1992): 1325–48.

Jackson, Kenneth T. *Crabgrass Frontier*. New York: Oxford University Press, 1985.

Jimenez, Ralph. Reporter, Boston Globe. Interview with Author, 17 August 1999.

Kanstoroom, Marci. "Do Courts Make a Difference? Courts and School Finance Reform." Ph.d. diss. Harvard University, 1998.

Kehler, David. "The Trenton Tea Party: The Story of New Jersey's Tax Revolt." *Policy Review* 60, Spring (1992): 46–49.

Kerr, Peter. "Florio Proposes New Spending Plans." *New York Times*, 25 May 1990a, B2.

Kerr, Peter. "Teachers and Bergen Democrats Attack Florio Budget Plan." *New York Times*, 14 June 1990b, B1.

———. "Florio School-Aid Package Gains Final Approval." *New York Times*, 22 June 1990c, A1.

———. "The 1990 Elections: New Jersey—A Governor's Response." *New York Times*, 8 November 1990d, A1.

———. "Legislator Offers Option on Taxes and School Subsidy in New Jersey." *New York Times*, 21 February 1991a, B2.

———. "Florio School Aid Plan Cut; Homeowners Get Tax Relief." *New York Times*, 12 March 1991b, B3.

———. "Florio Shifting Style to Let Legislators Set the Agenda." *New York Times*, 27 March 1991c, B1.

Kincaid, John. "Foreword: The New Federalism Context of the New Judicial Federalism." *Rutgers Law Journal* 26, 4 (1995): 913–48.

Kinder, Donald R., and David O. Sears. "Prejudices and Politics: Symbolic Racism versus Racial Threats to the Good Life." *Journal of Personality and Social Psychology* 40 (1981): 414–31.

King, Wayne. "Teachers Flunk Democrats (And Vice Versa) in Jersey." *New York Times*, 1 September 1991a, 5, sec. 4.

———. "Republicans Ready to Mount Attacks on Florio Program." *New York Times*, 7 November 1991b, A1.

Kirp, David L., John P. Dwyer, and Larry A. Rosenthal. *Our Town: Race, Housing and the Soul of Suburbia*. New Brunswick, N.J.: Rutgers University Press, 1995.

Klagholz, Leo. "There's No Clear Definition of 'Thorough, Efficient.'" *Star-Ledger*, 26 February 1995a.

———. "Schools Alone Can't Solve All of Society's Problems." *Star-Ledger*, 5 March 1995b.

———. "Plan Does Not Seek Absolute Social Uniformity thru Draconian Controls." *Star-Ledger*, 12 March 1995c.

Klarman, Michael J. "How *Brown* Changed Race Relations: The Backlash Thesis." *Journal of American History* 81, 1 (1994): 81–118.

Kozol, Jonathan. *Savage Inequalities*. New York: Crown Publishers, 1991.

Lankford, Hamilton, and James Wyckoff. "Why Are Schools Racially Segregated? Implications for School Choice Policies." Paper presented at the School Choice and Racial Diversity Conference, Teachers College, Columbia University, 7 May 2000.

Lehne, Richard. *The Quest for Justice*. New York: Longman, 1978.

Levin, Daniel Lessard. *Representing Popular Sovereignty: The Constitution in American Political Culture, SUNY Series, American Constitutionalism*. Albany: State University of New York Press, 1999.

Levinson, Sanford. *Constitutional Faith*. Princeton, N.J.: Princeton University Press, 1988.

Lowery, David, and William E. Lyons. "The Impact of Jurisdictional Boundaries: An Individual-Level Test of the Tiebout Model." *Journal of Politics* 51, 1 (1989): 73–97.

Lutz, Donald S. "Toward a Theory of Constitutional Amendment." *American Political Science Review* 88, 2 (1994): 355–70.

———. "Patterns in the Amending of American State Constitutions." In *Constitutional Politics in the States*, edited by G. Alan Tarr, 24–46. Westport, Conn.: Greenwood Press, 1996.

MacFarquhar, Neil. "Cut Government Spending at Expense of Schools?" *New York Times*, 23 November 1995a, B7.

———. "New Jersey Schools Adding Up Parity Proposals." *New York Times*, 4 December 1995b, B1.

———. "Whitman Adminstration Is Sued on School Spending." *New York Times*, 23 April 1996a, B5.

———. "Whitman Offers Fiscal Plan for Parity in Schools." *New York Times*, 17 May 1996b, 1.

MacInnes, Gordon A. "Opinion." *The Record*, 1 October 1996, L15.

Maltz, Earl M. "Lockstep Analysis and the Concept of Federalism." *Annals American Academy of Political and Social Science* 496 (1988): 98–107.

Massey, Douglas S., and Nancy A. Denton. *American Apartheid: Segregation and the Making of the Underclass*. Cambridge, Mass.: Harvard University Press, 1993.

McCann, Michael. "Reform Litigation on Trial." *Law and Social Inquiry* 17, 4 (1992): 715–43.

McDermott, Kathryn A. *Controlling Public Education: Localism versus Equity*. Lawrence: University Press of Kansas, 1999.

McGrath, Mary. "Senator Offers Compromise to Whitman Education Reform." *The Record*, 4 October 1996, L02.

McKenzie, Evan. *Privatopia: Homeowner Associations and the Rise of Residential Private Government*. New Haven: Yale University Press, 1994.

McLarin, Kimberly J. "Budget's Losers Display a Touch of Resignation." *New York Times*, 24 January 1995, B5.

McLaughlin, John. "Dealing for Dollars." *Star-Ledger*, 22 December 1996b, Perspective sec., 1.

McLaughlin, John. "They've Got a Wealth of Complaints." *Star-Ledger*, 25 February 1996a, 1.

Metz, Mary Haywood. *Different by Design: The Context and Character of Three Magnet Schools*. New York: Routledge & Kegan Paul, 1986.

Moore, Wayne D. *Constitutional Rights and Powers of the People*. Princeton, N.J.: Princeton University Press, 1996.

Morantz, Alison. "Money and Choice in Kansas City." In *Dismantling Desegregation*, edited by Gary Orfield, Susan E. Eaton, and Harvard Project on School Desegregation, 241–63. New York: The New Press, 1996.

Murnane, Richard J. "Interpreting the Evidence on 'Does Money Matter?'" *Harvard Journal on Legislation* 28, 2 (1991): 457–64.

Murray, Sheila E., William N. Evans, and Robert M. Schwab. "Education-Finance Reform and the Distribution of Education Resources." *American Economic Review* 88, 4 (1998): 789–812.

National Center for Education Statistics. *Digest of Education Statistics, 1998*. Washington, D.C.: U.S. Department of Education, 1998.

Natriello, Gary, and Morgan Collins. "Necessary but Not Sufficient: The Quality Education Act and At-Risk Students." Center for Education Policy Analysis, Rutgers University, 1993.

New Jersey Department of Education. "Comprehensive Plan for Educational Improvement and Financing: An Interim Report," 28. Trenton, N.J., 1995.

New Jersey Legislature. *Quality Education Act of 1990*, 1990.

————. "The Legislative Hearing on Public School Funding." Newark, N.J., 14 August 1996. Available at http://www.njleg.state.nj.us/Pubhear

New Jersey State Law Library. "Remarks of Governor Christine Todd Whitman Bill Signing for School Funding Plan." In *Legislative History of 1996 Comprehensive Educational Improvement and Financing Act, NJSA 18A:7F-1 to 34*. Trenton, N.J.: State of New Jersey, 1996.

New York Times. "Metro News Briefs: State Says Schools Plan Could Cost $811 Million." *New York Times*, 9 December 1997, B2.

Newman, Maria. "Anger against Governors Reflected in 3–State Poll." *New York Times*, 22 November 1991, A1.

Orfield, Gary. *Must We Bus?* Washington, D.C.: Brookings Institution, 1978.

Orfield, Gary, and John T. Yun. *Resegregation in American schools* [Web page]. Civil Rights Project, Harvard University, June 1999 [cited May 16 2000]. Available from http://www.law.harvard.edu/civilrights/publications/resegregation99.html.

Ostrom, Vincent, Charles M. Tiebout, and Robert Warren. "The Organization of Government in Metropolitan Areas: A Theory Inquiry." *American Political Science Review* 55, 4 (1961): 831–42.

Palmer, William S. Superintendent, Essex Falls School District, Essex Falls, N.J., letter to residents, January 1994.

Paris, Michael. "Legal Mobilization and Social Reform: A Comparative Study of School Finance Litigation in New Jersey and Kentucky." Ph.d. diss., Brandeis University, 1998.

Parker, Wendy. "The Future of School Desegregation." *Northwestern University Law Review* Summer 94, (2000): 1157–1227.

Percy, Stephen L., and Brett W. Hawkins. "Further Tests of Individual-Level Propositions from the Tiebout Model." *Journal of Politics* 54, 4 (1992): 1149–57.

Percy, Stephen L., Brett W. Hawkins, and Peter E. Maier. "Revisiting Tiebout: Moving Rationales and Interjurisdictional Relocation." *Publius* 25, 4 (1995): 1–17.

Peterson, Iver. "On Politics: Turning Back the Clock Is a Waste of Time." *New York Times*, 10 December 1995, Sec. 13NJ, 2.

Pitler, Robert M. "Independent State Search and Seizure Constitutionalism: The New York State Court of Appeals' Quest for Principled Decision-Making." *Brooklyn Law Review* 62 (1996): 1–117.

Polinard, J. L., Robert D. Wrinkle, and Tomas Longoria. "Education and Governance: Representation Links to Second Generation Discrimination." *Western Political Quarterly* 43, Sept (1990): 631–46.

Pollock, Stewart G. "State Constitutions As Separate Sources of Fundamental Rights." *Rutgers Law Review* 35, 4 (1983): 707–22.

———. "Adequate and Independent State Grounds As a Means of Balancing the Relationship between State and Federal Courts." *Texas Law Review* 63, 6, 7 (1985): 977–93.

Preston, Jennifer. "Three More Months to Answer a Twenty-Year-Old Riddle." *New York Times*, 15 September 1996, sec. 13NJ 2.

Pride, Richard A. "Public Opinion and the End of Busing." *Sociological Quarterly* 41, 2 (2000): 207–25.

Pristin, Terry. "School Plan Is Protested." *New York Times*, 4 June 1996, B1.

———. "New School Spending Figures." *New York Times*, 4 June 1997, B1.

Pyatt, Graham, Chau-Nan Chen, and John Fei. "The Distribution of Income by Factor Components." *Quarterly Journal of Economics* 95, 3 (1980): 451–73.

Racine, John. "Texas Lawmakers Get Second Chance As Court Develops School Finance Plan." *Bond Buyer*, 2 April 1991, 1.

Rae, Douglas, Douglas Yates, Jennifer Hochschild, Joseph Morone, and Carol Fessler. *Equalities*. Cambridge, Mass.: Harvard University Press, 1981.

Reed, Douglas S. "The People v. the Court: School Finance Reform and the New Jersey Supreme Court." *Cornell Journal of Law and Public Policy* 4, 1 (1994): 137–98.

———. "Democracy v. Equality: Legal and Political Struggles over School Finance Equalization." Ph.D. diss., Yale University, 1995.

———. "Popular Constitutionalism: Toward a Theory of State Constitutional Meanings." *Rutgers Law Journal* 30, 4 (1999): 871–932.

Reilly, Matthew. "Lawyer Fighting School Funding Law Drops Teacher Pension Challenge." *Star-Ledger*, 17 July 1992, A1.

———. "Governor Says Spending Must Translate to Success in Class." *Star-Ledger*, 24 February 1995a.

———. "Klagholz Says Penalized School Districts Can Afford Fines." *Star-Ledger*, 28 February 1995b.

———. "Judge Halts Takeover of Newark Schools." *Star-Ledger*, 6 July 1995c.

Rivkin, Steven G. "Residential Segregation and School Integration." *Sociology of Education* 67, 4 (1994): 279–92.

Rosenberg, Gerald N. *The Hollow Hope*. Chicago: University of Chicago Press, 1991.

Rossell, Christine H. *The Carrot or the Stick for School Desegregation Policy: Magnet Schools or Forced Busing*. Philadelphia: Temple University Press, 1990.

———. "The Convergence of Black and White Attitudes on School Desegregation Issues." In *Redefining Equality*, edited by Neal Devins and Davison M. Douglas. New York and Oxford: Oxford University Press, 1998.

Rossell, Christine H., and David J. Armor. "The Effectiveness of School Desegregation Plans, 1968–91." *American Politics Quarterly* 24, 3 (1996): 267–302.

Rostow, Eugene V. *The Sovereign Prerogative: The Supreme Court and the Quest for Law*. New Haven: Yale University Press, 1962.

Rugeley, Cindy. "'Robin Hood' Not Greeted Merrily." *Houston Chronicle*, 10 April 1993, A1.

Rugeley, Cindy, and Melanie Markley. "School Finance Foes Wage Low-Budget War." *Houston Chronicle*, 11 April 1993, A1.

Ryan, James E. "Sheff, Segregation and School Finance Litigation." *New York University Law Review* 74, 2 (1999): 529–73.

Salmore, Barbara G., and Stephen A. Salmore. "New Jersey: From Political Hacks to Political Action Committees." In *Interest Group Politics in the Northeastern States*, edited by Ronald J. Hrebenar and Clive S. Thomas. University Park: Pennsylvania State University Press, 1993a.

————. *New Jersey Politics and Government: Suburban Politics Comes of Age*. Lincoln: University of Nebraska Press, 1993b.

Sanders, Francine. "*Brown v. Board of Education*: An Empirical Reexamination of Its Effects on Federal District Courts." *Law and Society Review* 29, 4 (1995): 731–56.

Scheiber, Harry N. "Federalism and Legal Process: Historical and Contemporary Analysis of the American System." *Law & Society Review* 14, 3 (1980): 663–722.

Schneider, Mark, Paul Teske, Christine Roch, and Melissa Marschall. "Networks to Nowhere: Segregation and Stratification in Networks of Information about Schools." *American Journal of Political Science* 41, 4 (1997): 1201–23.

Schneider, Mark, Paul Teske, and Melissa Marschall. *Choosing Schools: Consumer Choice and the Quality of American Schools*. Princeton, N.J.: Princeton University Press, 2000.

Schofield, Janet Ward. *Black and White in School*. 2d ed. New York: Teachers College Press, 1989.

Schwaneberg, Robert. "State Submits Its Figure on Per-Pupil Cost; Whitman Aides Say It's $8,285." *Star-Ledger*, 18 May 1996, 1.

Sears, David O. "Symbolic Racism." In *Eliminating Racism*, edited by Phyllis A Katz and Dalmas A Taylor, 53–84. New York: Plenum Press, 1988.

Sears, David O., Carl P. Hensler, and Leslie K. Speer. "Whites' Opposition to 'Busing': Self-Interest or Symbolic Politics?" *American Political Science Review* 73, 2 (1979): 369–84.

Sen, Amartya. "Equality of What?" In *The Tanner Lectures on Human Values*, edited by Sterling M. McMurrin, 195–220. Salt Lake City: University of Utah Press, 1980.

Senate Budget and Appropriations Committee. "Statement to Senate Committee Substitute for Senate Committee Substitute for Senate No. 40." In *Legislative History of 1996 Comprehensive Educational Improvement and Financing Act, NJSA 18A:7F-1 to 34*, edited by New Jersey Legislature. Trenton: State of New Jersey, 1996.

Shearman, J. Craig. "Florio Wins NJEA Endorsement." *United Press International*, 28 August 1989.

Smith, Kevin B., and Kenneth J. Meier. "Public Choice in Education: Markets and the Demand for Quality Education." *Political Research Quarterly* 48, 3 (1995): 461–78.

Spring, Joel H. *Conflict of Interests: The Politics of American Education*. New York: Longman, 1988.

Stewart, Angela. "Court Backs Seizure of Newark Schools." *Star-Ledger*, 23 December 1995.

Stewart, Joseph, Jr. "Policy Models and Equal Educational Opportunity." *PS* 24 (1991): 167–73.

Sturm, Albert L. "The Development of American State Constitutions." *Publius* 12 (1982): 57–98.

Stutz, Terrence, and Christy Hoppe. "Senate Approves School Measure." *Dallas Morning News*, 13 November 1992, 23A.

Tarr, G. Alan. "The Past and Future of the New Judicial Federalism." *Publius* 24, 2 (1994): 63–79.

———. *Understanding State Constitutions*. Princeton, N.J.: Princeton University Press, 1998.

Tedin, Kent. "Self-Interest, Symbolic Values and the Financial Equalization of the Public Schools." *Journal of Politics* 56, 3 (1994): 628–49.

Teske, Paul, Mark Schneider, Michael Mintrom, and Samuel Best. "Establishing the Micro Foundations of a Macro Theory: Information, Movers and the Competitive Local Market for Public Goods." *American Political Science Review* 87, 3 (1993): 702–713.

Thompson, Neal. "Whitman: Link Aid, School Performance." *The Record*, 17 February 1995, A1.

Thro, William E. "Note: To Render Them Safe: The Analysis of State Constitutional Provisions in Public School Finance Reform Litigation." *Virginia Law Review* 75, 8 (1989): 1639–79.

———. "The Third Wave: The Impact of Montana, Kentucky, and Texas Decisions on the Future of Public School Finance Reform Litigation." *Journal of Law & Education* 19, 2 (1990): 219–50.

———. "The Significance of the Tennessee School Finance Decision." *Education Law Reporter* 82 (1993): 11–26.

———. "Judicial Analysis during the Third Wave of School Finance Litigation: The Massachusetts Decision As a Model." *Boston College Law Review* 35, 3 (1994): 597–617.

Tiebout, Charles M. "A Pure Theory of Local Expenditures." *Journal of Political Economy* 64, October (1956): 416–24.

Tractenberg, Paul L. "Reforming School Finance through State Constitutions: *Robinson v. Cahill* Points the Way." *Rutgers Law Review* 27, 3 (1974): 365–463.

Trent, William T. "Outcomes of School Desegregation: Findings from Longitudinal Research." *Journal of Negro Education* 66, 3 (1997): 255–57.

Tushnet, Mark. *Taking the Constitution Away from the Courts*. Princeton, N.J.: Princeton University Press, 1999.

United States. National Commission on Excellence in Education. *A Nation at Risk: The Imperative for Educational Reform: A Report to the Nation and the Secretary of Education, United States Department of Education*. Washington, D.C.: The Commission: Supt. of Docs. U.S. G.P.O. distributor, 1983.

Verhovek, Sam Howe. "Texans Reject Sharing School Wealth." *New York Times*, 3 May 1993, A12.

Walters, Laurel Shaper. "U.S. Schools Watch Busing-by-Income Program in Wisconisn." *The Christian Science Monitor*, 9 November 1993, 10.

Weiher, Gregory R. *The Fractured Metropolis*. Albany: State University of New York Press, 1991.

Wells, Amy Stuart. "Reexamining Social Science Research on School Desegregation: Long- versus Short-Term Effects." In *Brown v. Board of Education: The Challenge for Today's Schools*, edited by Ellen Condliffe Lagemann and LaMar P. Miller, 91–106. New York: Teachers College Press, 1996.

Wells, Amy Stuart, and Robert L. Crain. "Perpetuation Theory and the Long-Term Effects of School Desegregation." *Review of Educational Research* 64, 4 (1994): 531–55.

———. *Stepping Over the Color Line: African-American Students in White Suburban Schools*. New Haven: Yale University Press, 1997.

Whittington, Keith E. *Constitutional Construction: Divided Powers and Constitutional Meaning*. Cambridge: Harvard University Press, 1999.

Williams, Robert F. "Equality Guarantees in State Constitutional Law." *Texas Law Review* 63, 6, 7 (1985): 1195–224.

———. *The New Jersey State Constitution: A Reference Guide*. Westport, Conn.: Greenwood Press, 1990.

———. "Foreword: The Importance of an Independent State Constitutional Equality Doctrine in School Finance Cases and Beyond." *Connecticut Law Review* 24, 3 (1992): 675–702.

Witte, John F. *The Market Approach to Education: An Analysis of America's First Voucher Program*. Princeton, N.J.: Princeton University Press, 2000.

Woodward, C. Vann. *The Strange Career of Jim Crow*. 3d rev. ed. New York: Oxford University Press, 1974.

Wrinkle, Robert D., Joseph Stewart, Jr. and J. L. Polinard. "Public School Quality, Private Schools, and Race." *American Journal of Political Science* 43, 4 (1999): 1248–53.

Yearwood, John, and Steve Scott. "Many Bet a Buck, Hope for a Bundle." *Dallas Morning News*, 2 May 1993, 39A.

Young, Charles. "Proposal on School Funding Won't Fly; Unconstitutional, Critics Tell State." *The Record*, 6 December 1995, A1.

INDEX